Marketing the e-Business

Second Edition

By

Lisa Harris and Charles Dennis

Routledge
Taylor & Francis Group

NEW YORK AND LONDON

First published 2002 by Routledge
This edition published 2008 by Routledge
270 Madison Ave, New York, NY 10016

Simultaneously published in the UK
by Routledge
2 Park Square, Milton Park, Abingdon, Oxon OX14 4RN

Routledge is an imprint of the Taylor & Francis Group, an informa business

Typeset in Adobe Caslon, Copperplate Gothic and Trade Gothic by EvS Communication Networx

Printed and bound in the United States of America on acid-free paper by Edwards Brothers, Inc.

Library of Congress Cataloging in Publication Data
Harris, Lisa, 1968-
Marketing the e-business / by Lisa Harris and Charles Dennis. -- 2nd ed.
p. cm. -- (Routledge e-business series)
Includes bibliographical references and index.
ISBN-13: 978-0-415-96500-2 (hardback : alk. paper)
ISBN-10: 0-415-96500-4 (hardback : alk. paper)
ISBN-13: 978-0-415-96501-9 (pbk. : alk. paper)
ISBN-10: 0-415-96501-2 (pbk. : alk. paper)
[etc.]
1. Internet marketing. 2. Electronic commerce. I. Dennis, Charles (Charles E.) II. Title.
HF5415.1265.H376 2008
658.8'72--dc22
2007038216

ISBN 10: 0-415-96500-4 (hbk)
ISBN 10: 0-415-96501-2 (pbk)
ISBN 10: 0-203-93316-8 (ebk)

ISBN 13: 978-0-415-96500-2 (hbk)
ISBN 13: 978-0-415-96501 -9 (pbk)
ISBN 13: 978-0-203-93316-9 (ebk)

Contents

List of Diagrams and Tables

Tables

Contributors

Lisa Harris is a Senior Lecturer in Marketing and Director of the Marketing Analytics MSc at the University of Southampton School of Management. She is a Chartered Marketer and a member of the Chartered Institute of Marketing International Board of Trustees. Before joining the education sector she worked for 10 years in marketing roles within the international banking industry. Lisa teaches online marketing courses in the UK, Germany and Switzerland and she is also an e-tutor for the online MBA programme of the University of Liverpool. She is currently running a research project investigating how small firms are maximising their marketing effectiveness with Web 2.0 tools.

Dr Charles Dennis was elected as a Fellow of the Chartered Institute of Marketing (CIM) for work helping to modernise the teaching of the discipline. He is a Chartered Marketer and Senior Lecturer in Marketing and Retail Management at Brunel University, London, UK. The combined research/textbook *e-Retailing* (Dennis *et al.*, 2004) was published by Routledge in the present series; and the research monograph *Objects of Desire: Consumer Behaviour in Shopping Centre Choice* (Dennis, 2005) was published by Palgrave.

Acknowledgements

The authors thank Christine Hallier of Brunel University for contributing her work on corporate blogs (in Chapter 12); Hugh Griffiths of O2 for his insight into recent developments in mobile communications (in Chapter 7); Bill Merrilees and Tino Fenech of Griffith University for input from *e-Retailing* (in Chapters 5 and 10) Lands' End and My Virtual Model for the screenshots in Diagrams 5.2 and 5.3. George, Flash, K8e and Mary for patience and inputs far beyond the call of duty!

Introduction

Aim

The aim of this book is to demonstrate to both marketing students and practitioners how marketing efficiency and effectiveness can be improved through the use of the Internet.

Rationale

E-marketing is rapidly growing in significance and is having a direct impact upon traditional marketing strategy and operations. It requires planning and innovation to make it work, implying organisational commitment and effective management, supported by technology, process and structure.

Relatively few companies (with the exception of the 'pure-play' or 'dotcom' brigade) are able to start with a 'clean sheet of paper' so far as e-business is concerned. For most companies, setting up online operations requires significant cultural and structural change. It also usually means running both 'traditional' and 'new' business alongside each other, and developing an appropriate degree of integration between them to create useful synergies. Although a number of lessons can be learned from the bursting of the dotcom bubble (and these are considered where relevant), the main focus of this text is upon the challenges faced by 'bricks and mortar' organizations as they introduce and develop their online operations alongside their established business activities and attempt to keep up with the latest developments in technology.

Lessons from History and Cautionary Tales

Much has been written about the 'revolutionary' business implications of the Internet, to the extent that some authors have argued that a new business 'paradigm' has emerged, as a result of the scope of the potential applications of Internet technology. However, Palmer (2001) noted that the difficulties experienced by dotcom businesses once the initial euphoria wore off indicated that there has actually been little change in the underlying beliefs and values of the business world. E-businesses therefore operate within the same environment as conventional businesses and hence are subject to the same rules. Similarly, Dutta and Biren (2001) proposed that the key role of Internet technology was not to revolutionise business practices but instead to seek efficiency improvements through 'e-enabling' the current activities of the firm in a 'low risk' approach to innovation that is consistent with existing organisational culture. In addition, Phillips (2001) calculated that the application of technology to improve the efficiency of current operations may represent as much as 72 percent of all IT developments.

The information 'revolution' prompted by the Internet is often discussed as though it is without precedent. It can be tempting to conclude that the rate of innovation and technological change puts extraordinary and unique pressure on companies as they struggle with the demands of a '24/7' economy. Kanter (2001) provided a welcome dose of reality among the hordes of Internet evangelists:

> Many discussions of the New Economy take place in an historical vacuum. Mention the Internet, and intelligent people sometimes act as if they have had a portion of their brain removed—the memory.... As we search for the new and different things that occur in the wake of revolu-

tionary communications technology, it is also important to recall what can be learned from previous waves of innovation. (Kanter: 3–4)

She went on to highlight the key theme of her book, namely that in our enthusiasm to keep up with the ways in which the world is changing, we often fail to notice just how much remains the same:

> History demonstrates that new channels tend to coexist with old ones and sometimes even join them. Yes, the technology is revolutionary, network economics are different, and all the wheels must turn a lot faster, but the problems of leadership, organization and change are similar to those we have experienced for decades. (ibid.: 5)

Hanson drew some uncanny parallels between the Internet and the growth of radio in the 1920s. He demonstrated that change is always with us, however radically we might think that the Internet is altering marketing practices at the moment. His description of radio developments highlighted that they made a huge impact on the society of the 1920s, reminding us that radio 'so captured the public's imagination that commentators claimed it would revolutionise culture, education and commerce' (2000: 2). Similarly, David (1991) compared the growth of information technology to the early days of electricity, which was also labelled 'revolutionary' when first made available. He showed how it took several decades for people to learn how to make the most of the new technology and overcome their preference for 'traditional' and familiar alternatives. The same argument has been used persuasively by Simon (1987) in his study of the steam engine. Jardine (1999) looked further back into history, and claimed that the emergence of the printed book in the fifteenth century was equally radical in its impact on contemporary life. Interestingly, however, she noted that it took some fifty years for the printing business to become profitable, with a number of prominent early market entrants going out of business along the way. If a common pattern from these historical examples is not yet obvious, the following quotation from Charles Fraser (written in 1880, reproduced in *The Economist* in June 2000) should clinch matters: 'An agent is at hand to bring everything into harmonious co-operation, triumphing over space and time, to subdue prejudice and unite every part of our land in rapid and friendly communication…and that great motive agent is *steam*'.

It is often suggested that e-Business is just about technological change, but there arc greater difficulties in implementing the intellectual, cultural and structural shifts necessary to succeed in a much more interactive business environment. Firms set up specifically to operate through the Internet (the so-called dotcoms) were ideally placed to recruit suitable staff and deal with customers in the most effective way, although many dotcoms were lost in the crash of 2001. Established firms, however, may have a whole history of embedded working practices and customer relationships that require significant change if e-business is to be implemented successfully. Some of the qualities required for success are a lack of 'baggage' (in the shape of established business processes), a deep understanding of how technology can serve business strategies, and a flair for implementing these strategies.

It is easy to get carried away about the potential of the Internet, but several problems remain:

- The sheer volume of traffic can cause delays and lockouts.
- Security breaches by hackers and viruses hit the headlines regularly.
- A large proportion of the population still do not have Internet access.
- High-speed access is necessary to support the latest multimedia features

Throughout the book we look at the difficulties associated with Internet marketing and suggest how potential problems might be overcome. Even when an Internet initiative is organised, with appropriate leadership, its multidisciplinary demands test an organisation's communication channels. This is particularly true in bureaucratic companies that are still organised around traditional business functions. Internet initiatives require integration between strategic, marketing, technical, graphic design, communications, publishing and operations capabilities. The organisational challenge of assembling, managing and empowering such teams is immense.

Structure of the Book

This book adopts a methodical approach to the development, implementation and control of Internet marketing strategies. The relevance of the chapter's subject matter to that of the book as a whole, a summary of the key lessons that will be learned, and an ordered list of subtopics to be covered are set out at the start of each chapter. Feedback is provided at the end of each chapter on a number of self-assessed questions and activities presented in the text, together with a list of specific web-based sources and book references.

Chapter 1 History, Definitions and Frameworks

- Discusses how the Internet has developed over the past 30 years.
- Explains the meaning of basic e-marketing related terminology.
- Explains how the basic infrastructure of the Internet is constructed and the relationship between the component parts.
- Discusses the marketing implications of macro-issues such as e-governance policy and recent developments such as Web 2.0.

Chapter 2 The e-Business Environment

- Discusses and evaluates the key issues prevailing in the current e-business environment, specifically with regard to:
  - The inter-relationship between legal and ethical considerations
  - Intellectual property rights
  - The 'digital divide'
  - Data protection
  - Online payment systems.

Chapter 3 e-Marketing Research

- Explains the basic principles of marketing research.
- Discusses the increasingly central role played by research in effective marketing.
- Discusses how to choose the most appropriate method to address a particular research task.

- Explains how the Internet can be applied to add value to the research process.
- Discusses the legal and ethical issues raised by online research in terms of data protection and privacy.

Chapter 4 e-Marketing Strategies

- Discusses the importance of creating the 'right mix of bricks and clicks'.
- Explains how e-marketing strategy can add value to a business.
- Evaluates the key models of online marketing strategy that have emerged to date.

Chapter 5 e-Consumer Behaviour

- Why consumers e-shop (or do not e-shop).
- How consumers achieve satisfaction (or not) from e-shopping.
- How consumer satisfaction from e-retailing compares with satisfaction from in store shopping.
- What factors are inhibiting the growth of e-shopping?

Chapter 6 Customer Relationship Marketing

- Discusses the relationship between internal marketing and customer relationship marketing.
- Explains the critical role of information in the implementation of effective relationship marketing strategies.
- Describes how the Internet permits relevant marketing data to be acquired, stored, analysed and managed.
- Explains how the information derived from this data can be applied in order to build and sustain customer relationships.

Chapter 7 Multi-Channel Marketing

- Discusses the characteristics of the various online channels now available to marketers

- Evaluates the internal challenges posed by multi-channel marketing strategies and explain how such issues can be addressed.
- Discusses the implications for service quality of automating channel communications.

Chapter 8 Online Branding

- Evaluates the broad scope of branding decisions.
- Discusses the range of online branding strategies available.
- Compares and contrasts issues of 'global' versus 'local' branding.
- Discusses the emerging challenges inherent in multi-channel branding.

Chapter 9 Online Marketing Communications

- Discusses the purpose of marketing communications.
- Explains the relationship between online consumer behaviour and effective marketing communications.
- Describes the range of tools available for online communications.
- Explains the importance of effective integration of online and offline communications.

Chapter 10 e-Retailing: From 'Clicks' To 'Clicks and Bricks'?

- What e-retail is, advantages and disadvantages for retailers.
- The success factors for e-retail (and the 'no-nos').
- The e-retailing strategic options for retailers.
- The growing importance of multi-channel retailing.
- The tools and techniques of e-retailing—the e-retail mix.

Chapter 11 e-Marketing Planning

- Critically evaluates the effectiveness of the planning cycle for e-marketing operations.

- Demonstrates how an online marketing plan is constructed by:
    - Carrying out a marketing audit
    - Setting SMART objectives
    - Segmentation and choice of strategy
    - Implementing the chosen strategy through the marketing mix
    - Applying suitable metrics to evaluate success
- Explains the implications of e-marketing for organisational structures and internal business processes.

Chapter 12 The Future of e-Marketing

- Maximising the opportunities of Web 2.0:
    - RSS
    - Blogs
    - Podcasts
    - Online networking
- Where are we now? Successes and failures
- What does the future hold?

1

HISTORY, DEFINITIONS AND FRAMEWORKS

Introduction

In this scene-setting chapter we will review the history of the Internet and briefly describe the physical makeup and protocols which control it. You will then be introduced to some recent developments that will be covered in more detail later in the book. We will also examine some basic e-marketing terminology and discuss the key models of contemporary online business activity.

Topics Covered in this Chapter

- A brief history of the Internet
- Internet components, protocols and security
- Overview of recent developments
    - Governance
    - Access
    - Web 2.0
- Key e-marketing definitions
- Boo.com case study.

Learning Objectives

By the end of the chapter you should be able to:

- Discuss how the Internet has developed over the past 30 years.

- Explain the meaning of basic e-marketing related terminology.
- Explain how the basic infrastructure of the Internet is constructed and the relationship between the component parts.
- Discuss the marketing implications of macro issues such as e-governance policy and recent developments such as Web 2.0.

Recommended Reading

Cellen-Jones, R. (2003) *Dot.bomb: The Strange Death of Dotcom Britain*, London: Aurum

Berners-Lee, J. (1999) *Weaving the Web. The Past, Present and Future of the World Wide Web by Its Inventor*, London: Orion Publishing

Kuo, J. D. (2001) *Dot.Bomb, Inside an Internet Goliath from Lunatic Optimism to Panic and Crash*, London: Little, Brown

A Brief History of the Internet

In 1969 the Internet was just a demonstration project linking up four university campuses in the US but by the end of 2004 there were in excess of 934 million users across the world, according to the *Computer Industry Almanac*. This figure is predicted to grow to 1.35 billion users by 2008. The latest statistics of Internet growth can be found at the Clickz Network (see www.clickz.com). In addition to these fixed hosts that link individual desktop computers to the Internet, there will be mobile hosts linking up mobile phones using wireless technology.

The Internet was based on an original concept developed by the Rand Corporation in the early 1960s. The objective of the research was to provide the US with a communications network that would survive in the event of a nuclear conflagration. The project was codified into a set of protocols (eventually called TCP/IP) by Vinton Cerf during the mid-1970s and deployed across all the inter-linked networks in 1983. Growth between 1980 and 1987 shows numbers of hosts in the tens of thousands.

After 1987 when the US funding body NSF (National Science Foundation) started to work with the Internet, growth leapt into the hundreds of thousands. Many non-US academic sites and scientific and research bodies linked up at this point. It was inherent in the technology that new nodes could easily be added to the Internet, and this has permitted the exponential growth of users. Secondly, all messages were to be treated equally—there was no inherent prioritisation of messages—so no matter which computer was being used, all messages have equal rights regardless of whether the user is an employee of a large corporation or an individual accessing the Internet from home.

No single entity owns the Internet or is wholly responsible for its functioning. It is a decentralised network whose operation is influenced by a number of bodies, not least large commercial interests such as Cisco and Microsoft which help drive ICT standards and innovation in the marketplace itself. The ethos underpinning the Internet at this point was one of not-for-profit, and the lack of packet prioritisation underpinned an essentially democratic spirit amongst its user communities. It was only with the emergence of the World Wide Web (WWW) that individuals with little knowledge of such protocols could participate in this electronic medium. By use of hypertext (embedded links within electronic documents) and a pointing device such as a mouse, navigation amongst a series of web pages was made possible for novice users. The development of the web browser Mosaic in 1993 meant that rapid colonisation of the network by commercial interests began. It is from this point that online trading (or e-commerce) really took off.

Earlier forms of e-commerce include Electronic Data Interchange (EDI) which is the exchange of information and orders by trading partners using technically-defined templates. EDI originated in 1969 when a US rail freight company sought to optimise its freight shipments by using cabling alongside its tracks to link up with customers. The succeeding decades saw many large corporations taking up EDI (based on value-added networks operated by private sector organisations such as IBM) to the point where by 1995 there were in excess of 30,000 EDI networks in Europe alone.

As opposed to the Internet which uses protocols that are *open* and *non-proprietary*, these EDI systems are *closed* or *proprietary* systems which are open only to invited participants. These technical problems and restricted functionality contrived to ensure that EDI as a whole never achieved widespread credibility. The lack of a common standard for document formats meant that companies tended to get locked in to one supplier. It has taken the growth of the Internet with its universal standard to project electronic trading into mainstream commercial credibility, by allowing businesses to connect throughout the value chain, exchange real-time information and streamline business processes both internally and externally.

For more detail on the development of the Internet, Hobbes' Internet Timeline identifies a chronology of events and the individuals behind them at www.zakon.org/robert/internet/timeline

Internet Components, Protocols and Security

The Internet as we know it to-day consists of small area networks belonging to individual organisations (Local Area Networks or LANs), networks spread across large geographic areas (Wide Area Networks or WANs) and individual computers. To connect to the Internet, a computer or network uses the TCP/IP protocol. Internet Protocols are rules that govern the transfer of data within computer networks.

The Internet itself usually utilises the UNIX operating system. Within the Internet there are more networks. These include:

- Backbone networks (e.g. the NTSNET system)
- Commercial networks (businesses with direct links to the Internet)
- Service providers who offer smaller firms with an Internet connection
- Non-commercial networks belonging to educational/research organisations
- Gateway networks provide their subscribers with access to the Internet.

Most Internet sites have an address or 'domain name' that performs the role of being the telephone number for individuals wishing to reach them. Transfer of information uses FTP (File Transfer Protocol). These files can contain images, video clips, sound recording, text or graphics. In short, the Internet is capable of transmitting anything that can be put in digital form. This means the cost of information transfer is becoming negligible, distance is increasingly irrelevant and content can be accessed almost immediately. For a relatively small outlay on a computer, a suitable telecommunications link (e.g. via a phone line and modem), and an online account provided by an Internet Service Provider, individuals located across the globe can access this massive network.

For the small business user, the physical components of the Internet are likely to look like this:

- Browser on computer
- Modem on computer
- Telephone line (dial-up or broadband) into telephone company (e.g. BT) network
- Internet account with Internet Service Provider (ISP).

Larger firms might look more like this:

- Browser on computer
- Computer connected to corporate server(s)
- Corporate server connected to corporate router
- Telecoms link from corporate router to telephone company
- High speed Internet account with ISP.

Benyon-Davies (2004) notes that customer concern over security breaches has been the most significant barrier to the growth of e-business. According to www.nielsen-netratings.com (November 2006) almost half of Britons online (45 percent) still have concerns about the handling of their credit card and personal information when shopping online. People over 55 are the most likely to have these concerns, 16–24 year olds the least likely. However, the latest online trading predictions from Nielsen/Netratings indicate that such fears are receding, with people dedicating 55 percent of their total Christmas gift spending to online sources—an average of £237 online and £197 on the high street per person. Despite this increased confidence, no credible business can afford to ignore Internet security issues. In summary:

- From a corporate perspective, Internet security is a subset of information security.
- The Internet was originally designed as an open network to guarantee the ability to share information.

- As it moved from the military and academic arenas into the corporate world where information and knowledge is an asset, the need to 'protect' the Internet became a key feature of global Internet access.

The following points should be borne in mind in order to help prevent security breaches:

- A prominently displayed security policy to ensure user awareness
- Restricted access to certain types of content or message attachments
- Secure computer rooms
- Password controlled access to the system
- Encryption of data in sensitive areas; for example, where credit card details are held
- Firewalls to protect the system from unauthorised access
- Specialist security detection software (e.g. virus software)
- Security alerts and reports
- Engage a reputable firm to perform attack and penetration tests.

Overview of Recent Developments

Internet Access

The UK government, which is committed to putting all government services online, has so far spent around £8bn on obliging its departments and the wider public sector to comply with its targets. It was originally estimated that 24-hour e-access to government services would save £3.5 billion per year, and a target date of end 2005 was set to 'e-enable' all public services. A special government department, the 'Office of the e-Envoy' employing 400 people was created to deliver on this promise. The 2005 target was met in terms of creating online channels into government, but the underlying government bureaucracy remains largely unchanged. According to Colin Muid, who ran the early 'skunkworks' programme examining how government could be changed through technology: 'Back in 1996 we were saying "let's clear up this mess". Now, we've got a digital interface to that mess' (Cross, 2006).

There is certainly little evidence as yet that all customers want or need online transactions, let alone any sign of payback from the government's investment (Vincent 2004). E-government spending to date will be dwarfed in the next few years by projects such as the NHS National Programme for IT and the integration of Customs and Excise and Inland Revenue information systems. Historically, the success rate for implementation of large-scale computer projects is reported to be around 17 percent. The dotcom crash is another recent example of the consequences of 'blind faith' in new technology without consideration of the social implications, and it would appear that the UK government is now exercising some cautious optimism with the statement that 'some of the newer technologies today will be mainstream by 2011 and the time will be right to roll out their widespread exploitation' (Transformational Government Enabled by Technology, 2006: 19).

Diagram 1.1 shows how the profile of Internet access in the UK has changed since the mid-1990s. The rate of growth in Internet use has recently slowed significantly and is starting to plateau at around 60 percent of the population. A report from the Office of National Statistics (Oxford Internet Institute 2005) highlighted that of the 32 percent of UK adults who had still never used the Internet, 43 percent had no interest in doing so and 33 percent felt that they lacked the knowledge or the confidence to do so. These findings suggested the need for new features to attract users to existing channels, investment in new channels such as digital television and mobile, and a government policy focus on access incentives and training if online channels were to become truly mainstream.

Diagram 1.2 illustrates the take up of a range of technologies in terms of the extent of their penetration into mainstream usage. It highlights significant potential for growth in technologies such as VOIP and 3G mobile. Business demands on the Internet are for increasing speed and greater bandwidth. Recent improvement in the availability of broadband has helped to drive e-business by offering rapid transfer rates to open up multimedia delivery to small and medium-sized firms (SMEs) and individuals.

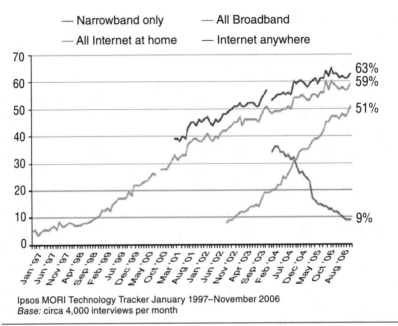

— Narrowband only   — All Broadband
— All Internet at home   — Internet anywhere

Ipsos MORI Technology Tracker January 1997–November 2006
Base: circa 4,000 interviews per month

Diagram 1.1 Internet access mechanisms. http://www.ipsos-mori.com/technology

We will examine these issues further in Chapter 7.

Currently more than one billion people around the world have Internet access but the distribution across countries is anything but even. Why does the digital economy appear to be flourishing more

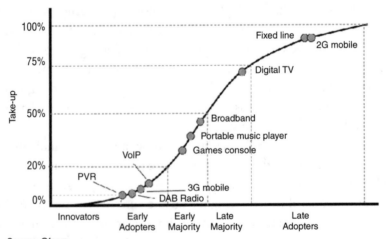

Source: Ofcom
Note: Pentetration of DAB radio, 3G mobile and VoIP are based on individuals; other technologies are based on households

Diagram 1.2 Adoption curve for communications services and devices, Q1 2006.

in some countries than others? The obvious answers concerning the health of the economy and the sophistication of the telephone infra-structure do not tell the whole story. For example, in France, one of the wealthiest economies in the world, only 39 percent of the population can be classified as 'active' Internet users, compared with 45 percent in the UK. Culture may provide one answer—the accepted language of the Web is English, which is less than popular in France. Scandina-vian countries are known for their language skills, and active Internet penetration in Sweden is 55 percent. In Asia, the sheer diversity of languages and cultures has slowed the spread of the Internet. It may cross national borders with ease, but linguistic barriers are proving harder to negotiate. For this reason, Latin America is predicted to be a major online force in the years to come, because only two languages separate the entire continent. It is also evident that countries respect-ing individualism and entrepreneurship are more likely to embrace e-commerce. In some Middle East countries, even public access to the Internet is difficult, with systems heavily policed by the government.

However, the most important ingredient for increasing Internet penetration is a modern telephone system. The impact of mobile phones is also likely to be pivotal in the next generation of web devel-opments. Wireless transmission has brought speedy communications to countries which were too poor to build traditional telephone net-works. Uruguay for example, is not saddled with crumbling analogue cabling, and it now has one of the most advanced digital networks in the world.

Activity 1.1

Examine the resources of ClickZ (now available at www.clickz.com/stats) which also give details of the level of Internet access in a number of different countries. This picture is incomplete with-out an understanding of the different demographics that apply within each country (age, sex, income, geographical region). See www.mori.com/technology/techtracker.shtml for UK demo-graphic data. What does this add to your understanding of UK Internet users?

Web 2.0

Web 2.0 is not an actual technology but instead it describes a sea change in how we use the Internet. It facilitates interaction, social networks, community-based ranking systems and a rich user experience through emerging web technologies such as Really Simple Syndication (RSS). It also offers users open data formats that are cheap, sharable and easily editable. According to Tim O'Reilly, organiser of the first Web 2.0 Conference, Web 2.0 is 'an attitude not a technology', suggesting that it reflects a cultural change in the Web's development. But how can marketers maximise the opportunities inherent in these developments for the benefit of their brands, particularly when seeking interaction with experienced web users who resent intrusive and repetitive advertising? These are key themes that we will be addressing throughout the book, particularly in Chapters 9 and 12.

Some early examples of successful Web 2.0 sites are Jobster (www. Jobster.com) which uses social networking to fill employment positions and American Express (www.amex.com) which uses Web 2.0 technology throughout to improve the user experience.

Key e-Marketing Definitions

This section introduces you to some of the key Internet terminology and new business frameworks that you will encounter in this book.

Intranets

An intranet can be defined as:

> A network within a single company which enables access to company information using the familiar tools of the Internet such as web browsers and e-mail. Only staff within a company can access the intranet, which will be password protected. (Chaffey 2004: 26)

Intranets are becoming increasingly popular within organisations as a communication tool to collect and disseminate information. Firewalls (special security software applications) are necessary to prevent access to confidential information, such as employee records, which can then be accessed by password only. Like the Internet itself, an intranet can work all over the globe for a company that has offices based in several countries, meaning that it is not constrained by geography.

The main benefits of an intranet to the organisation are improved competitiveness through operational efficiency and productivity. An Intranet can also create a culture within the firm that is conducive to information sharing and collaboration.

The advantages of intranets can be summarised as follows:

- Inexpensive to implement (an intranet can be established on a company's existing network with little training needed)
- Easy to use, just point and click (this is because it works on the same technology as a web page—thus employees already know how to navigate around sites)
- Saves time and money by providing better information faster (information which has been previously locked away in cupboards or in the heads of key staff is now accessible to all at the click of a mouse)
- Based on open standards (the key to the intranet is freedom of information)
- Scaleable and flexible (an intranet can be managed and changed instantly)
- Connects across disparate platforms (an intranet can work for a business which has various regional offices within or outside a country)
- Puts users in control of their data (an intranet can allow and enable users to update their data)
- Improved decision making due to the fact that employees now have access to far more information at their fingertips and so can make more informed and thus better decisions
- Empowered users (if they are allowed to by management, users can edit and control their data and thus begin to become empowered)
- Builds a culture of sharing and collaboration (this is created through the intranet's ability to enable documents to be shared and online collaboration of projects to happen)

- Facilitates organisational learning (developed through the culture that the intranet creates and achieved via the data that the intranet provides for everybody to see)
- Breaks down bureaucracy (mainly achieved through the reduction in paper required, but also by the empowering of users)
- Improved quality of life at work (an intranet creates this not only through the modified culture, but by empowering the users and creating a sense of ownership for them)
- Improved productivity (this is the sum of both the tangible and intangible benefits described).

However, problems can also occur with the use of intranets:

- They have to be continually updated to be credible, which is a resource-intensive job.
- Intranets which merely mimic existing inefficient processes will not add much value.
- Poor design can mean that information is hard to find, and the resource will be under-utilised.
- If there is no means of control over Intranet content, chaos can result through over-use.
- Responsibilities for development and maintenance must be clearly understood.

Extranets

'An extranet is formed by extending the intranet beyond a company to customers, suppliers, collaborators or even competitors. This is again password-protected to prevent access by general Internet users' (Chaffey 2004: 26).

Activity 1.2

Jakob Nielsen specialises in usability, particularly web usability. Take a look at his website www.useit.com. What rules regarding intranet design can you find?

Activity 1.3

Initially, the only language used for the web was HTML. However as the need for data exchange has grown, other languages have taken off. Take a look at www.xml.com/—why do you think XML has become so popular?

Extranets are a rapidly developing area and significant cost savings can be generated by companies that are linked electronically through extranets along the supply chain. They also offer the opportunity to cut out intermediaries in some cases, (disintermediation) while introducing new types of intermediary (reintermediation) in others. Kodak (www.kodak.com) has spent considerable resources on developing an extranet. When first set up in 1999, the site had links to about 25 external organisations. Once set up, they were adding sites at the rate of two per week. The extranet is primarily used for information exchange with dealers, contractors, joint-venture partners and key suppliers.

e-Commerce or e-Business?

There are many definitions of e-commerce. The narrowest definitions refer to it simply as the buying and selling of goods online, though Zwass defines e-commerce more broadly:

> the sharing of business information, maintaining business relationships, and conducting business transactions by means of telecommunications networks. (Zwass 1998: 157)

Chaffey treats e-commerce as a subset of e-business because the former does not include intra-business functions such as the processing of a purchase order. He quotes the following definition of e-business:

> When a business has fully integrated information and communication technologies (ICTs) into its operations, potentially redesigning its business processes around ICT or completely reinventing its business model....e-business, is understood to be the integration of all

these activities with the internal processes of a business through ICT. (Chaffey 2006: 8)

In its broadest form therefore, e-commerce can be regarded as synonymous with IBM's expression 'e-business' which is a holistic concept covering the full range of business functions and structures effected by the Internet, and this is the approach taken here. Agonising over definitions is probably a waste of effort as these terms are likely to be transitory as the Internet becomes an integral part of business activity. In fact, they can be likened to early descriptions of the motor car as a 'horseless carriage'.

The principal driver for the take up of e-commerce is economics. For example, the cost of processing a financial transaction online can be as little as 1 percent of doing the same at a bank branch using traditional paper methods. So once fixed costs such as equipment and telecommunications lines are covered, the marginal cost of servicing online transactions can be very low.

Fischer (1999) described the scope of e-commerce revenue under headings that can be summarised as the '5Cs':

- *Connection*—AOL, for example (www.aol.com), as an Internet Service Provider (ISP) obtains its revenues from connecting customers to the Internet.
- *Commercials*—Some companies obtain revenue from displaying advertisements for other companies. Key sites such as Yahoo! with millions of visitors can charge high fees. Smaller, more specialist websites can attract advertisers with relevant products or services to offer; for example, an estate agent's website might carry advertisements for removal companies or solicitors.
- *Commerce*—Goods or services are sold directly to customers online.
- *Content*—Some sites can charge for content that can be accessed from the site. For example a market research firm may offer research reports for sale.
- *Community*—Specialist online community sites may be able to charge a membership fee for access and discussion participation.

Business to Consumer (B2C) e-commerce refers to the selling of goods and/or services directly to consumers by businesses. The classic example is Amazon (www.amazon.com) which retails in excess of 1.5 million book titles online and has extended its sales into other products including music CDs, videos, and games.

Business to Business (B2B) e-commerce refers to the selling of goods and/or services by one company to another as part of their supply chain (see, for example, www.marshalls.com).

Consumer to Consumer (C2C) refers to the selling of goods and/or services between individuals; see, for example, the auction house eBay (www.ebay.com).

Consumer to Business (C2B) refers to consumers generating trade with businesses; for example, www.letsbuyit.com allows consumers to come together and aggregate purchasing power to command discounts normally reserved for large organisations.

Activity 1.4

New descriptors like these are appearing on a regular basis, can you think of any more?

To give you a flavour of the scope of e-business, it is worth introducing the dominant models of e-business strategy in the marketplace today (Lumpkin and Dess 2004). We will be covering these models in more detail in Chapter 4:

- Commission-based businesses provide services for a fee; for example, www.eBay.com.
- Advertising-based businesses provide content and charge fees to advertisers wishing to target the viewers of the content; for example, www.yahoo.com.
- Markup-based businesses acquire products, mark up the price and resell at a profit; for example, www.amazon.co.uk.
- Production-based businesses convert raw materials into specific products, often customised by the end user; for example, www.dell.com.

- Referral-based businesses direct customers to another company for a fee; for example, www.yesmail.com which generates leads through e-mail marketing.
- Subscription-based businesses charge a fee to viewers for providing content; for example, www.ft.com.
- Fee-for-service based businesses are a 'pay as you go' system; for example, www.eproject.com provides virtual workspaces to allow online collaboration.

Case Study—Amazon

Amazon.com is often regarded as a template for successful e-business. Amazon's success is based on its disintermediation of the supply chain by combining the role of wholesalers and retailers, acting as a single-link online intermediary between publishers and individual consumers. The web-based business model offers easy purchasing, a huge selection and fast delivery. The cost savings that Amazon's model achieves also allows it to sustain a price advantage over many traditional booksellers. Amazon is in fact not so much a force of disintermediation, as a cybermediary merchant fulfilling informational, transactional and logistical operations. Part of the reason for Amazon's success is because it has been able to establish a trust role in the marketplace by creating a strong brand name. Although customisation of its products is at best highly limited, its software enables it to achieve a higher degree of personalisation of its service. For example, on re-entering the website, returning customers are met with a personal greeting and suggested purchase offerings. Amazon also facilitates some customer-to-customer (C2C) interaction. This is not direct C2C interaction, but takes the form of customer reviews of books. Customers are invited to review a book or CD, and these reviews are published alongside the price and ordering information for each prod-

---

Activity 1.5

Amazon is not the only company to encourage C2C interaction of this kind. What other examples can you find?

uct. In this way, Amazon uses its customers to spread 'word of mouth' recommendations about its products.

Case Study: The Rise and Fall of Boo.com

Between 1998 and 2000 many traditional UK and European financial institutions began a surge of investment into new high technology business start-ups. Investment euphoria could be largely attributed to the commercial possibilities of the Internet. The Internet was not only regarded as a new channel for commerce but as an entirely new era in the retail industry. A huge rush of B2C dotcoms then ensued, supported by a pack of hungry venture capitalists determined to make millions from the 'new economy'. Unfortunately, misconstruing online ventures as a replacement for more traditional business has meant that many dotcoms tripped at the first hurdle and millions have been wasted.

Perhaps the most hyped of all the failures is that of Boo.com. This infamous company finally managed to launch after five failed attempts, squandered £90 million in investment capital and then went into receivership after only six months of trading. Boo was positioned as a leading site in fashion selling premium designer sports wear collections through the concept of 'geek chic'. The site was vastly over-ambitious, it operated out of a number of countries and contained ground-breaking innovations such as a virtual hostess, 3-D imaging and a virtual magazine called *Boom*.

What Went Wrong?

To be objective in this analysis we must also consider the business environment at the time of Boo. The whole of the UK was buzzing with talk of the fantastic opportunities of the new economy. As a result, the first valuations for dotcom start-ups were ridiculous as business credibility was measured through site traffic, click-throughs and page views rather than purchases and profit. Boo's biggest mistake was to misconstrue the new economy as a 'get rich quick' scheme. This attitude meant that valuable knowledge and experience accrued in traditional bricks and mortar retail was snubbed.

Boo's founders Ernst Malmsten (artist and poet) and Kajsa Leander (former model) had little business experience but were very inspirational characters. Before Boo they had founded a pioneering online bookstore in Sweden called Bokus. A good concept, however, is not enough in itself. Although charisma is an essential part of entrepreneurial management style, Malmsten and Leander lacked a basic understanding of business principles. They began to consider product diversification at a very early stage: 'We had invested millions in building a global retailing platform, we had established a powerful brand name, so why stop at clothes?' (Malmsten *et al.* 2001).

Once Malstem and Leander had raised enough capital to begin making strategic partnerships with headhunters, tax consultants and technology providers, they started a heavy PR strategy. Building a brand before a business platform is in place is risky, and Boo had over 230,000 registrations before the site was launched. As a result, they were unable to test their platform properly and had to invest over a million pounds just to ensure the site did not collapse due to high density of traffic. The international aspect of the site's growth was also problematic, although many of the issues involved could have been resolved with careful planning. For example, Boo discovered only through experience that Portugal needed every delivery package hand stamped with serial numbers and in Canada all returns were taxed.

Boo's culture was centred on the concept of youth, exuberance and creativity. The founders insisted that Boo was a lifestyle and not just a company. The company encouraged extravagant alcohol-fuelled nights out at top nightclubs and celebrity parties. Many of the staff were young and inexperienced yet were expected to perform well with little guidance. For example, the founders hired an ex-club DJ to coordinate the opening of their new Paris operations. It would seem a ludicrous decision to employ someone with no management experience to open and coordinate overseas operations, just because their personality complemented the brand image.

If they had received proper scrutiny from their financial advisors and prospective investors, Boo's founders would have been forced to be more realistic and substantiate their amateurish business plan with suitable research, costings, checks and balances. Any business start-up needs a strong plan complete with a business and marketing strategy, objectives, financial co-ordination and resource allocation. A full environmental, competitive and customer analysis is an essential component of such a plan.

Boo managed to spend $30 million even before the site launched five months late in November 2000. Company finance paid for the founders' executive apartments, first class travel, expensive business trips and hotels, holidays, and living expenses. At this point it was realised that 'sales would be less than 10% of the promised target' (Malmsten *et al.* 2001). This revelation meant that Boo needed another $20 million to enable it to continue trading until February 2001. It was only after investors would not release more capital in March that Boo management started to discuss spending cuts. Despite the fact that the company managed to save $27 million in cut-backs and that their weekly revenue was higher than that of Amazon, they failed to secure further funding and Boo went into receivership.

A misunderstanding of what constituted good marketing was also a large factor in Boo's demise. Abel Harpen of Texas Pacific, one of Boo's investment contacts, said Boo had only two assets, 'brand and back-end logistics' (Malmsten *et al.* 2001). Boo's brand strength was no accident. Kajsa and her team went to great lengths to ensure that Boo built an extremely strong brand in only six months as a result of a dedicated and creative promotional campaign. External promotion was also complemented by *Boom*, the online fashion magazine which they hoped would transform Boo into a 'lifestyle choice' rather than just a place to shop.

Brand image was so important that the smallest detail was considered even if it was costly. Boo's rationale for its average monthly spending of $10 million was that the expenditure was necessary to create a multi-national company with the strongest brand. For example, Boo paid for the world's most famous hair-stylist, Eugene Souleman to sit with a graphics designer for a day and design the hairstyle of the site's virtual hostess Miss Boo. This seems like an expensive extravagance that served no purpose, especially because the hairstyle was changed at a later date....

One of the most important aspects of marketing for a new business is market research. Boo's founders felt that such 'old economy' rules no longer applied, but research might actually have prevented one of

Boo's biggest mistakes, which was to overestimate the technical capabilities of its potential customers. The site was so technically advanced that to view the graphics customers had to use special software (plugins). Not being able to view the site gave many potential customers a rational reason not to revisit it. The founders believed that after six months of trading they would have a loyal customer base of 50,000. This figure had no validity and seemed to have been plucked from thin air. Boo also relied on groundless estimates of the amount of supplier discounts that could be obtained, which impacted adversely on pricing policy.

Boo was a good concept, but the project was too ambitious because the market, systems and customers were not sophisticated enough to maximise the potential of the technology. The strategy may have been more successful if they had started small, building the brand more slowly over time. The virtual magazine *Boom*, the virtual shop assistant Miss Boo and the 3D imaging should have been introduced gradually as the site developed a loyal customer base. If Boo is compared with successful fashion websites there are many differences. For example, Zoom.com has managed to survive due to its unique positioning and a strong strategy. The site is trendy yet accessible and manages to combine simple navigation and shopping processes with desirable products. Lessons about tight budgeting, gradual development in a climate of uncertainty and substantial customer research can also be learnt from traditional retailers' commercial sites such as Next.com and Debenhams.com.

It can also be argued that Boo's experienced investors and contractors could have helped control the company rather than watch it head rapidly towards destruction. Unfortunately, in line with the spirit of the times, the venture capitalists concentrated on getting a high valuation for a company that was no more than a creative concept, with the hope of selling it on at a huge profit. Therefore, they were concerned with short-term profit rather than long-term success.

Under new management Boo became a content-only site used as an advertising platform for established fashion brand home sites. Fashionmall.com bought the Boo brand and has sold its assets (state of the art technology in which millions was invested) for just £250,000.

Activity 1.6

With the increase in computer power and broadband access, if Boo.com were launched in 2007, do you think they would they have been more successful?

Summary

This broad-ranging chapter has set the scene for more detailed discussion of specific topics later on in the book. You should now have an appreciation of where the Internet has come from, understand how its scope as a business tool has evolved over the past 10–12 years and also be aware of the 'bigger picture' within which e-marketing takes place. These environmental issues will be considered in more detail in Chapter 2.

It is easy to get carried away about the potential of the Internet, but several problems remain:

- The sheer volume of traffic can cause delays and lock-outs.
- Security breeches by hackers and viruses hit the headlines regularly.
- A large proportion of the world's population still do not have Internet access.

Questions

Question 1.1

What would you see as a major danger for societies inherent in the varying levels of Internet access in different parts of the world?

Question 1.1 Feedback

Evidence is mounting that the world may be dividing along the lines of the 'information haves' and the 'information have-nots', meaning that people without Internet access become increasingly disadvantaged and disenfranchised.

Question 1.2

Despite the benefits listed in the chapter, why do you think companies might still be reluctant to make full use of an intranet?

Question 1.2 Feedback

A cynic might claim that 'information is power' and that individuals in possession of certain important information have a vested interest in keeping such data to themselves. Senior management may be reluctant to disclose details of strategy in the belief that it is a mark of status to have access to privileged information. Fortunately, attitudes like this appear to be less common these days because traditional hierarchies of management are being broken down in many firms.

Question 1.3

Can you anticipate any problems associated with operating through extranets?

Question 1.3 Feedback

The issue of exactly who should be allowed access to data could be problematic. Imagine, for example, a situation where customer e-mail addresses have been collected and each partner company wants to make use of them to implement an e-mail marketing campaign.

Question 1.4

What particular benefits does e-commerce offer the business customer?

Question 1.4 Feedback
- Lower purchasing overheads
- Greater choice
- Faster fulfilment cycle time
- Greater ability to supply information
- Lower cost than EDI
- Ease of swapping between suppliers

Question 1.5

What particular benefits does e-commerce offer the consumer?

Question 1.5 Feedback

- Demands for increased choice
- Demands for information
- Demands for inter-active, online support
- Avoidance of travel and search costs
- 24-hour availability

Question 1.6

Why do you think the ethos of not-for-profit was so important to the uptake of the Internet?

Question 1.6 Feedback

One of the key features of the World Wide Web is that anyone can use the standards developed by the World Wide Web consortium. Tim Berners-Lee (who is credited as the inventor of the web) is adamant that if users had been charged for using the technology developed then it would have never taken off as it did, despite the fact that it could have made him a multi-millionaire!

Question 1.7

One security concern that comes up in the media time and time again is computer viruses. Why do you think viruses cause so much fuss?

Question 1.7 Feedback

Computer viruses can range from displaying an annoying message on your screen to wiping entire computer systems. Clicking on what looks like a harmless e-mail message can lead to hours of recovery efforts, if not irreparable damage. One recent example is the 'Mydoom' worm. It is estimated that this worm infected approximately a quarter-million computers in a single day. In March 1999, the 'Melissa' virus was so powerful that it forced Microsoft as well as a number of other large companies to turn off their e-mail systems until the virus could be contained.

Feedback on Activities

Activity 1.1

Knowing the number of online users in a particular country is just the starting point. Much more detail is required for a business that is considering whether to develop its online marketing channels; for example, the following questions need to be asked:

- How many of these users can be classified as 'active'?
- What percentage of users have high speed Internet connections?
- Are users concentrated in a particularly wealthy geographic region; for example the South East of England?
- What is the percentage breakdown of Internet access channels used by the population (PC-based, mobile, digital television)?

Activity 1.2

Some of Nielsen's 'best practice' rules include:

- Encouraging employees to self-publish content
- Keeping the intranet up-to-date
- Supporting factory-floor employees
- Collaborating with clients through an extranet
- Customer relationship management
- Consistent navigation
- Multilingual intranets; supporting international employees
- Online video; executive communications
- Collaboration tools and discussion boards
- E-learning features on intranets
- Intranet as driver for corporate culture and to promote corporate values
- Intranet search
- Development process for intranet redesigns

- Promoting intranet launches; campaigns to encourage use of new features
- Staffing of intranet teams; where they report in the organization
- Updating and maintaining standards and guidelines for intranet design.

Activity 1.3

The problem with HTML is that the language is all about how information is presented on the screen. All the instructions ('tags') are set out by the World Wide Web consortium (www.w3.org) . XML on the other hand is a much more flexible language. Anyone can define what the tags mean. This allows for a much greater flexibility when it comes to data exchange. Thus companies wishing to exchange data do not have to rely on alternative standards (such as EDI) when they can simply agree on an XML format between them. For example XML is used in the 'Open eBook' standard which allows publishers to use this common format to place texts online.

Activity 1.4

Other examples include the government; for example:

- G2C—Government-to-Citizen or Customer: this would include payment of taxes, for example.
- G2B—Government-to-Business: although this becomes very similar to B2B in some cases.

Activity 1.5

There are many examples of this kind of product review available. The computer components company e-buyer (www.ebuyer.com), for example, allows customers to review all its productions with a rating and a comment. The Internet Movie Database (uk.imdb.com), for example, relies heavily on user reviews to keep its site up-to-date. More generally, sites such as Wikipedia, My Space and YouTube are maintained entirely with user generated content. Interestingly, Amazon did not initially allow customer reviews of its products; this was left to an editorial department. However, as the number of books available from

Amazon increased, it become impossible for the staff to give all books a review and they therefore allowed customers to review books as well. Eventually, only the user reviews remained.

Activity 1.6

Obviously, it is impossible to accurately predict what would happen with the current higher speed Internet connections. However, it is important to note that companies are still making similar mistakes by offering highly graphical or flash sites with no alternative to those Internet users who either have slower connections or lack the software to run such sites. Indeed, while broadband is becoming both faster and more popular in the UK, many Internet users still use a dial-up connection. Net-savvy companies are now offering both high and low speed alternatives so as not to put off any potential customers (e.g. www.bbc.co.uk).

Web Links

www.clickz.com
   Latest statistics of worldwide Internet growth
www.durlacher.co.uk
   Quarterly research reports on Internet usage from a UK perspective
www.intranetroadmap.com
   Useful student resource with definitions, links and examples
www.ebusinessroadmap.org
   Useful student resource with definitions, links and examples
www.whatis.com
   Directory of Internet terminology
www.whatis.com/tour.htm
   An introduction to how the internet works
www.butlergroup.co.uk
   Reports on latest developments in electronic commerce from a UK perspective
www.kpmg.co.uk
   Produces regular free reports on the latest trends in e-commerce
www.startups.co.uk
   Allows subscription to a new monthly paper-based magazine containing up to date case studies and updates on latest trends
www.w3.org
   An organisation responsible for defining worldwide standards for the Internet

2

THE e-BUSINESS ENVIRONMENT

Introduction

The environment within which a company is operating will impact significantly upon the e-marketing strategies that it develops and implements. In this session we examine the influence of the 'big picture' by breaking it down into its component parts through 'PEST' analysis. PEST is a framework for evaluating the political, economic, social and technological environments within which the business is operating.

Topics Covered in this Chapter

- The role of PEST analysis
  - Political and legal factors
  - Economic factors
  - Social factors
  - Technological factors
  - Ethical factors.

Learning Objectives

By the end of the chapter you should be able to:

- Discuss and evaluate the key issues prevailing in the e-marketing macro-environment, specifically with regard to:
  - The inter-relationship between legal and ethical considerations

- Intellectual property rights
- The 'digital divide'
- Data protection
- Online payment systems.

Recommended Reading

Woolgar, S. (2003) *Virtual Society?* Oxford: Oxford University Press

PEST Analysis

From a company's perspective, the macro-environment is comparatively remote from the day to day activities of the business. While the company has some degree of control over its immediate stakeholders, it cannot directly influence the 'bigger picture' of the macro-environment. PEST analysis allows the company to monitor and be aware of the implications of likely changes in the macro-environment, even if it cannot directly control them. We will now examine the various components in turn.

Political and Legal Factors

A comprehensive international legislation system that applies to global online trading does not exist at present and is not expected in the foreseeable future. Even within the United States, which is comparatively advanced in its use of the Internet, legal issues such as the validity of digital signatures have caused significant disagreements. Organisations such as the United Nations on International Trade Law have been actively calling for global co-ordination of appropriate legal structures.

Beynon-Davies (2004) notes that there are currently unresolved tensions between two schools of thought on the relationship between e-business and legislation:

- Entirely new laws are required to cover the practical implications of e-business operations which are regarded as entirely unique business activities.

- e-business is just the latest in a long line of new technologies which companies have adopted. Existing laws still apply and they will evolve as necessary to cover the specific requirements of e-business.

It seems that neither of these viewpoints has yet come to dominate. In this section we will highlight some recent legal developments from around the world.

Intellectual Property   Because the copyright legislation on the Internet is complex and vague, many website operators are re-using information from other sites. Comparison-shopping sites such as www.moneysupermarket.com, for example, rely heavily on aggregating information existing on other sites and presenting it in a comparative format.

Another contentious issue concerns domain name conflict. There have been a number of cases whereby individuals (known as 'cybersquatters') have registered domain names that resemble established brands or generic terminology and then attempted to sell the right to use that name to the company concerned; for example, Chen (2001) notes that the address 'business.com' was sold for $7.5 million and 'wine.com' for $3 million. The author goes on to describe the UK case of *Marks and Spencer* v. *One in a Million Limited* and others, in which M&S sued for infringement of its trademark after the defendant registered the domain name marksandspencer.com and demanded money in exchange for handing it over. The courts found in favour of M&S and One in a Million was prevented from using the name or trying to sell it to anyone else.

This example also illustrates that copying anything from a website is very easy—merely a matter of cutting and pasting the code—so that protection of any intellectual property is very difficult. A famous example concerns the ongoing dispute over the piracy of music on MP3 sites, which are file compression formats allowing songs to be freely transmitted over the web and downloaded to an individual's computer. Peer-to-Peer (P2P) sites such as www.napster.com allowed users to share the content of their computer's hard drives and this technological innovation makes the world-wide sharing of music files even easier.

Napster was first released in 1999 by a student, Shawn Fanning, who wanted to share his music collection with his friends. Napster allowed users to share their music collections via the Napster central servers. By February 2001 the number of Napster users peaked at over 13 million. However, as the majority of the songs shared were copyrighted the music industry filed suit almost immediately. The service was shut down in July 2002 despite Napster users arguing that this action would only mean replacement by an alternative peer-to-peer (P2P) service. At its bankruptcy auction the Napster brand was sold to Roxio Inc, and Napster 2.0 was re-released in 2004 as a legitimate 'paid-for' music download service.

Activity 2.1

Take a look at www.napster.co.uk now. Given its origins and history of troubles with the traditional music industry, how might this adversely affect the brand image of Napster 2.0?

Case Study: BitTorrent

BitTorrent is a peer-to-peer file sharing protocol that can be used to download any form of electronic file—from application software to MP3s and films. The advantage of BitTorrent is that it dramatically reduces the pressure on servers as files can be downloaded from other users rather than a central point. There are many uses for this technology—both legitimate and not so legitimate. Many companies that produce open-source software encourage users to download their software via BitTorrent rather than directly from their own servers. Examples include OpenOffice.org (www.openoffice.org) and Linux distributors SUSE (www.novell.com/linux) and Fedora (www.redhat.com/fedora/).

However, BitTorrent also receives a great deal of negative press as it can be used for illegal downloads. Sites such as Azureus (azureus.sourceforge.net) place no restrictions on what files can be downloaded. As a result it can be used to download a wealth of copyrighted material such as films, TV programmes, books, and music. This has led many BitTorrent sites, such as Legal Torrents (www.legaltorrents. com) to promote the use of legal downloads only.

The music and film industries are starting to see the benefits of legitimately using the BitTorrent technology, although it has not yet been taken up by any of the principal music or film producers. Sub Pop Records is a small label that has released its 1000 or so albums via BitTorrent. Many individual bands have also started to use the technology to make live performances and videos available for free. While many companies have not made full use of the BitTorrent technology, many still make content available via their own websites. As a result of the pressure from illegal downloads, many US TV companies have started to provide a great deal of content online (quite a bit of it free with some advertising). The US network ABC currently shows some of TV's most popular programmes such as "Desperate Housewives", "Grey's Anatomy" and "Lost". From their streaming website (dynamic.abc.go.com/streaming/landing) it is possible to view six of their most popular programmes for free (as long as you're in the US). Each programme has three 30 second ad breaks as you watch the show. Similar services are available for music such as www.pandora. com and www.last.fm.

Contractual Agreements Electronic contractual agreements are part and parcel of e-commerce. The registration procedure is part of the purchasing process and requests the buyer to scroll through a set of contract terms. The purchase sequence is only completed when the buyer has clicked his agreement to the terms and conditions presented. The validity of such an electronic contract has been tested already through the US courts but it is not certain that it is globally acceptable. Consumer protection laws vary from country to country and the global operator must be aware of differing obligations that could impact on the validity of the transaction performed.

The importance of keeping track of changes in legislation that will affect e-business cannot be under-estimated. Certain legislation such as the law passed by the European Union regarding e-mail marketing could have far reaching consequences. Effective from 1st March 2001 this law states that if a dispute occurs between a consumer and an online retailer in any of the 15 countries of the EU, the consumer may file a suit in his or her own country. In addition, the Privacy and Electronic Communications Regulations (2003) made 'opt out' marketing communications to individual consumers illegal, but many companies still continue to operate in this way. This issue will be explored further in Chapters 6 and 9.

The European Union's Distance Selling Directive 2000 (updated April 2005) offers protection to consumers buying goods online. The retailer must now provide:

- Clear information about the goods or services offered.
- Written confirmation of this information after a purchase is made.
- A 'cooling off' period during which an order can be cancelled without any reason and a full refund made.
- A full refund if the goods or services are not provided within 30 days.

Full details of recent UK legislation impacting upon e-business can be found at www.informationcommissioner.gov.uk and www.dti.gov.uk. There will of course be differences between the e-business legislation passed in various parts of the world and the applicable government website is usually a good starting point if you are trying to identify the regulations pertaining to a particular country.

Small firms that have historically thrived from the relative freedom offered by the Internet may well find it harder now to maintain control over their direct e-mail marketing campaigns in this increasingly legislative environment.

Another new piece of legislation which impacts upon the Internet is the US crackdown on online gambling. American firms are no longer allowed to accept bets placed over the Internet in an attempt to restrict organised crime and money laundering. Online gambling has been a huge growth area in recent years, but this new legislation could put a stop to that. The UK government's position is to regulate online gambling rather than prohibit it, with the Gambling Commission approving UK-based sites which meet best practice guidelines. Operators will not be allowed to target children and they must keep customers informed about how much money they have spent.

Activity 2.2

Take a look at www.informationcommissioner.gov.uk. What guidance is available regarding data protection?

Data Protection   In the UK the Data Protection Act 1984 (and later amendments) focuses on the information that companies hold on customers and how individuals can access it and ensure it is correct. Although of course this act pre-dates the Internet the principles involved are exactly the same.

Economic Factors

It is important that an online sales effort should also take into account the variety of currencies and country linked value added tax (VAT) systems. Prospective customers may be reluctant to commit to an online transaction in a 'foreign' currency due to the uncertainty presented by the daily fluctuation of exchange rates. A simple solution is to add an interactive currency calculator to the site, which will give the customer a rough idea of the cost of the product or service and an indication if it is worth proceeding with the purchase.

A better solution would be to offer a payment system that not only performs currency calculations but also calculates VAT by country and product or service category. The best systems currently available automatically update the currency conversion and tax rates, (relieving the website operator of a daily burden) and can be used with any payment system on the market. An example of such a multi-currency payment system is WorldPay (www.worldpay.com) which offers the website operator the facility of offering products or services in more than 100 currencies. By having the exchange rate updated daily, the customer will see the real value of purchases and be able to make a meaningful comparison with local stores. Paypal (www.paypal.com) is another popular payment system, allowing over 100 million worldwide users to either send or receive financial payments safely and securely. With many country specific sites (for example, the UK site www.paypal.co.uk) it has a particularly popular way to pay for items on auction sites such as eBay. More recently, Paypal Mobile has allowed users to make payments via their mobile phone.

Transportation within European countries has historically been burdened with rules and regulations. For example, a trucker transporting goods from Glasgow to Athens used to spend 30 percent of its time on border crossings, waiting and filling out up to 200 forms. These inefficiencies are mercifully now a thing of the past. In order to move goods between EU member states, only one simplified transit document is required and many of the custom formalities have been eliminated. Payment systems within Europe have now largely been standardised with the Euro. These developments are encouraging more firms to take advantage of the Internet's market development capabilities, meaning the ability to extend their geographic reach at relatively low cost and risk.

Social Factors

The Digital Divide   At a local as well as a global level, access to the Internet is far from universal. In 2005 it was estimated that 1.08 billion people had Internet access (www.clickz.com/stats). This may seem a lot, but in fact it is just 16.7 percent of the world's population, and furthermore 50 percent of the global population have yet to make a telephone call, let alone access the Internet. More than 80 percent of those with Internet access are in North America and Europe. So rather than being a social leveller, the Internet is potentially yet another divide between rich and poor, the 'haves' and 'have-nots', the networked and the non-networked. Furthermore, the gap between the advantages associated with being online and the disadvantages of not being online is continuing to widen.

The 'digital divide' is confirmed by a report from the US Digital Divide Task Force (www.ntia.doc.gov) which notes that:

- Disabled people are only half as likely to have Internet access as the able-bodied.
- Access is less common in households with low income levels.
- There are large differences in penetration rates between different ethnic groups.

- No significant differences exist between male and female users.

According to the UK's National Statistics Omnibus Survey (2006) the percentage of households able to access the Internet varied between different parts of the country. The region with the highest percentage was the South East with 66 percent. The area with the lowest access level was Scotland with 48 percent. Overall, 40 percent of UK households, or 69 percent of households that had Internet access, had a broadband Internet connection. London had the highest level of households with broadband Internet access at 49 percent and Northern Ireland had the lowest level at 28 percent. The annual increases in the level of broadband access vary from 17 percentage points in London and the East of England to 4 percentage points in the West Midlands.

There is still a large divide between the young and the old, with 83 percent of the 16 to 24 age group regularly accessing the Internet

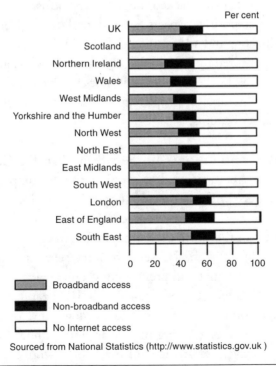

Per cent

Broadband access

Non-broadband access

No Internet access

Sourced from National Statistics (http://www.statistics.gov.uk)

Diagram 2.1   Percentage of UK households with Internet access, 2006.

	Percentage of UK Households
Don't need Internet because not useful, not interesting etc.	24
Lack of skills	24
Equipment costs too high	14
Access costs too high (telephone etc.)	11
Other	9
Have access to Internet elsewhere	7
Privacy or security concerns	5
Don't want Internet because content harmful etc.	3
Physical disability	2

Sourced from National Statistics (www.statistics.gov.uk)

Diagram 2.2   Reasons why UK households do not have Internet access, 2006.

compared with 15 percent of the 65+ age group. This is also supported by data that show there are now only 10 percent of the 16 to 24 age group who have never used the Internet, compared with 82 percent of the 65+ age group. Of the 43 percent of households that did not have Internet access, 24 percent said that they didn't need the Internet and 24 percent said that they lacked the necessary skills.

There are also positive aspects to the digital divide. Look up www.thehungersite.com and add your 'click' to help feed the world's poor. This site is sponsored by large global corporations who pay fees to the charity according to the number of visitors received. In other words, the greater the number of people exposed to the advertisements, the more the charity benefits.

Inappropriate Website Content   In the US in 1996 the Communications Decency Act attempted to prohibit the online publication of 'indecent' material. The degree of success achieved is evidenced by the fact that some of the most frequently visited and effectively marketed websites in the world are pornographic in content. Legislation recently introduced in the US seeks to force schools to use web-filtering technologies that will prevent children viewing such material. The Children's Internet Protection Act (CIPA) targets three types of visual depictions: obscenity, child pornography, or in the case of minors, content that is 'harmful to minors'. Under CIPA, every school that receives certain federal funds or discounts must install a technology protection measure such as Internet blocking software to block student access to these types of images. The definitions of these categories are very specific and limited, guided by court precedent. Civil liberty organisations objected to this new law, claiming that parents should take responsibility for supervising their children's viewing. After all, one of the key drivers behind the early development of the Internet was the ability to share information freely and without censorship. For example, www.netnanny.com allows parents to restrict access to particular sites and prevent credit card or contact details being given out by children in chat rooms by automatically breaking the Internet connection if prohibited actions are instigated. It also keeps a record of all activity undertaken on the computer for monitoring purposes.

In 2001 a US court ruled that Yahoo! could ignore a French court ruling restricting the auction of Nazi memorabilia on the Yahoo! website. This case was critical because it indicated that national laws (in this case French anti-hate speech laws) could not be applied more broadly on the Internet. The judge ruled that the French order violated Americans' constitutionally-protected right to free speech. The case highlighted the growing tensions involved in regulating cyberspace, given the Internet can be accessed globally.

Chen (2001) noted a number of cases of government action taken in an attempt to control Internet content, for example:

- The Chinese government has installed software to filter foreign websites in order to remove any anti-communist information.
- In the United Arab Emirates the state telecommunications company Etisalat censors websites deemed to breech local moral values by disconnecting offending customers.

Case Study: Google China

In January 2006 Google was allowed to set up a Chinese site (www.google.cn), but with heavy restrictions. These restrictions included putting a stop to many of Google's most popular products such as Google News and its communication tools—e-mail (Google-mail), blogging (Blogger) and Internet Messaging (Google Talk).

However, it was criticised most for filtering its search results, a policy which was picked up very quickly by the blogging community and the mainstream press. For example, doing a Google image search for 'Tiananmen' produces entirely different results depending on whether you use the Chinese Google site or not. Indeed in June 2006, China went so far as to block the main Google homepage (www.google.com).

Google are not the only company to have these problems, Yahoo has also had issues in China. According to the *New York Times* (15 February 2006):

> The company [Yahoo], which has been providing web services in China since 1999, has been criticized for filtering the results of its China-based search engine. But its bigger problems began last fall when human rights advocates revealed that in 2004, a Chinese division of the company had turned over to Chinese authorities information on a journalist, Shi Tao, using an anonymous Yahoo e-mail account. Mr. Shi, who had sent a government missive on Tiananmen Square anniversary rites to foreign colleagues, was sentenced to 10 years in prison.

Technological Factors

One of the biggest technical concerns about online business activity is the issue of security. Developing the ability to protect information resources from unwanted access by hackers or viruses is a major headache for many organisations. The growth of the mobile Internet (see Chapter 7 for more detail), which enables employees increasingly to access company databases, and other internal information while on the move has piled additional pressure on security systems.

From a customer's perspective, the main worry involves the risk of credit card fraud if their details are stored electronically, although this risk is little different from that associated with other forms of credit card transactions. A number of research projects have found that reassurance over security is the primary factor in turning online browsers into buyers.

The attitude of customers towards new technology is critical to the success of e-business operations. Think, for example, of the ill-fated

Activity 2.3

Thinking about your own attitudes to technology, which of Rogers' classifications would you place yourself in—innovator, opinion leader, early majority, late majority or a laggard?

online retailer Boo.com profiled in Chapter 1, which squandered an impressive brand by making the technical features of the company website too advanced for its customers to deal with. At the time of Boo's launch in 2000 the vast majority of customers were restricted to slow dial-up Internet access, so a website which was based upon sophisticated technology was soon going to hit problems.

Rogers (1962) produced a classic bell-shaped curve to illustrate how new technologies became adopted by the different segments of the population. For any new invention, he classified 2.5 percent of the population as 'innovators' who were eager to try out something new, 13.5 percent as 'opinion leaders' who were early to market and encouraged others to follow their lead, 34 percent as 'early majority' who constituted the 'mass market', 34 percent as 'late majority' who were conservative in their tastes and 16 percent as 'laggards' who would hang onto the old ways for as long as possible. Knowing which group (or groups) that customers fit into is therefore essential when designing the scope and style of e-business operations.

Chapter 7 will consider the business implications of new online channels such as Digital TV and the mobile Internet in more detail. In Chapter 12 we will discuss the growth of Web 2.0 technologies such as blogging and social networking which are now making a large impact on the collaborative aspects of Internet use.

Ethical Factors

Overview   Companies have realised that competitive advantage can be gained by behaving (or in some cases being seen to behave!) in an ethical way. For example, NatWest bank has run an advertising campaign emphasising the abandonment of its branch closure programme. This follows considerable negative publicity accusing banks of disadvantaging the elderly or disabled by shutting branches in rural areas. The new policy indicates that NatWest is accepting a wider social responsibility by not taking branch closure decisions solely on economic grounds, and at the same time differentiating itself from its competitors. Such policies can in fact pay off in economic terms, because the value added to the brand and additional business gained from customers impressed by the company's standpoint can more than offset the costs of implementing socially responsible policies.

Internet communications have some important and distinctive ethical characteristics:

- The ease of communicating with many anonymous people simultaneously; for example, sending an unsolicited e-mail to a group can be construed as 'spamming'.
- The disembodied nature of electronic communication, which takes place in text, and hence does not convey tone of voice or other non-textual clues, although 'symbols' are increasingly used to convey, for example, a joke or happiness :)=☺, or sadness: (=☹. It is easy, therefore for the 'meaning' of the message to be misinterpreted.
- Where a common language is understood, communication of images, documents and complex ideas can be made across the world as long as the technology is available.
- Cyberspace is not secure. This means that transactions on the web can be accessed by those not party to the transaction. Security is improving, however, and of course terrestrial transactions are not 100 percent secure either.
- The 'borderless' nature of the Internet makes control extremely difficult. Attempts at national controls, such as prohibiting the purchase of Adolf Hitler's *Mein Kampf* over the Internet in Germany, have failed.
- Communication in cyberspace has extraordinary archiving capabilities. Internet sites accessed are recorded and firms can also track the cyberspace activities of those who have visited their website. There are clear implications here for consumer privacy, a topic to which we will now turn.

Privacy The rise of the Internet, which permits companies to get information about customers more easily than ever, has brought privacy issues to the centre stage. Consumer protection groups fear that businesses will use the opportunity to capture information about people who visit their websites. By merging this data with a wide range of publicly available information such as credit histories, phone calls and medical records, companies can accumulate vast databases of knowledge about their customers. This information can quite legitimately be used to develop relationships with the customer based on serving their specific needs, but the data could also perhaps be sold on to other interested parties for a significant fee.

'Cookies' are small text files which are planted on a user's computer when they visit a particular website as electronic tags. The purpose is to identify the customer in order to target him or her with specific promotional information. When you make a return visit to www. amazon.co.uk and are greeted with a personalised message, then a cookie is hard at work. It is possible to disable cookies as some customers consider them to be an invasion of privacy rather than a legitimate marketing tool. For more information about cookies see www. cookiecentral.com.

Kelly and Rowland (2000) reported that three privacy groups (Electronic Privacy Information Centre, Junkbusters and Privacy International) were able to force Intel, the world's largest computer chip maker, to allow consumers to switch off the user-identification features built into Intel chips. Although Intel claimed that its technology enhanced security on computer networks, critics claimed that it allowed merchants to build up electronic dossiers on customers and their transactions to a level of unacceptable detail.

To demonstrate to customers that they take their moral obligations seriously, firms can:

- Include a clearly displayed privacy policy on the website, explaining what information will be collected about the customer and how it will be used, and stating clearly that customer lists will not be sold on to third parties.
- Prevent unauthorised access by providing a secure section of the site within which collection of data and transactions can occur.

BoxActivity 2.4

Look up www.network-tools.com and try the following demonstrations:

The 'Privacy.net tracking demo' hotlink shows how cookies are placed on your system.

The 'website log files' hotlink shows what types of visitor information can be captured.

The fictional network of 27 sites illustrates how your online activity is tracked across the entire network and linked to your identity.

- Give customers the option of opting out or correcting information that is held about them.
- Sign up with an organisation such as www.truste.org which audits a website's privacy policies and provides a 'kitemark' to those meeting specified criteria.

A full list of privacy issues is covered by Which? Web Trader Code and can be found at www.which.net/trader.

Codes of Conduct Computer Professionals for Social Responsibility 'Electronic Privacy Principles' (1996) suggest that:

- Each employer should provide and act on clear policies regarding the privacy implications of the computing resources used in the workplace. The policies should explicitly describe:
- Acceptable use of electronic mail and computer resources, including personal use;
- Practices that may be used to enforce these policies, such as the interception and reading of electronic mail or scanning of hard disks;
- Penalties for non-compliance with these policies.

Codes of conduct can be criticised on the grounds that they are only for public relations purposes and just add to bureaucracy, that they ignore context and deny individual responsibility and moral diversity.

They do, however, have the advantage of offering some guidance in a chaotic Internet environment that so far lacks any common understanding of appropriate use.

SPAM (Sending Persistent Annoying Messages)   Unsolicited electronic junk mail known as 'SPAM' now makes up about 70 percent of all e-mail throughout the world, according to www.messagelabs.com. The practice is heavily frowned upon in the online community and offenders are known to be vulnerable to bulk retaliation that can be large enough to crash their systems. The Messagelabs website has some interesting statistics and free articles on both viruses and SPAM. Sending SPAM is a lucrative business. It costs spammers next to nothing to send out millions, even billions, of e-mail messages. If even a tiny percentage of a hundred million people buy something in response to a junk message, that can still add up to significant revenue.

Spammers steal, swap, or buy lists of valid e-mail addresses (and the addresses of people who have responded to spam command a premium). Spammers also build their own lists using special software that rapidly generates millions of random e-mail addresses from well-known providers, such as MSN Hotmail and others, and then sends messages to these addresses. Invalid e-mail accounts return e-mail to the sender, so the software very rapidly records which e-mail addresses are active and which are not. Some spammers also gather or harvest addresses from websites where people sign up for free offers, enter contests, and so on. Harvesters may also use programs (known as web bots) that trawl for e-mail addresses anywhere they're posted for all to see—on Internet white pages, job postings, newsgroups, message boards, chat rooms, and even personal web pages.

Spam can also potentially be dangerous to computers, an individual's bank account, and to privacy. Spammers can overwhelm a recipient with offers to buy things (real or fake). They may pretend to be a

Activity 2.5

Take a look at spam.abuse.net for advice on how to tackle SPAM. What tips are useful for reducing the problem?

trusted company, such as a bank, to entice people to reveal personal or financial information. This practice is known as 'phishing'.

As noted earlier, the EU's Distance Selling Directive allows consumers to 'opt out' of unsolicited e-mails but no protection is given to business recipients, and financial service contracts are also exempted, even in the B2C arena. Technological solutions to this problem have emerged, for example Hotmail (www.hotmail.com) has a filtering service that re-directs junk mail to a separate folder. A US Internet Service Provider called Community Connexion has developed a free product called the Anonymizer (www.anonymizer.com) which allows users to remain anonymous while surfing the Web.

'Spamdexing'   Williams (2005) notes the growth of 'spamdexing' or 'search engine spamming' which is the practice of deliberately and dishonestly modifying web pages to increase the chance of them being placed higher up the list of search engine results. Many designers of web pages try to get a good ranking in search engines and design their pages accordingly. Spamdexing refers exclusively to practices that are dishonest and mislead search and indexing programs to give a page a ranking it does not deserve, leading to unsatisfactory search results for users of that search engine. Many search engines check for instances of spamdexing and will remove suspect pages from their indexes.

Legitimate search engine optimization to maximize a website's ranking in the results lists is a rapidly developing marketing tool which will be discussed in Chapter 9. Inevitably there is a 'grey area' between these two extremes as to when effective marketing becomes dishonest business practice.

Summary

This chapter has considered the broader macro-environmental issues that affect all companies seeking to develop e-business activities, including the wider implications of Internet developments for society as a whole. It is important to recognise the inter-relationship between many legal and ethical issues pertaining to online marketing and to appreciate that in many as yet untested cases both the legal and ethical position remains uncertain. We have demonstrated that customers

Activity 2.6

How is your impression of a brand affected when you receive unwanted SPAM e-mails from a company?

are increasingly demanding the highest standards of ethical behaviour from companies with which they will do business, and so being seen to be 'ethical' can lead to competitive advantage in many markets, such as retail banking.

Questions

Question 2.1

How might a firm turn its online ethical policies to competitive advantage?

Question 2.1 Feedback
In view of the fact that Internet security has been identified as a major inhibitor to the growth of e-commerce, companies which are proactive and demonstrate how seriously they take such issues may well be rewarded with increased customer loyalty. They may also persuade people to transact online who have thitherto been reluctant to do so. Have a look at Amazon's privacy policy, which is clear and comprehensive (www.amazon.co.uk). There are also some interesting case studies on www.howpersonal.com.

The famous US retailer L.L. Bean (www.llbean.com) has a very clear and comprehensive privacy policy which clearly demonstrates the value of effective communications in this area. Note the prominence of the endorsement by TRUSTe and the clear explanation of cookie usage to help alleviate customer concerns about the privacy of their data:

Question 2.2

The collection of information about customers is not a new activity, so why do you think there is so much concern about online privacy?

Question 2.2 Feedback

Businesses have always kept records of customer preferences and purchasing behaviour, although of course they had to keep paper-based records until relatively recently. Many would argue that such information allows them to provide a better quality of service to their customers. What is new is the level of detail that can be routinely captured by increasingly sophisticated technology and the extent to which it can be combined and integrated to build up personal profiles, leading customers to feel they have lost control over how and where their data is used.

Question 2.3

How can multi-currency payment systems like WorldPay add value to both buyer and seller?

Question 2.3 Feedback

These proactive customer-sensitive methods are likely to reduce the number of order cancellations or returned goods, as well as building trust as the customer is fully informed of the local currency cost implications and cannot claim to have been misled.

Question 2.4

Keeping up with the law for companies involved in e-business is an essential if time-consuming process. What possible solutions to this problem might the Internet offer?

Question 2.4 Feedback

Certainly it is a problem for firms to keep up with any changes in the law. However, the Internet can be used to good effect here. Information for companies on their situation is easy to keep up-to-date via the Internet. Not only is much of the legal documentation available on the Internet, there are also many information based sites, such as www.cyberspacelaw.org

Question 2.5

There has been a great deal of media attention regarding the digital divide, but why do you think that it is so important to close the gap?

Question 2.5 Feedback

There are a number of arguments for closing the digital divide. These chiefly include economic equality, democracy, social mobility and economic growth. This issue is further discussed in an online paper: Davison, Elizabeth and Shelia R. Cotten (2003). Connection discrepancies: Unmasking further layers of the digital divide. *First Monday*, v.8, n.3. Available from: firstmonday.org/issues/issue8_3/davison/index.html

Feedback on Activities

Activity 2.1

Napster is still a brand that is synonymous with online music given its early start-up and media attention. Ultimately it is perhaps too early to tell whether or not this will have a negative association for the brand.

Activity 2.2

There is an almost overwhelming amount of information available from this site. A good place to start is the three-page data protection 'fact sheet' which is available in the 'data protection' topic area.

Activity 2.3

A good example to pick here is mobile phone technology. Do you have one? When did you first get one? At what point did you adopt a WAP phone? Do you have a 3G phone? In the UK there are actually more mobile phones than there are people, indicating that some people must have more than one! You should be able to categorise yourself based on how important the latest technology is to you personally.

Activity 2.4

Some of their tips include:

- Never respond to spam.
- Filter it out using free software from reputable ISPs.
- Complain to the ISP.

Activity 2.5

Your impression is highly likely to be negative, because the sheer volume of SPAM messages hitting inboxes mean that consumers are becoming increasingly intolerant, particularly if they have already asked to be removed from a particular list but the messages keep coming, or if they try to unsubscribe to a list but find it difficult to find the right location on the website to post their request.

Activity 2.6

Web Links

www.bcs.org.uk
   Website of the British Computer Society, which includes the BCS Code of Conduct.
www.ccsr.cse.dmu.ac.uk
   Centre for Computing and Social Responsibility. Comprehensive webpage covering a wide range of information relating to Computer Ethics. Takes the perspective of the responsibilities of Information Systems professionals.
www.cpsr.org
   Computer Professionals for Social Responsibility: A public-interest alliance of computer scientists and others concerned about the impact of computer technology on society.
www.cyber-rights.org
   Website of a not-for-profit civil liberties organisation, Cyber-Rights and Cyber Liberties (UK).
www.ico.gov.uk
   Latest legislation covering the types of customer information which companies can hold with and without permission. The free seminar provides practical guidance.
www.digitaldivide.gov
   Includes full text of 'Falling through the Net: Digital Inclusion Report 2001'. The Commerce Department's National Telecommunications and

Information Administration (NTIA) has established this site to publicise the US government's activities regarding access to the Internet and other information technologies.

www.findlaw.com

Information resource on legal issues, with section on cyberspace law (US based).

www.ispa.org.uk

The Internet Services Providers Association. Includes a Code of Conduct.

www.netnanny.com

Site allowing parents to monitor and control their children's web surfing.

www.privacy.net

Provides demonstrations of how cookies are set and a user's surfing behaviour monitored.

www.thehungersite.com

Charity site which harnesses the power of the web to raise funding and attract corporate sponsorship.

www.truste.org

Provides an audit of a site's privacy policies and allocates a 'kitemark' to those meeting specified criteria.

www.untied.com/www.ual.com

The 'vigilante' site and the offending original, United Airlines.

www.which.net/trader.

A full list of privacy issues covered by Which? Web Trader Code.

www.wipo.com

World Intellectual Property Organisation which aims to harmonise intellectual property legislation and procedures.

www.w3.org

The World Wide Web Consortium (W3C) develops inter-operable technologies (specifications, guidelines, software and tools) to lead the web to its full potential as a forum for information, commerce, communication and collective understanding.

3

e-MARKETING RESEARCH

Introduction

This chapter will introduce you to the basic principles of marketing research and explain how research is becoming increasingly central to marketing activity, particularly with regard to effective personalisation and customisation and the evaluation of promotional activities. While the Internet itself is clearly an extensive resource of secondary data, developments in technology mean that there are increasing opportunities for companies to carry out primary research online, and the chapter goes on to review these techniques.

Topics Covered in the Chapter

- The importance of research
- The research process
  - Sources of data
  - Data collection methods
  - Sampling methods
  - Problems with research data
- Using the Internet for marketing research
  - The Internet as a source of secondary data
  - The Internet as a means of collecting primary data
  - Problems with Internet research
  - Ethics of online research.

Learning Objectives

By the end of this chapter you should be able to:

- Explain the basic principles of marketing research.

- Discuss the increasingly central role played by research in effective marketing.
- Discuss how to choose the most appropriate method to address a particular research task.
- Explain how the Internet can be applied to add value to the research process.
- Discuss the legal and ethical issues raised by online research in terms of data protection and privacy.

Recommended Reading

McDaniel, C. and Gates, R. (2003) *Marketing Research: The Impact of the Internet*, New York: Wiley

The Importance of Research

McDaniel and Gates (2002) define marketing research as 'the planning, collection and analysis of data relevant to marketing decision-making and the communication of the results of this analysis to management' (6).

Research is particularly important for:

- Understanding a particular problem, and identifying what actions can be taken to bring about improvement;
- Providing managers with feedback on the effectiveness of current marketing strategy or tactics and indicating the nature of any changes that might need to be made;
- Allowing new market opportunities to be identified and evaluated;
- The choice of research method is critical: to structure an understanding of the problem situation, help collect relevant information about it, and provide analysis to aid decision making. An understanding of research methods can ensure that:
  - The work is carried out systematically—in that it is planned and executed in a clear and well-thought-out way;
  - The data collected are reliable. In other words, they:

- Reflect the (subjective) views and meanings of people interviewed, and/or
- Describe the (objective) phenomena that have been examined;
- Consistently measure the same thing,
- The resulting knowledge claims are valid—meaning that the arguments and statements are actually supported by the data and theory covered in the research.

A good way of illustrating the difference between reliability and validity is to think about the example of a thermometer which consistently informed you that water boiled at 80 degrees Celsius (at sea level): it would be reliable, but not valid. A thermometer which gave a temperature reading for the boiling point of water as 99 degrees one day but 101 degrees the next would be more valid but not very reliable.

Research, in a broad sense, is becoming increasingly central to marketing strategy. Think of the trend towards mass customisation, in which customers can specify their exact requirements and the production process is customised accordingly. See www.levi.com for a classic example. Detailed knowledge of customer needs is essential here if the goods are to be produced on an individual basis. Another example concerns permission marketing (which will be discussed in more detail in Chapter 6), where specific services are provided to customers based entirely on 'permission' that the customer has given the company. This means that a travel company may be given permission by a customer to send them promotions that relate only to self-catering holidays in Florida in the month of October—and nothing else. The company will need to be able to process and act upon this information (which of course is research data about customer preferences) and not just send the customer a general brochure that includes all of the company's holidays. More recently, social networking sites such as MySpace have become a rich source of information for marketers about such diverse issues as musical tastes, product preferences and lifestyle choices. We will examine the growth and importance of social networking in Chapter 12.

Loyalty, and hence customer retention, is based upon a thorough understanding of customer needs that can be established and maintained only by research. The economic benefits of customer retention are obvious: revenues and market share grow through repeat business and referrals, while costs fall through economies of scale and the reduced amount of effort that needs to be spent on customer acquisition and the servicing of familiar customers. McDaniel and Gates (2002) describe the example of British Airways, which researched the preferences of first-class passengers and found them to be—sleep! So, as an alternative to receiving a series of intrusive services during the flight, such passengers can now have dinner in the lounge before take-off and then enjoy an uninterrupted flight.

The Research Process

The research process can be summarised as follows:

- Research objectives and plans need to be set. Setting them will help to focus the research, sharpen the questions and problems to be examined, and possibly also derive hypotheses that the research will set out to test.
- Appropriate data collection and sampling methods should be chosen.
- The questions or problems are then pursued by going out and obtaining relevant data.
- Depending on the methods used, data will be produced in a number of forms (e.g. interview transcripts, statistics and archive papers).
- The data are then examined using suitable analytical techniques such as 'data mining'.
- An account of the findings is then produced.

But this is not necessarily the end of the research. The analysis may well lead to new questions or problems, or suggest that existing ones need to be refined. We can see, then, that the research process is likely to be iterative rather than linear. It may involve several circuits before the research is complete. It might also be that a number of stages are executed simultaneously (for example, data may still be being collected while analysis and a review of theory take place).

Research is often interpreted very narrowly by companies, some of which may operate with just a small 'research' section within a marketing department, or contract out specific research tasks to agencies as required and undertake no in-house research at all. To companies using this approach, only data collection and moments of insight based on those data are thought of as research. This approach can be likened to the core of an apple. Thinking of research in terms of an onion illustrates a broader approach. An onion has many layers which are all integral constituents, but no core as such. Likewise, in a piece of research, all the activities involved are important and have a bearing on success. A researcher must be skilled at all of them—from persuading people to take part in interviews, to setting goals and targets and making sure they are met. In this context, the very nature of what actually constitutes research is also much more inclusive. For example, as will be described in the next section, ongoing research is critical to the development and maintenance of relationship marketing strategies where all employees are expected to take responsibility for identifying and meeting customer needs. Here, research becomes part of an individual's normal way of working rather than an isolated task.

Sources of Data

Secondary data are information that has been collected earlier for a different purpose, but which may still be useful to the research project under consideration. Census data are a good example of secondary data, and of course the Internet can be searched by key words entered in search engines to obtain secondary data on a huge range of subjects. Finding the information needed to answer a particular research question from secondary data avoids the need to spend time and money on primary research, but the likelihood of an ideal match is remote.

Primary data are information that is being collected for the first time in order to address a specific research problem. This means that it is likely to be directly relevant to the research, unlike secondary data, which may be out of date or collected for a totally different purpose. Ideally, an effective research project should incorporate both primary and secondary data.

Data Collection Methods

- Questionnaires can be self-administered (as with postal or e-mail questionnaires), or carried out by telephone or face to face.
- Structured interviews are interviews in which the interviewer asks a standard set of questions, often by phone but also face to face, but with some opportunities for open-ended discussion.
- In-depth interviews allow for a more open-ended discussion, perhaps based around broad themes or questions (such interviews are commonly referred to as 'semi-structured').
- Observation is a technique in which the researchers engage directly with the phenomenon under study (for example, by watching and recording group processes in a product development team). Observation can be done as either a 'participant' or a 'non-participant' in the real-world activity, and is the method that gets 'closest' to the object under study.
- Focus groups are unstructured, free-flowing interviews with a small group of people. The supermarkets are big users of focus groups; for example, to canvass the opinion of customers concerning proposed changes to store layouts. The approach is flexible, and a skilled group moderator can draw in all the participants and allow the critical issues to arise from the discussions to create synergies.

Gummesson (1991) contrasts common research methods in terms of their 'access to reality'. His concern is how close they get to the real-world phenomenon under study. The key challenge is to choose methods of research that gain insights into how the world 'really is'. Often, he notes, researchers focus on issues they think are important, but because they have relied too heavily on second-hand accounts, they gain a false impression of the phenomenon under study and focus on issues that might not be the most pertinent to the research. Gummesson likens the problem to the exploration of an iceberg, in that certain research projects will require methods that 'get beneath the surface' of the phenomenon.

By flying over, sailing by or landing on the iceberg, you are going to get only basic facts, and may simply achieve a superficial impression of what the iceberg is like. This may be fine, of course, where you are clear about the things you are interested in, and their dynamics are well known. This is akin, we could say, to the use of questionnaires and structured interviews. The presumption here is that the phenomenon under study is reasonably understood and that deep investigation is not required. For that reason, a structured set of closed questions is sufficient to gain insight into the issues at hand. These methods are useful, therefore, when researchers do not want to look at something in depth, and instead wish to compare a set of characteristics across a large sample. This might be the case if you were to examine the relationship between marketing priorities in small firms and the industry in which those firms are located. In this case, the questions would be reasonably straightforward and 'objective'. They might only ask about the:

- Range of marketing activities undertaken
- Number of employees in marketing roles
- Total number of employees
- Products and services produced
- Industry sector to which the firm belongs.

Such information could easily be obtained over the phone. And because the study might be seeking to establish the picture across a broad population (say, all small firms in London), the sample of firms contacted could run into the hundreds or thousands. In this case, then, the methods used are an efficient way of finding out a 'little' (just those five data items) about a 'lot' (a large sample size). Data in these studies tend to be reasonably *quantitative*. In other words, phenomena are defined so they can be measured or counted, with the data then collated so that items can be compared and contrasted across the data set as a whole. This is quite different from research carried out using in-depth interviews, focus groups or observation.

In-depth interviews, focus groups or observation are used when the researchers want to approach research phenomena in a more *qualitative* way. They lead to a 'richer' understanding of the things under study and thus—to use the iceberg metaphor—help to get beneath the surface. You often need to do this in research when a superficial grasp will not do; the thing under study needs to be examined in depth. Accordingly, you need to do the research in a way that tells you 'a lot' (something rich and detailed) about a 'little' (a few instances or cases). Qualitative approaches to research make fewer assumptions about research phenomena. They require you to observe people in action and capture their experiences and meanings. As a result, you are able to conceptualise what is happening and provide a new way of thinking about and describing it. For example, a study into 'the difficulties of implementing relationship marketing strategies at the shop-floor level' may work best where you can get close up to the people who do this kind of work and find out, first hand, what sort of problems they face. You could then explore how they solve these problems and examine the sources of invention that allow them to do this. By observing people and asking them to reflect, in depth, on the way they work, you may even provide an account of their working practices about which they themselves are only tacitly aware. Such an account could then be generalised to these situations more broadly.

As can be seen, then, no one method is superior to another. It really depends on the context of use. Indeed, it is common for projects to involve both qualitative and quantitative methods. For example, qualitative methods may be used to look—in depth—at issues that have arisen from the exploration of quantitative data. In contrast, qualitative methods may be used first—to sharpen the issues and problems (providing a better conceptualization of the phenomenon under study) with quantitative methods then being employed to explore these in a broader population.

Sampling Methods

It is rarely possible to interview or survey the entire target population (the UK's national census, conducted just once every ten years, is a famous exception). For most research projects, a compromise needs to be reached between, on the one hand, obtaining the number of respondents necessary for accuracy and, on the other, the time and cost involved in dealing with them.

The terminology of different sampling methods is confusing, so a brief explanation will be given. Probability sampling is where individual respondents are drawn at random from the population. The key alternatives are:

- *Simple random sampling*, in which individuals are randomly selected from the population at large;
- *Stratified random sampling*, which first divides the population into groups based on criteria such as age or gender. Individuals are then randomly selected from within these groups.
- *Non-probability sampling* is where individuals are selected by the researcher on the basis of predefined criteria. The key alternatives are:
  - *Judgment sampling*, in which the researcher uses their judgment to select individuals that they feel are representative of the population or have a particularly useful expertise which should be drawn upon;
  - *Convenience sampling*, where time and resources are saved by choosing respondents on the basis of convenience (a very common method!);
  - *Quota sampling*, in which the researcher selects a predetermined number of individuals from groups based on gender, age etc.

For a detailed discussion of sampling methods, see McDaniel and Gates (2002).

Problems with Research Data

So far we have concentrated upon the benefits of research, but of course there could also be a number of disadvantages:

- The research might not be objective. For example, if it were seeking to save money by cutting back on online activities, a company might be tempted to present the results of research into the contribution made by online trading in as negative a light as possible.
- Research may be used to justify a decision that has already been taken. This means that a company may have a predetermined 'result' established and then takes steps to 'influence' the results of the research to ensure that the findings reflect the required position. Some types of research might not be ethical. Think, for example, of the practice of 'mystery shopping',

whereby the performance of sales staff is assessed by researchers posing as customers. This controversial research method is now also spreading to the Internet; see, for example, www.emysteryshopper.com.

- It is possible to 'over-research' so that decision making is stifled by a perceived need to check out everything first—a situation known as 'analysis paralysis'.
- The cost of conducting the research may exceed the benefits obtained from it.
- The results might be unexpected, and unwelcome! For example, research conducted into the failure of a new product launch might point the finger of blame at certain individuals.

Using the Internet for Marketing Research

The Internet is becoming an increasingly important *source* of research data (known as secondary data) as well as providing a cost-effective new *medium* for the research process itself; for example, as an alternative means of collecting data by completion of an online questionnaire rather than from telephone or face-to-face interviewing (known as primary data).

The Internet as a Source of Secondary Data

The best way to find information on the Internet is to key in the unique Uniform Resource Locator (URL) which will take you directly to the page required, without the need to rely upon search engines. Organisations can promote their URL address on company stationery, on the side of vehicles or buildings or in other increasingly innovative ways.

If you are looking for information without knowing the exact source, then a key word search on Google or one of the other major search engines is the best strategy to adopt. The exponential growth of the Internet is making the task of search engines increasingly difficult because of the sheer volume of new sites and information being placed online. McDaniel and Gates (2002) provide a list of sites that are of specific relevance to market researchers. You might also like to try www.netskills.ac.uk for an online tutorial guide to searching the Internet, or www.researchbuzz.org, which has news on new information sources and search engines, or www.searchenginewatch.com which explains how search engines work.

Information available online is increasingly diverse. For example, exporters now have the opportunity to resolve historical information gaps when contemplating trading internationally that previously may have dissuaded firms from pursuing such strategies due to the uncertainties involved. Details of market access, exchange control regulations, costs of import duties, etc. are now much more transparent on the Web. Some media organisations such as the *Financial Times* (www.ft.com) are competing to offer quality content online, thereby enhancing their brand image and encouraging repeat visits and recommendations for research purposes. Many of the traditional sources of market information are now available online; for example, annual reports, large-scale market surveys, government reports and economic data. While there are valuable data freely available, care needs to be taken because the Internet of course also carries vast amounts of poor quality data. As with traditional market research, appropriate questions to ask include these:

- Is the data relevant?
- Is the data accurate?
- Is it up to date?
- What sampling techniques have been used to collect the data?

The Internet as a Means of Collecting Primary Data

There are a number of primary research tasks that can be effectively carried out online; for example:

- measuring the effectiveness of a firm's Internet strategy;
- measuring customer satisfaction levels;
- obtaining customer feedback on new product/service ideas;
- polling consumers for information about any subject you can think of (see mini case study 'The Internet Survey Industry'.

Activity 3.1

Compare the information that is available from the Websites of the following market research agencies and consider the questions below:

www.forrester.com
www.acnielsen.co.uk
www.mori.co.uk

Do you notice any similarity in terms of the way in which research data are made available by the respective companies? Are some more generous with their data in terms of what they give away? Which sites are easiest to navigate to find what you are looking for? Why do you think this is?

Undertaking primary research to measure the effectiveness of a company's website is a critical aspect of the evaluation of its online marketing strategy. The following questions may be asked;

- Are the objectives of the site being met?
- Is the corporate message getting across?
- How effective arc the various promotional techniques used to attract visitors to the site?
- What changes need to be made to improve the quality of customer service offered?
- Is the site easy to use?
- How many sales are resulting from online contacts?
- How many visitors are coming back to the site?
- How much new business has resulted from the website (as opposed to it merely offering an additional channel to existing customers)?
- How does the site compare with those of competitors?

Chaffey *et al.* (2006) recommends five specific categories of measurement:

- Channel promotion measures assess why customers visit a site. Key questions are: which sites have they been referred from, or which offline adverts did they see? From this analysis it should be possible to measure the percentage of customers whose enquiry was prompted by online and offline means respectively, thereby guiding the nature of future promotional campaigns.

- Channel buyer behaviour measures assess which aspects of the website content are visited, the times of day and the duration of the visit. This analysis enables 'stickiness' to be measured; for example, the average length of a visit, and the proportion of first-time to repeat visitors. It can also suggest changes to site structure and content.

- Channel satisfaction measures evaluate customers' perception of online service quality issues such as e-mail response times. It is also possible to use services such as Gomez (www.gomez.com) to benchmark service quality against the competition.

- Channel outcome measures compare the number of site visitors to the number of actual purchases made; in other words, how many visitors leave the site without buying anything. For example, if 10 purchases result from 100 visits, the conversion rate is 10 percent. Channel profitability measures are a critical test of success. How much does the online channel contribute to business profit after taking account of the costs incurred?

In addition to evaluating existing marketing strategy, research can also play a more proactive role through identifying changes in the market and customer needs, thereby suggesting future strategic directions for the firm. Asking customers what they expect from a company's site and obtaining feedback on current promotions can provide important information to aid market segmentation and other marketing applications. For example, Honda now has different sites for male and female customers, following a research exercise that established how men preferred detailed graphics emphasizing different aspects of car performance, while women preferred brief factual information.

Company intranets can also be used effectively to gather research data from staff, a key group of stakeholders whose importance is now increasingly recognized by the designation 'internal customers' (see Chapter 6 for detailed discussion of managing stakeholder relationships). Staff opinions are a valuable source of research data that can be sought and collated through an online questionnaire.

There are a number of methods by which primary data can be collected online:

Specialist Software To measure website effectiveness, increasingly sophisticated software is now available to assess the number of visitors by measuring site visits (where one or many pages may be viewed) or page impressions (one person viewing one page). It is now also possible to assess,

- which parts of the site are most popular;
- what times of the day people visit the site;
- which search engines people are using to find the site;
- the route people take through the site;
- how long they spend there (a measure of the so-called 'stickiness' of the site).

Also, a number of businesses such as www.hitbox.com or www.webtrends.com are being established to capitalize on this technological capability. Firms can install a free link to Hitbox and it will calculate how many times their pages are viewed, and offer a real-time display of this information in a password-protected area on the firm's site. Hitbox also provides information about:

- Visitor domains
- Country of origin
- URL of referring sites
- Browser type
- Operating system
- Visitor frequency
- Entry and exit pages
- Session duration.

Information about the configuration of visitors' browsers can be very useful in guiding a company's site design parameters. For example, there would be no point in building elaborate graphics into a website if analysis of visitors showed that few had the technical capacity to appreciate their full glory. There is no charge for the Hitbox service because the company now has animated links to itself on thousands of websites that have taken advantage of the service, so it gets plenty of visitor traffic to attract advertisers and build banner advertising revenue.

Website Registration In order to identify and assess individual visitors to its website, a firm can request registration details. If a company knows the identity of visitors who are browsing the site, they can be contacted directly through other means; for example, to arrange a sales visit, Persuading visitors to register their interests by supplying their e-mail address and personal information requires a suitable incentive, such as useful free information, and sufficient trust on the part of the visitor that the information supplied will not be misused. The danger is that a site visitor may be put off by the request to register before accessing the site and look elsewhere to resolve their query.

Questionnaires Questionnaires distributed via e-mail or over the Web are quick, inexpensive, have a broad geographical reach and the data received can be input directly into a database for the purposes of recording and analysis. There are two major ways of conducting such research:

- For e-mail customers quote an URL in the text of the message that customers can click on at their own convenience to link to an online questionnaire.
- Include a 'pop-up' box on the website that customers can complete while they are actually viewing the site online.

DealerNet (www.dealernet.com) offered customers the chance to win a free car if they answered a few short questions asking about the year, make and model of their current car and signed up to receive a free monthly e-mail newsletter. Processing this small amount of information enabled the company to very specifically and effectively customise subsequent e-mail newsletters sent to these customers.

Companies now exist which allow researchers to design and administer an online survey without the need to purchase expensive software. Take a look at www.websurveyor.com, which allows a survey to be created, published on a website, data collected, results analysed and then printed out as a report.

Internet surveys have a number of specific advantages over more traditional data collection methods:

- The results can be broadcast quickly and cheaply to a large number of respondents on a global basis.
- Increasing the number of respondents does not necessarily add to costs or the time taken to conduct the research.
- Messages can be personalised to increase the chances of response.
- 'Hard to reach' groups can be accessed.
- Surveys can be completed and returned at the respondent's convenience.
- Because it is a relatively new data collection medium, people tend to be more tolerant of online research than they are of telephone or postal surveys, although of course the novelty may not last too long!

e-Satisfy's (www.e-satisfy.co.uk) Site Monitor allows companies to interview visitors when they enter or leave their website. It uses survey modules to gather general, commerce or visitor profile information. Try the demonstration—by answering the questions posed, you are giving e-Satisfy feedback on its products in the same way that a company could use the service on its own site to collect data from visitors. When a visitor arrives at or leaves a page, Site Monitor pops up and asks if they would answer a few questions about the site. If the visitor agrees to answer questions by clicking 'Continue', they are informed that it will take only a few minutes to complete the survey. A series of questions is then asked in short sets, and the visitor clicks on the 'Next' button when they have completed each set. The final page thanks the respondent, asks for additional comments and an (optional) e-mail address. Survey information is automatically captured into e-Satisfy's secure database where the company can:

- review aggregated reports of visitors' and customers' responses;
- review trends to monitor activity/service/opinion over the course of the survey's project life;
- download the raw data and visitor's comments to analyse/ review using its own software/reporting methods.

Added value in terms of building trust and brand equity can then be achieved by displaying the results of the survey on the site.

Web Marketing Today (www.wilsonweb.com) has a free monthly e-mail newsletter distributed to some 140,000 people worldwide. From the website potential subscribers can sign up without supplying vast amounts of data about themselves. A few basic questions were posted on the site, along the lines of 'What is your job?' and 'Why do you find the newsletter useful?' Analysis of the results allowed the business founder to segment his customers and redesign the site around the needs of the five major segments identified, creating several different versions of the same newsletter. Subsequently, a customer who was identified as a student would receive the next newsletter in a very different style and focus compared with a customer identified as a consultant. Subscription rates improved significantly as a result.

Online Focus Groups   Online focus groups are still rare in the UK but increasingly popular in the US. There, bulletin board discussion groups on the company website are used to collect real-time feedback from a selected group of customers in response to questions from the focus group leaders. Customers may be asked to comment on particular aspects of the company's business and respond to points made by other members of the group in an online version of a 'round-table' discussion. One of the leading companies offering this service is www.zoomerang.com. Zoomerang creates virtual gatherings, which increases geographic representation and allows diverse connections to be quickly made. As well as providing the technological infrastructure, Zoomerang sources qualified participants, experienced moderators and provides transcripts of the focus group sessions.

The respective merits of online and offline focus groups are currently the subject of much debate. The advantages of online focus groups are:

- There is a lack of geographic barriers.
- Costs are lower.
- They can be administered quickly.
- Respondents are less likely to be intimidated by more opinionated group members or the discussion moderator than when groups meet face to face.

- They provide access to 'hard-to-reach' market segments such as time-pressed professionals who would not make the effort to attend a face-to-face session.
- It is hard for one overbearing individual to dominate an online group.
- People tend to be more direct and honest in their responses.
- Unrelated small talk and time-wasting are unusual.
- 'Emoticons' (for example '☺') can be used to convey emotions (albeit in a rather primitive way!).
- www.vrroom.com has an ejection feature to remove participants who try to sabotage the online discussions.

There are, however, also a number of disadvantages:

- Non-verbal input such as facial expression and body language is impossible to detect.
- Participants may not give the session their full attention for the required time span.
- The ability of the moderator to draw in all group members is limited online.

Kiosk-Based Computer Interviewing Kiosk-based computer interviewing is an innovative way of gathering data about customers' buying experiences. Multimedia touch-screen computers are set up in kiosks and can be programmed to administer surveys, show images, and play sound and video clips in order to ascertain and capture customer feedback. They are becoming increasingly common in new retail shopping centres (see Chapter 10 for more detail in this area).

Feedback Buttons to E-mail Comments or Queries You can see from the screenshot in Diagram 3.1 that Southwest Airlines (www.southwest.com) does not accept e-mail feedback. Cynics claim that this is because the airline receives so many complaints about poor service that it could not manage the volume of e-mails that might be received. However, it does seems that Southwest Airlines is missing a valuable research opportunity to check out what its customers think about the company—what do you think? We will return to this example when discussing customer communications in Chapter 6.

Internet Panels   The use of TV panels as a method of analysing viewer behaviour has been common for many years. Panels such as those operated by Neilsen/NetRatings (www.neilsennetratings.com) provide the firm's customers with online access to comprehensive Internet audience information. The Internet population is profiled by NetRatings on a regular basis using random sampling techniques that ensure that representative sampling can be generalised to the entire Internet user population. Households are recruited to the panel through analysis of census data, and they are then given a 'box' to attach to their computers that tracks and stores their online behaviour. NetRatings customers can then interrogate the data to answer such questions as 'Which banner advertisement best reached my target audience in October?' or 'Where are my competitors advertising?'

Cookies   A cookie is a text file that contains a unique user identifier. When a visitor accesses a website, the site's server can place a cookie in the user's browser. As the visitor navigates the site, the cookie transmits the path taken back to the server so that the movement of the visitor through the site can be tracked. The cookie is associated with the browser rather than the individual user, so, for example, if you access www.amazon.co.uk from a different computer, you may find

Diagram 3.1   Southwest Airlines contact information.

that the usual personalized 'welcome' greeting is missing. There are, of course, ethical issues here regarding invasion of privacy in the collection of such data, as discussed in Chapter 2.

The European Parliament has outlawed the use of cookies without *explicit* prior consent. Until then, many businesses had relied mainly upon *implied* consent by using privacy statements to inform visitors that cookies were being used to collect personal data, but this is no longer sufficient. Explicit consent requires the user to agree in advance to the gathering and use of information. This means being informed as to what information is going to be gathered and exactly how it will be used. The consent process needs to take place on each occasion when data are collected, meaning, for example, that the whole buying experience will be slowed down and complicated, whereas for most people the attraction of online shopping is speed and simplicity.

Mystery Shopping   It was noted earlier in the chapter that one of the growth area of online research is e-mystery shopping. See www.emysteryshopper.com for an example and demonstration. Mystery shoppers can check out a company's website to test:

- site usability
- fulfilment
- response times
- impact on traditional brand.

Would you like to earn some extra money whilst surfing on the Web? If you check out the eMystery Shopper website they are on the look-out for new members to join their self-employed team of eMystery Shoppers—monitoring and assessing websites and reporting on their usability, effectiveness and customer service performance. So, if you enjoy surfing the Web, why not make money doing so, and help to improve the services offered on the Internet at the same time!

Problems with Internet Research

Earlier in the chapter we discussed some of the problems that can occur when conducting research, and these issues are just as pertinent for web-based research. There are, however, a number of new problems that are specific to online research:

- Websites requiring a lengthy registration procedure may provide the company with excellent research data, but only if visitors can be bothered to complete the process.
- Customers may be reluctant to supply their e-mail address for fear of such personal details being sold to third parties and a deluge of junk e-mails set in motion.
- Access to the Web can still be slow or interrupted.
- A sample of customers surveyed online may well be representative only of that section of the company's online customers who have the time and the inclination to respond to surveys. This approach can lead to what is called 'selection bias' in the data. The respondents are in any case very unlikely to be representative of the entire customer base, because not everyone has Internet access, or indeed, a willingness to respond to surveys.

Nancarrow *et al.* (2001) warned of what they called the seven deadly Internet research sins:

1. *Excess*—leading to respondent burn-out if 'over-surveyed';
2. *Omission*—failure to take note of the shortcomings of online research;
3. *Exposure*—innovative research techniques or market insights falling into the hands of competitors;
4. *Intrusion of privacy*—through use of cookies, as discussed above;
5. *Negligence*—in protecting the confidentiality of data;
6. *Off-loading costs*—expecting respondents to pay for the cost of completing a survey online;
7. *Complacency*—in failing to take the consequences of the above sins seriously.

Ethics of Online Research

Gaining respondents' confidence is crucial for research to go ahead with any kind of openness. Assuring people that their comments can remain confidential will be an important starting point. It will also be important to discuss issues of 'anonymity' with respondents. For example, where their words might subsequently appear in print, they might be promised that a pseudonym will be used, thus ensuring that their comments will not be attributed to them as individuals. It is therefore crucial that researchers:

- Respect confidentiality, whether explicitly or implicitly promised;
- Do not misuse data and other findings—in other words, do not use them for (potentially damaging) purposes for which the data were not provided in the first instance;
- Recognize the 'wider implications' of actions taken, for both individuals and organizations—does your report, for example, recommend changes that may cost people their jobs?
- Abide by both the large and the small print of privacy policies.

Summary

In this chapter, we have considered the basic principles of marketing research and how to choose the most appropriate method to address a particular research task. We have emphasised the increasingly central role played by research in evolving online marketing activities such as one-to-one marketing and permission marketing, topics which will be considered more detail in Chapter 6. It should also now be clear to you how the Internet can add value to marketing research more generally through such innovations as online questionnaires and focus groups. Finally, it is important to bear in mind the legal and ethical issues raised by online research in terms of data protection and privacy.

Questions

Question 3.1

What sources of secondary data can you think of, from both inside and outside an organization?

Question 3.1 Feedback

Internally published data sources include financial records, sales records, customer database, production records, internally conducted research projects, customer complaints and staff suggestions. Externally published data sources include market research reports, government statistics, trade journals, newspapers, CD ROM databases, the Internet and company annual reports.

Question 3.2

List the advantages and disadvantages of secondary data in comparison with primary data.

Question 3.2 Feedback

Advantages
- Saves time and money.
- Time series studies are possible (examining the history of a particular problem to highlight changes over time).
- Data is easy to access.
- Can tell in advance whether the data is going to be useful or not.

Disadvantages
- The data has been collected for a different purpose, so the formats and categories used may differ from what is now required.
- Data may be out of date.
- Data may be inaccurate.
- There may be information overload, particularly if the Internet is used.

Question 3.3

What method of data collection would be best suited to the following projects?

a. Finding answers to 'closed' questions about customer satisfaction levels in order to test a set of hypotheses about service quality in high-tech businesses.
b. Investigating how cabin crew maintain service quality while having to deal with drunk and difficult passengers on airlines.
c. Exploring the difficulties established companies face when introducing online channels to market.

Question 3.3 Feedback

a. Closed questions and hypothesis-testing involve a quantitative approach, and the search for 'objective', 'factual' data. For that reason, questionnaires would be the most efficient method to use. Structured interviews might also be appropriate.
b. Observation, ideally as a 'participant' (i.e. as another member of the cabin crew), would be most appropriate here. It would allow you to get close to the action and see how problems are dealt with in the context of action. Slightly less effective, though more straightforward to earth-bound researchers, would be in-depth interviews. Questionnaires or structured interviews would not be appropriate because this method is usually used to collect quantitative data, and the situation here calls for 'richness': understanding the dynamics of practice, as well as the experiences of the cabin crew involved.
c. The challenge here is to get managers to reflect on, and contrast, their experiences of online and offline marketing. They might not always be conscious of the greatest difficulties they face, and are even less likely to be conscious of why they face them. In-depth interviews would give you the freedom to explore the richness of these issues. Observation would be less effective because the data needed stretch across domains of experience (in time and space). You could observe what someone is doing here and now, but this would not help you to make connections with their earlier experiences in previous jobs.

Question 3.4

Why might data collected from an online questionnaire not be representative of the population as a whole?

Question 3.4 Feedback
The obvious answer is because not everyone has access to the Internet, but there are more subtle problems as well. The type of person inclined to respond to an online questionnaire is likely to be technology literate and have time on their hands. Such individuals may make up only a small segment of a firm's customer base, and their views may well differ from those of more mainstream customers. The problem can be addressed by the use of screened Internet samples when collecting data. This means that quotas based upon particular sample characteristics such as age or income bracket are imposed on self-selected sample groups. Alternatively, panels of respondents may be drawn upon who have agreed in advance to participate and therefore have been pre-selected and categorised into demographic segments.

Question 3.5

Can you think of any other problems in connection with Internet survey research?

Question 3.5 Feedback
There are increasing concerns about privacy and security on the Internet. People are worried that the personal details they supply when responding to surveys may be misused. It is also possible that survey results may be skewed by individuals submitting multiple replies to a questionnaire which is posted on the Web for anyone to see. To get around this problem, unique passwords can be supplied to participants that will access the survey form only once.

Question 3.6

Can you think of a way in which the arguments for and against online focus groups can be resolved?

Question 3.6 Feedback

Perhaps a combination of methods might be a suitable compromise. For example, offline group sessions can be recorded and then broadcast to senior management over the Internet.

Web Links

www.busreslab.com
> This is a useful specimen of online questionnaires to measure customer satisfaction levels, and tips on effective Internet marketing research.

www.marketresearch.org.uk
> The Market Research Society. Site contains useful material on the nature of research, choosing an agency, ethical standards and codes of conduct for research practice.

www.statistics.gov.uk
> Detailed information on a variety of consumer demographics from the Government Statistics Office.

www.privacy.net
> Useful information and demonstrations of online privacy issues.

www.esomar.nl
> The World Association of Opinion and Marketing Research Professionals site; it contains detailed guidelines on conducting online research and managing privacy policies, plus a useful glossary of marketing research terminology.

4

E-MARKETING STRATEGIES

Introduction

This chapter considers the role played by e-marketing strategy in the development of competitive advantage. Of particular importance is the way in which businesses are re-structuring in order to maximise the value from their e-business operations. Various models of e-marketing strategy are summarised in order to demonstrate the increasing scope of online marketing and the level of innovation that is taking place as the technology matures.

Topics Covered in the Chapter

- The importance of strategy
- Alternative organisational structures for e-business strategy
- Models of e-business strategy
- Key differences between B2B and B2C online strategies
- The long tail.

Learning Objectives

By the end of this chapter you should be able to:

- Discuss the importance of creating the 'right mix of bricks and clicks'.
- Explain how e-marketing strategy can add value to a business.
- Evaluate the key models of online marketing strategy that have emerged to date.

Recommended Reading

Cellen-Jones, R. (2003) *Dot Bomb: The Strange Death of Dotcom Britain*, London: Arum

Lindstrom, M. (2001) *Clicks, Bricks and Brands*, London: Kogan Page

The Importance of Strategy

By setting realistic goals and assessing whether they have been achieved, a company can evaluate the contribution its online strategy is making, and then use this information to guide the choice of future strategy and its implementation.

Historically, writers have distinguished 'prescriptive' and 'emergent' approaches to strategic planning. The two forms are reviewed by Lynch (2000) as follows:

- Prescriptive models regard strategic planning as a pre-determined, sequential process moving from analysis to development and finally to implementation.
- Emergent models view the process as more chaotic with considerable overlap and re-iteration between the various stages.

The latter would appear to be most appropriate in a dynamic business environment. However, there has been criticism of traditional planning models since well before the Internet era. For example, Mintzberg (1994) argued that his extensive research involving observation of actual management practices found little correlation between the degree of planning and business profitability. Now, of course, it can be very tempting to abandon traditional planning models altogether in order to move at 'Internet speed', although the example of Boo.com in Chapter 1 illustrated the dangers of that approach.

Gale and Abraham (2005) have reviewed the extent of organisational transformation brought on by e-business strategies in the 'first ten years' of online trading. They concluded that virtually all aspects of business structure and internal process have been affected across a range of industry sectors, with evidence of significant organisational change in the form of power shifts and the job re-design. This chapter will now go on to summarise how e-business strategies have evolved over this period.

Alternative Structures for e-Business Strategy

The Mix of 'Clicks and Bricks'

Internet developments provide a powerful incentive for established firms to experiment with new ways of structuring their operations, in order to compete with more flexible new market players such as dotcoms that are not burdened by legacy computer systems and entrenched operational routines. For example, Kalakota and Robinson put consideration of new forms of organisational structure at the heart of Internet strategy:

> Maintaining the status quo is not a viable option. Unfortunately too many companies develop a pathology of reasoning, learning and attempting to innovate only in their comfort zones. The first step to seeing differently is to understand that eBusiness is about structural transformation. (1999: 5)

Many companies try to maintain traditional structures when developing their online strategies, and hence become victims of new firms with better alignments of structure and strategy. Effective Internet strategy, however, calls for a re-engineering of processes and structures in order to focus on key customer groups, rather than product or service divisions. It is essential that firms understand how to manage change effectively in order to sustain competitive advantage. This issue will be addressed in Chapter 11.

A number of frameworks can be drawn upon to examine the range of alternative Internet strategies that firms are currently pursuing. At a corporate level, alternatives for the web can be categorised in order of increasing commitment as follows:

- Information only
- Interactive communications tool
- Channel to market (e-commerce)
- Separate online business
- Integration with traditional business strategy
- Transformation of traditional business to the Web.

As the degree of commitment increases, issues concerning organisational structure become more important. In this section the basic structures considered are:

'Bricks and mortar'—traditional business model; website is brochureware only.

'Clicks and mortar'—company pursues online and offline marketing and transactions.

'Clicks only'—entire business model is online, little or no physical
presence (also known as dotcoms or pure-plays).

Gulati and Garino (2000) discuss the need for a company to get
'the right mix of bricks and clicks'. 'Bricks and mortar' firms obtain
all their revenue from traditional means and the website is used purely
for providing information; hence little change to established strategy
is required. At the other end of the scale, 'pure-play' Internet firms
obtain the majority of their revenue online and in some cases may
need no physical presence at all. For an established firm this strategy
requires radical change and offers little flexibility to customers, so it
is more likely that the intermediary category of 'clicks and mortar'
combining both online and offline strategies will apply.

Companies such as Easyrentacar (www.easyrentacar.com) have
tried to reduce costs and hence prices by providing an 'Internet only'
car hire service. This cost-driven approach means that even e-mail
responses are standardised by computers sending pre-prepared replies
generated by key words in the text, which may well not exactly con-
form to the enquirer's request. A number of well-publicised customer
service disasters caused by technical hitches have led to an upgrading
of the more 'traditional' telephone call centre.

Kumar (1999) suggests that a firm should decide whether the
Internet will primarily *replace* ('clicks only', or 'pure-play') or alternatively *complement* other channels to market ('clicks and mortar').
In the former scenario, it is important that sufficient investment is
made in the necessary infrastructure to achieve this. It is a critical
decision because it forces the company to think about whether the
Internet is just another channel to market, operating alongside traditional methods, or whether it will fundamentally change the way that
the company interacts with its customers, as it is transformed into
an Internet pure-play. He suggests that replacement is most likely to
happen when:

• Customer access to the Internet is high.

- The Internet offers a better value proposition than other media.
- The product can be standardised, and ideally also delivered over the Internet (e.g. software).

The attitude of the senior management team will be critical in establishing the degree of commitment to the Internet, and therefore in choosing the most appropriate strategy given the resources available. In many cases, companies are reluctant to commit to providing Internet channels to market because of a fear of 'cannibalising' their existing business. They fear that if they provide alternative channels to customers it will add to costs, as existing customers take advantage of the ability to switch at will between different ways of dealing with the firm, without any new business being generated by the existence of the new channel. This is undoubtedly a risk, but the alternative of not providing the channel at all may mean that customers go elsewhere— to competitors who do provide the choice. So while the Internet channel may not generate additional business (at least in the short term) it should at least help to ensure that existing customers do not defect.

In Chapter 7 we will consider the topic of multi-channel marketing in detail, but it is worth noting here that many companies are struggling to meet customer expectations. For example, RS Components has won many awards for the significant investment made in its innovative and highly successful website, but the firm admits that the volume of paper catalogues it produces has merely stabilised, and not decreased as might be expected.

Bricks and Mortar Brochureware websites, a novelty and hence a distinct competitive advantage in the mid-1990s, are now often derided as reflecting an unimaginative approach to Internet strategy, as the company concerned continues to rely largely on an established 'bricks and mortar' business model. When dotcom fever was at its height early in 2000, the fear amongst established firms was that new, flexible online business models would render 'old economy' firms obsolete. Many organisations that felt threatened in this way rushed to catch up and develop their own online strategies. Since the dotcom crash, companies that adopted a 'wait and see' approach are now reaping the benefits of learning from their competitors' mistakes before testing the online waters.

Dotcoms   Dotcoms have received considerable adverse publicity, due to a number of spectacular failures in the crash of 2001. These firms were established specifically for Internet trading, and the classic examples are Amazon.com and eBay, which has each built up a massive customer base in just a few years.

Clicks and Mortar   A combination of 'old' and 'new' business practices. The term is derived from the established expression 'bricks and mortar' that symbolises a wholly physical presence. Firms such as WH Smith (www.whsmith.co.uk) exemplify the trend towards 'clicks and mortar' operations whereby synergies can be generated by the availability of a choice of delivery mechanisms through both traditional and Internet channels. Stores in prime high street locations throughout the country can promote special Internet dealing offers, provide terminal access to online ordering for products not held in store, and also act as a collection point for returned goods that were delivered direct to the home. WH Smith is now experimenting with digital television as a communications channel.

Sawhney and Zabin (2001) note that there are certain products and services (an obvious example being the refuelling of vehicles) that will always rely on physical delivery. Others will vary in the degree to which the Internet channel can contribute to delivery. They suggest a number of factors that influence the extent of online contribution:

- Complexity of the exchange.
- Degree of asset specialization; for example, certain chemicals may require low pressure transportation.

Activity 4.1

Try and find your own examples of 'bricks and mortar', 'clicks and mortar' and 'clicks only' companies. See if you can list three or four examples of each.

- Level of reseller fragmentation; powerful distributors may be able to resist manufacturer efforts to sell direct to customers.
- Knowledge of customer needs; if this largely resides with channel partners they will be difficult to circumvent successfully.

The authors quote the example of the furniture maker Herman Miller that introduced a direct selling channel while maintaining the co-operation of its retail partners. The company is a market leader and 90 percent of its sales are still made through the traditional channel that is relied upon by the retailers. The mutual dependence means that both producer and retailer are prepared to be flexible.

For clicks and mortar companies, one of the key debates about Internet strategy concerns the implications for organisational structure. According to Gulati and Garino (2000), the advantages of creating of a separate Internet division are more focus and flexibility for innovation, avoidance of legacy system integration and opportunities to float as a separate business. Abbey National Bank has pursued this strategy in the UK with the development of Cahoot (www.cahoot.co.uk) On the other hand, the advantages of integration include leverage of existing brands, generation of economies of scale and sharing of information.

Sawhney and Zabin recommend that Internet operations should initially be separated from the rest of the organisation, but over the longer term there should be a clear integration plan. They note: 'Remember that e-business is a crutch, not a leg. It is useful to separate it from the lines of business when you are learning to walk, but eventually it needs to become an integral part of the business' (2001: 27). The authors describe how, in 1999, Bank One launched WingspanBank.com in an early example of separating out online business activities. The new venture was promoted under the tagline 'If your bank could start over, this is what it would be'. In practice, while the parent bank offered both online and offline access to its customers, in order to keep the new venture completely separate from the parent, WingspanBank's customers were not allowed to use Bank One branches. As a result, the parent bank gained more 'online' customers than its 'Internet only' venture did, despite huge promotional spending. A 'U turn' was performed and Wingspan was brought back into the core business.

Activity 4.2

It is not only Bank One and Abbey that have entered into online banking. Take a look at other UK banks' websites, how have these traditional banks adapted to the Internet?

Models of Internet Strategy

Michael Porter has updated his classic model of industry structure and competitive forces influencing company strategy to consider the impact of the Internet. He argues:

> The Internet has created some new industries, such as on-line auctions and digital marketplaces...its greatest impact has been to enable the reconfiguration of existing industries that have been constrained by high costs for communicating, gathering information or accomplishing transactions. (2001: 66)

Porter predicts that successful companies will be those viewing the Internet as a complement to existing operations and not as a separate course of action.

Hackbarth and Kettinger (2000) distinguish three levels of Internet strategy:

Level 1—Individual departments develop isolated applications serving parochial interests that are not co-ordinated into corporate strategy.

Level 2—Functional departments integrate Internet resources to support existing business strategies. Electronic links are also established with customers and suppliers to reduce costs and enhance relationships across the network.

Level 3—Internet strategy drives corporate strategy. New revenue streams are developed as partners (including competitors) are incorporated into a seamless network generating 'win win' opportunities.

Many organisations will recognise themselves at Level 1. Some, for example, Tesco (www.tesco.co.uk), are now reaping the benefits of committing the resources necessary to reach Level 2. To date, very few have reached beyond Level 3, with the possible exception of Dell Computers (www.dell.com).

The implication from all of these models reviewed above is that organisations should progress over time towards more and more integration of Internet activities. However, the priorities will vary depending on the type of business model. For example, a consultancy firm will place more emphasis on building online customer relationships or recruitment of staff than the procurement of its own supplies. A firm operating through a reseller network will focus primarily on developing electronic links with its partners, whereas an industrial manufacturer will be more concerned with sourcing raw materials online. These priorities will dictate the direction and emphasis of online developments and not necessarily lead to a 'complete' solution as implied by stage models.

Activity 4.3

Take a look at the Tesco website (www.tesco.co.uk). What evidence is there that Tesco have reached Level 2 of Hackbarth and Kettinger's criteria?

The traditional Ansoff Matrix (categories summarised below) is also useful for considering alternative Internet strategies:

- Market penetration
- Market development
- Product development
- Diversification.

Market penetration, whereby the firm focuses on selling existing products in existing markets, is the 'safest' strategy but does not maximise the potential of the medium. For example, added value can be offered to existing customers by providing online contact options.

Because of its global reach, the Internet is ideal for market development strategies, where existing products can be offered in new markets without the need to establish an expensive physical presence in the country concerned. New market segments may also be drawn in if products are offered online. For example, consumer retailer Argos (www.argos.co.uk) now also attracts business customers and the business-focused RS Components (www.rswww.com) now attracts individual consumers online.

It may also be possible to develop new information-based products that provide added value to existing customers (product development). A common application here is the development of free 'white papers' or case studies providing useful information while also promoting the activities of the company itself (see www.rightnow.com). Online diversification is unusual because it carries the most risk. Unlike the other categories, both product and market are unknown quantities.

Chaffey et al. (2006) note that many companies have merely been reactive and followed a natural progression over time in developing a website to support their marketing activities:

Level 0—No website!

Level 1—Listing on online directory such as Yellow Pages (www.yell.co.uk).

Level 2—Basic 'brochureware' site contains contact details and product information.

Level 3—Simple interactive site that allows e-mail queries (www.brunel.ac.uk).

Level 4—Interactive site that supports transactions and customer services (www.whsmith.co.uk).

Level 5—Fully interactive site that provides relationship marketing and facilitating full range of marketing functions (www.amazon.co.uk).

The amount of effort devoted to Internet marketing strategy tends to be proportional to the position currently occupied by the company on this hierarchy, or, in other words, how central the Internet is considered to be to its marketing activities. This categorisation applies to what Chaffey *et al.* (2006) term 'sell-side' e-commerce, the process of selling to customers and collecting money for goods or services rendered. They note that a similar progression based on levels can be applied to 'buy-side' e-commerce, which is the sourcing of a firm's products through the supply chain (sometimes called 'procurement'):

Level 1—No use of the web for product sourcing or electronic integration with suppliers.

Level 2—Review and selection from competing suppliers using intermediary sites, B2B exchanges and supplier websites. Orders placed by conventional means.

Level 3—Orders placed electronically through EDI, intermediary sites, exchanges or supplier sites. No integration with supplier's systems. Re-keying of orders needed into procurement or accounting systems.

Level 4—Orders placed electronically with integration of company's procurement systems.

Level 5—Orders placed electronically with full integration of procurement, planning and stock control systems.

These models are most appropriate for transactional websites, but Chaffey and his colleagues point out that there are several other types of online presence in which collecting payment is not a direct priority:

- Service-oriented relationship building websites such as those operated by PricewaterhouseCoopers (www.pwcglobal.com) and other major consultancy firms focus on the provision of information rather than online transactions.
- Brand building sites such as www.guinness.com focus on supporting the offline brand.
- Portal sites such as www.yahoo.com provide gateways to a wide range of content across the Web that can be customised to individual preferences.

Chaston (2004) provides another perspective for categorising Internet strategy options:

Product performance—Customisation of products online (see, for example, www.levi.com).

Transactional excellence—Makes it easy to source and buy products, track progress of delivery (see Amazon's 'one click' ordering service at www.amazon.co.uk).

Relationship excellence—Focuses on personalisation based on order history to engender loyalty (again, see Amazon's 'recommendations' based on knowledge of reading habits gleaned from past purchases).

Price performance—Special offers for online transactions to maximise the cost effectiveness of the technology (see www. easyjet.com).

These categories are not mutually exclusive, as the inclusion of Amazon in two categories demonstrates.

A paper by Lumpkin and Dess (2004) notes that despite the undoubted potential offered by digital technologies, and several years of online experience, many companies are still struggling to establish exactly how the Internet can add value to their business. The authors note four distinct strategies that companies can follow in order to address this issue:

Search—The Internet has increased the speed and scope of information gathering at the same time as reducing search costs. This means that companies can find critical data online and can also themselves be more visible to prospective customers.

Evaluation—Alternative actions can be easily compared in terms of likely costs and benefits through price comparison services and customer reviews posted online. For example, www.bizrate.com rates a number of competing products to aid the evaluation process, and www.planetfeedback.com details customer feedback on a wide range of suppliers.

Problem-solving—Community sections of the website can add value by opening up customer service enquiries or technical support functions for all to see. In some cases customers start

Activity 4.4

Study the example sites above and then see if you can find other examples where the primary function of the site is not to sell goods or services and collect payment online. For each example you identify, consider whether it focuses on relationship building, brand building, information provision or perhaps something else entirely?

Activity 4.5

The amount of information freely available on the web is ever-increasing. As mentioned, companies can find information on competitors and customers can easily find information on companies. Go to a search engine that you usually use, type in the name of a high street company, and skim through the first few pages of results. How informative is this exercise?

to answer queries posed by other customers, see for example www.cisco.com.

Transaction—Online trading both lowers the cost of and speeds up the transaction process. Services such as Paypal provide a secure and efficient payment system and the auction mechanism exemplified by www.ebay.com is revolutionising pricing agreements between buyers and sellers.

To summarise this section, it is worth considering the dominant models of e-business in the marketplace today as identified by Lumpkin and Dess (2004):

- Commission-based businesses provide services for a fee; for example, www.ebay.com.
- Advertising-based businesses provide content and charge fees to advertisers wishing to target the viewers of the content; for example, www.yahoo.com.
- Markup-based businesses acquire products, mark up the price and resell at a profit; for example, www.amazon.co.uk.
- Production-based businesses convert raw materials into specific products, often customised by the end user; for example www.dell.com.
- Referral-based businesses direct customers to another company for a fee; for example, www.yesmail.com which generates leads through e-mail marketing.
- Subscription-based businesses charge a fee to viewers for providing content; for example www.ft.com.

Activity 4.6

Try to find your own examples of seven dominant models of e-business:

- Commission-based
- Advertising-based
- Markup-based
- Production-based
- Referral-based
- Subscription-based
- Fee-for-service-based

- Fee-for-service-based businesses are a 'pay as you go' system; for example, www.eproject.com provides virtual workspaces to allow online collaboration.

Key Differences between B2B and B2C Strategies

While a consumer is a single decision-making unit, a business may contain many people with an influence on the decision whether or not to buy a product because of financial control procedures. Questions that need to be addressed include:

- Who has the authority to make the purchase decision?
- How do the purchasing procedures differ from department to department?
- Which individuals might be willing to try a new product?
- Which individuals are the 'gatekeepers' who aim to maintain traditional buying behaviour?
- Are the users of the product the same people who are responsible for purchasing it?

It is difficult for a B2B company to generalise its clients into distinct segments because there may well be far fewer of them than in a B2C context, but still too many to treat as individuals.

Particularly in high technology markets, customers and suppliers have to exchange detailed information about product design, operation and service. There may be a long period of supplier comparison and evaluation. Because of these timescales and complexity, a B2B company is likely to focus on selling a broader range of products or services to existing customers rather than expanding the total volume of customers.

The means by which a B2B company connects with its customers through channel partners tends to be more complex than for a B2C company. Distribution channels might well be multi-tiered and global in scope. A B2B company may well need to focus on training its business customers on how to use the product most effectively, and indeed even convince them that they have a need for the product at all. A good example here is Dell Computer's 'Premier Pages' which are managed within an extranet and customised according to the needs of individual business customers (www.dell.com).

Actual purchase events by business customers may be rare, particularly if the products are high value, so maintaining customer relationships in between purchases can be quite a challenge. The composition of the B2B marketing communications mix is likely to place more emphasis on personal selling than advertising and promotion, and hence the Internet aids the purchase decision by providing easy access to technical information rather than transactional capability.

The complexity of B2B interactions means that providing added value beyond the actual product or service itself in terms of online information or support can help to differentiate a B2B company from its competitors. Cisco (www.cisco.com) has had considerable success with its online technical support functions because not only could customers easily find the information they were seeking, but they soon

Activity 4.7

Certainly much of the early attention for e-commerce was fixed on B2C; however, the B2B market is now much greater in size. Using an Internet statistics site such as Clickz Stats (www.clickz.com/stats) see what information you can find about the current size of the B2B market.

began to share experiences and answer each other's queries without the need for intervention by Cisco staff.

As noted in Chapter 1, there are of course new e-business models emerging on a regular basis. More recent developments include C2C (customer to customer) models such as eBay and C2B (customer to business) models such as Priceline.

The Long Tail

One of the major developments in online strategy over the past few years concerns the exploitation of the long tail. The Internet allows companies to sell a much wider range of products than has been practical in the past. Providing customer access to very low value or rare items is an example of this phenomenon, which was popularised in a widely cited article in *Wired* (Anderson 2004) and is illustrated in Diagram 4.1. Anderson argued that in the traditional, 'bricks and mortar' world the limitations of programming and the costs of physical store space restrict what can be profitably offered to the public to items which can guarantee a large number of people demanding that same item in a confined geographic space. In Anderson's words: 'An

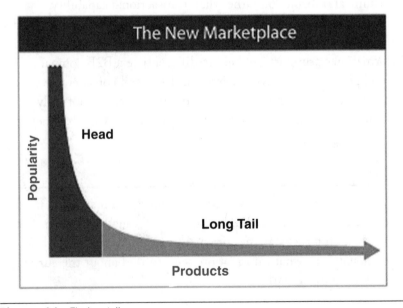

Diagram 4.1   The long tail.

average movie theatre will not show a film unless it can attract 1500 people over a 2 week run ... an average record store needs to sell at least 2 copies of a CD per year to make it worth carrying; that's the rent for a half inch of shelf space' (2004: 1).

This means in essence that they can only focus on sourcing and promoting 'hits'. What the online world has done is make it viable for organisations such as Amazon to carry a much longer 'tail' of products offering added value to customers and encouraging repeat business, and to make the same amount of money from each one:

> Wal-Mart must sell at least 100,000 copies of a CD to cover its retail overhead and make a profit. Rhapsody (by contrast) is a streaming music service that offers 735,000 tracks...once you get below the top 40,000 tracks which is the limit for a 'real' record store the top 400,000 tracks still stream several times a month. (2004: 2)

Brynjolfsson *et al.* (2006) analysed Amazon's sales patterns and found that 30 to 40 percent of sales were of books that could not usually be found in a traditional bookstore which was limited to the major titles by the physical storage space available on its shelves. Moreover, although Amazon heavily discounts the most popular titles, these items could be sold at a premium because of their restricted availability. The music industry has also benefited from the long tail phenomenon, and of course digital music can also be delivered to the customer electronically and it takes up no physical storage space at all.

Another factor which has contributed to the success of long tail items is the recent growth of social networking. This topic will be discussed in more detail in Chapter 12, but it is worth noting here that website features such as customer reviews, blogs and chatroom conversations can be powerful influencers of consumer behaviour due to the perceived lack of bias in comparison with company-generated content.

Case Study: Internet Banking Strategies

Electronic banking strategies are particularly attractive to banks because:

- There is no need to establish a physical presence in new areas, since growth can be accommodated centrally.
- The time-to-market for new products and services is reduced.
- Partnership arrangements (for example, with retailers) can provide added value for customers at little cost.
- Transactions and updates can occur daily.
- Customers can have access whenever and wherever it is convenient for them.

Retail banking customers are more sophisticated and demanding today than they were in the mid-1980s. Sophistication has come from a greater awareness of financial matters following saturation coverage in the media. Consumers are more demanding as they seek to maximise precious leisure time by leveraging technology in the pursuit of speedy and effective service. Today's customers require multiple products, a range of channels, seamless service and sound advice from a bank they can trust.

Segmenting a customer base in a meaningful way by clustering behavioural and attitudinal traits-lifestyle, familiarity with technology and levels of financial awareness reveals a marked difference in needs. Segmentation and targeting by wealth has revealed that affluent customer groups are more likely to hold a greater number of complex financial products with higher expectations of service excellence and seamless delivery across all channels. This segment is also taking up new technologies faster than the general population and is more active online, leading many banks to create 'high net worth' offerings. In addition, many offline purchases are actually driven by prior online research so that the benefit of building a 'virtual showcase' for financial products is greater than take up statistics would suggest, albeit difficult to quantify accurately.

In the early days of the Internet, many banks hoped online banking would allow them to cut costs dramatically by closing branches. They are now becoming increasingly aware that because customers expect a choice of channels, *absolute* customer numbers is not a reliable indicator of the success of an online offering, but that the number of *active* online customers is a more meaningful measure. Recognising that it will take much longer to realise the anticipated cost savings, banks are adopting various strategies to push customers online:

- Branches are used to educate customers in how to use online services.
- Reassurances over security issues are provided.
- Lower fees and higher interest rates are offered.
- Staff incentives are used to encourage customers to use online banking services.

The bricks-and-mortar bank branch, therefore, is unlikely to become redundant in the near future.

Generally speaking, traditional banks have not adapted products and prices or developed customised propositions for their online operations. 'Pure plays' (new Internet-only banks) have competed so far on the basis of products with aggressive pricing, innovative offerings and investments in new technologies. However, their efforts to win market share have been costly and will not be sustainable in the long-term. In a very crowded marketplace banks will increasingly try to 'poach' other online customers, which is a potentially more profitable strategy than getting their existing customers to migrate to the Internet. It is ironic that some online banks are now seeking to set up physical operations just as traditional banks create online ones.

A further structural dilemma for banks is to determine if their online operations should be integrated into the existing business or 'ring-fenced' as a separate division. Gulati and Garino note that the issue of integration or separation is not a zero-sum game, and that companies should 'strike a balance between the freedom, flexibility, and creativity that come with separation and the operating, marketing, and information economies that come with integration' (2001: 113). In 2002, Bank of Ireland decided to merge its previously separate Internet bank called F Sharp into its main operations after attracting just 2000 customers. The rationale was that the online operation could not offer the high level of customer service on its own that is necessary to support high net worth customers. Other banks with separate Internet operations such as Abbey National (www.cahoot.co.uk) and Coop Bank (www.smile.co.uk) have focused on less exclusive segments of the market with considerable success in terms of customer numbers, but also at significant cost to the bottom line.

Summary

It should now be clear to you that already the boundaries between the so-called 'old' and 'new' economies are blurring in the emphasis on integration of online and offline strategies to add value. The long tail is an interesting concept of online markets that we will return to again in later chapters.

Questions

Question 4.1

Can you think of any examples of well-known companies that have established separate Internet divisions?

Question 4.1 Feedback
British Airways is another high-profile organisation that recently set up a separate division. The objective was to mimic the speedy decision-making and organisational flexibility of an Internet start-up company without the constraints of established business structures and practices.

Question 4.2

Can you think of specific examples of companies where business priorities or industry structure dictate a more 'unusual' approach to Internet strategy?

Question 4.2 Feedback
Companies in the Fast Moving Consumer Goods (FMCG) sector, for example, will tend to focus on brand building rather than customer relationships due to the mundane nature of many such products, which is unlikely to stimulate significant consumer interest. Pharmaceutical companies can focus on innovation management by sponsorship of health-related online communities to learn more about rare diseases and add considerable value to research and development activities.

Question 4.3

Why do you think traditional banks are so keen to invest in online banking services?

Question 4.3 Feedback

If one bank does not offer its customers the choice then a competitor will be only too pleased to do so. In addition, competition in the banking and financial sector does not now only come from other bank institutions. Non-bank competitors use smart cards, Internet and software cryptography to reduce their market entry costs and steal a march on traditional banks. Retailers such as Tesco have more recent technological infrastructures and they have added financial services to their product portfolio.

Question 4.4

What advantages do 'clicks and mortar' companies have over 'dotcom' operations?

Question 4.4 Feedback

Established businesses usually have well-known brands, a loyal customer base, an established record of profitability, a network of industry contacts and experienced employees with detailed knowledge of the company and its history.

Question 4.5

What are the advantages of separating out e-business activities from the more traditional divisions of a 'clicks and mortar' company?

Question 4.5 Feedback

The UK retailer Debenhams (www.debenhams.co.uk) is an example of a successful 'clicks and mortar' company. It has set up a separate Internet division that is known internally as the 'pressure cooker', a reference to the prevailing frantic office atmosphere. Separate divisions allow the company to avoid conflicts between existing entrenched cultures and the new 'knowledge' mindset necessary for Internet success. By functioning independently, the new division is 'ringfenced' from the established, slow-moving and inflexible bureaucracy of its parent company, while still benefiting from association with the trusted brand image of the traditional Debenhams store.

Feedback on Activities

Activity 4.1

If you're finding it difficult to think of examples, simply try to categorise companies that you might use when shopping on the Internet or in the high street. Very few companies now operate totally on a 'bricks and mortar' basis; if you type a brand name into Google you can usually locate a website for all but the most basic of businesses these days. The strategic importance of the 'clicks' aspect to the business as a whole should also be evident from a scan of the website content.

Activity 4.2

The majority of more popular high street banks in the UK have adapted online banking in some form or other. However, it is interesting to note the different strategies. HSBC, for example, has its own online banking element (www.hsbc.co.uk) as well as a separate online banking entity First Direct (www.firstdirect.com).

Activity 4.3

Certainly, basic information can be gained from the website about products and services, as well as corporate and shareholder information. However, the site has been designed to enhance their relationship with their customers; for example, special sales information, Tesco club card online deals and music downloads. There is also information on other Tesco ventures; for example, Tesco's ISP service (www.tesco.net) and Tesco Finance (www.tescofinance.com).

Activity 4.4

Many examples of brand building websites exist in the motor industry where the majority of sales still currently occur offline. Ford (www.

ford.co.uk) is a good example of this; www.pg.com has a section for Crest toothpaste which is focused on children and educational in content—there is no option for purchasing a tube of toothpaste online!

Activity 4.5

For example, a Google search (www.google.com) on the supermarket Tesco brings back over three and a half million sites. Basic information can be gained from the company's own website (www.tesco.com, which comes top of the list) about products and services, as well as corporate and shareholder information.

There is also information on other Tesco ventures; for example, Tesco's ISP service (www.tesco.net) and Tesco Finance (www.tesco-finance.com). As well as thousands of reviews and reports on Tesco from other sites.

Activity 4.6

There are many examples you can use. Sometimes the categories overlap. Amazon (www.amazon.co.uk), for example, is principally mark-up based. However it also uses a commission-based approach for the Amazon Marketplace.

Activity 4.7

According to the US Department of Commerce, B2C only made up 8 percent of e-commerce in 2005, compared to B2B's 93 percent.

Web Links

www.amazon.co.uk.
>An innovator in online trading and customer relationship building

www.argos.co.uk
>Traditionally catalogue based, but now offers products through a range of online channels

www.cahoot.co.uk
>The Internet-only bank owned by Abbey National

www.cisco.com
>A market leader in online community building

www.dell.com
>The leading e-commerce company, Dell computers provides custom built computers to consumer specification

www.easyjet.com
A low cost airline which has migrated its business model to the Web
www.easycar.com
An Internet-only car hire service which has been forced to upgrade its offline channels to improve service quality and provide customer choice
www.guinness.com
The website supports the offline brand image but does not permit online sales
www.pg.com
Example of FMCG product website. A section on Crest toothpaste provides dental hygiene advice
www.rightnowtechnologies.com
Provides free white papers and case studies to build the brand and generate goodwill with potential customers
www.rswww.com
RS Components traditionally offered products via paper based catalogues, but now has award-winning Internet channels
www.smile.co.uk
The Internet-only bank owned by Co-op Bank
www.tesco.co.uk
Successful retailing site that integrates Internet resources to support offline business strategies
www.whsmith.co.uk
An excellent example of a clicks and mortar company now offering multi-channel services
www.yell.co.uk
Online directory version of Yellow Pages

5

e-Consumer Behaviour

Introduction

In this chapter we examine the evolving profile of the e-consumer, and consider both the advantages and disadvantages of an e-shopping experience.

Topics Covered in the Chapter

- Introducing e-consumers
- Disadvantages and advantages of e-shopping for consumers
- Image
- Security, privacy and trust
- Social and experiential aspects of e-shopping
- Differences between male and female shopping styles
- Geographical differences in e-consumer behaviour
- Web atmospherics
- Towards an integrated model of e-consumer behaviour.

Learning Objectives

After completing this chapter you will have an understanding of:

- Why consumers e-shop (or do not e-shop).
- How consumers achieve satisfaction (or not) from e-shopping.
- How consumer satisfaction from e-retailing compares with satisfaction from in store shopping.
- What factors are inhibiting the growth of e-shopping?

Recommended Reading

Cheung, C. M. K., Chan, G. W. W. and Limayem, M. (2005) 'A critical review of online consumer behaviour: Empirical research', *Journal of Electronic Commerce in Organisations*, 3 (4): 1–19

International Journal of Retail and Distribution Management (2007) Special issue on social and experiential retailing, , 35 (6)

Perea y Monsuwé T, Dellaert, B. and de Ruyter, K. (2004) 'What drives consumers to shop online? A literature review', *International Journal of Service Industries Management*, 15 (1): 102–121

Introducing e-Consumers

Researchers have been aware, since before creation of the World Wide Web, that shopping is not just a matter of obtaining tangible products but that it is also about experience and enjoyment (Martineau, 1958; Tauber, 1972). e-Shoppers were originally thought to be more functional and utilitarian than conventional shoppers (e.g. Dholakia and Uusitalo, 2002; Brown *et al.*, 2003), concerned more with dimensions such as usefulness and ease of use rather than with hedonic dimensions such as enjoyment. In line with 'Diffusion of Innovations' theory (Rogers, 1995), the 'innovators' and 'early adopters' of e-shopping tended to be of a higher educational level (Li *et al.*, 1999) and socio-economic status (SES) (Tan, 1999) than the average, with more experience of the Internet and more favourable attitudes to technology (Sui and Cheng, 2001) and more variety seeking (Rohm and Swaminathan, 2004). Donthu and Garcia (1999) characterised early e-shoppers as: more innovative in their shopping activities; convenience oriented; more impulsive; less brand conscious and less price conscious. They were originally more likely to be male (Korgaonkar and Wolin, 1999). e-Shoppers have always tended to be older than the average Internet user, perhaps reflecting higher disposable income (Swinyard and Smith, 2003), with 45- to 54-year-olds being the highest-spending UK e-shoppers (Royal Mail, 2006). e-Shoppers are now becoming much more mainstream (Swinyard and Smith, 2003), although there is still a bias towards more prosperous SES (Citizens Online, 2007; OxIS, 2005). As in the high street, UK women now spend more time and money e-shopping than men do (Kelcoo/NeilsenNetRatings, 2006).

Contrary to the expectation that the Internet consumer is a wholly different type of individual from the traditional shopper (e.g. Dholakia and Uusitalo, 2002), Jayawardhena and colleagues (2007) found that consumer purchase orientations in both the traditional world and on the Internet are largely similar. This is consistent with findings of researchers that multi-channel retailers have higher market shares of e-retail than do pure-plays (Min and Wolfinbarger, 2005). Jayawardhena and associates (2006) indicated that consumers' emotion—described as 'excitement'—strongly influenced re-patronage intentions. The four antecedent factors of excitement were: convenience; attributes of the website; merchandising; and involvement. Far from being solely motivated by utilitarian, convenience considerations, there is considerable evidence for the importance of social interaction (e.g. Parsons, 2002; Rohm and Swaminathan, 2002) and recreational motives (Rohm and Swaminathan, 2002).

Disadvantages and Advantages of e-Shopping for Consumers

Disadvantages

Consumers were initially slow to embrace e-shopping. Back in 1996, the UK's largest e-consultancy, Cap Gemini, carried out an employee survey. The disadvantages for shoppers included: 'Can't be in to receive delivery'; 'Premium charged for delivery'; and 'Can't see or feel the merchandise'. With years more experience, many e-retailers still do not have satisfactory answers to these problems. Many consumers are still uncomfortable with the lack of face-to-face contact, difficulties assessing product quality and with returning or exchanging goods (OxIS, 2005). Typical shopper comments have included: 'They left it in the garden and didn't tell me'; 'It's a 24-hour shopping service but only a 6-hour delivery service'; and 'Returning unwanted products is when it all goes low-tech' (consumer surveys from Vincent and colleagues 2000).

Lack of trust is one of the most frequently cited reasons for consumers not e-shopping (Lee and Turban, 2001). Swinyard and Smith (2003) elicited reasons why people do not e-shop by comparing questionnaire responses of e-shoppers with non-e-shoppers and found that

> **Box 5.1   Disadvantages of e-shopping for consumers**
> - Credit card and security worries
> - Lack of personal and social interaction
> - Can't see or feel the merchandise
> - Don't know how
> - Can't be in to receive delivery
> - Premium charged for delivery
> - Difficulties with returning goods for refund

the most substantial reason is fear, with concerns such as credit card fraud. E-shoppers are higher than non-e-shoppers on 'Internet shopping is easy and fun'. Non e-shoppers are higher than e-shoppers on: 'Don't know how to shop or find things on the Internet' and 'Internet shopping is a hassle'. According to Swinyard and Smith (2003), there is an issue with lack of training.

The disadvantages are typical of those that faced mail order traders a few decades ago. Given time, as sales grow, sellers work to overcome the customers' concerns, and consumers become more confident. In the United States, L. L. Bean (www.llbean.com) could claim to be the pioneer of mail order, selling goods to rural farmers since way back in the mid-1800s. Today the company has put their reputation for customer responsiveness, helpfulness, cheerfulness and reliability to use in becoming world leader in e-retailing outdoor equipment and clothing, with an efficient, award-winning site.

Advantages

Counterbalancing the disadvantages and the slow responses of many UK e-retailers to addressing them, there are a number of advantages for shoppers. In a survey typical of many others, Kittle (2007) found these to be (in ranked order): 'convenient'; 'ability to compare products and prices'; 'availability of products not found in stores'; 'free shipping'; 'promotions'; and 'ease of last minute purchasing'. Other commonly cited advantages include 'prices favourable' (e.g. Dennis *et al.*, 2002); 'live chat', 'loyalty programs' and 'customer reviews' (Freedman, 2007).

Box 5.2   Advantages of e-shopping for consumers

- Cost effective
- Convenient
- Easy
- Saves time
- Fits in with other activities
- Breadth and depth of products
- Easy search of many alternatives
- Personalisation of presentation and merchandise
- Prices favourable

Image

Researchers attempting to answer why people e-shop have tended to look to various components of the 'image' of e-retailing and specific e-retailers, in a similar way to measurements of the image of a bricks store (Wolfinbarger and Gilly, 2002). This may be a valid approach for two reasons. Firstly, 'image' is a concept used to mean our overall evaluation or rating of something in such a way as to guide our actions (Boulding, 1956). For example, we are more likely to buy from a store that we consider has a positive image on considerations that we may consider important, such as price or customer service. Secondly, this is an approach that has been demonstrated to work for bricks stores over many years (e.g. Berry, 1969; Lindquist, 1974) and it is largely the bricks retailers with strong images that are making the running in e-retail. According to Kimber (2001), shopper loyalty instore and online are linked. For example, Tesco's customers using both on and offline shopping channels spend 20 percent more on average than customers who only use the regular store. Tesco is well known as having a very positive image both instore and online, being the UK grocery market leader in both channels.

e-Retail image measurements that have been used by commercial marketing research studies include: ease of use; product selection; product information; price; on-time delivery; product representation; customer support; and privacy. There is empirical support for some of these dimensions of image; for example 'product selection' and 'ease of use' (Dennis *et al.*, 2002a; Dennis and Pappamattaiou, 2003 respectively) but in general the connection between the components of image and e-shopping spending behaviour remains an under-researched area. Perhaps the most extensive investigation to date has come from Wolfinbarger and Gilly (2003) who carried out focus groups and quantitative surveys to determine the components of e-retail quality. The qualitative analysis identified four factors: (1) fulfilment/reliability; (2) website design; (3) customer service; and (4) security/privacy. Fulfilment/reliability includes both the description of a product and efficient delivery. Website design includes navigation, search, and ordering. Customer service means responsive and helpful service, responding to customer enquiries quickly. The quantitative surveys indicated that these three factors were all significantly related to e-shoppers understanding of e-retail quality.

Security, Privacy and Trust

As mentioned in the 'disadvantages' section above, credit card security and privacy worries have often been reported as one of the most important reasons for not e-shopping. It is surprising, therefore, that the survey did not find this factor to be significantly associated with e-retail quality. Other studies have shown that as e-shoppers become more experienced, they tend to shop more and become less concerned about security (OxIS, 2005). In the case of the Wolfinbarger and Gilly study, those e-shoppers who were satisfied with e-retailers' reliability, website design and service may well have been more confident e-shoppers and therefore suffered less security worries, resulting in 'security/privacy' being swamped by the other factors in the analysis. When shopping outcomes are satisfactory, consumers are more likely to continue e-shopping, both in general and from the specific e-retailer (Shim *et al.*, 2001). This illustrates the importance for e-retailers of turning e-shoppers into loyal, repeat buyers (Weber and Roehl, 1999).

Social and Experiential Aspects of e-Shopping

For decades retailers and researchers have been aware that shopping is not just a matter of obtaining tangible products but also about experience and enjoyment (Martineau, 1958; Tauber, 1972). Research has drawn attention to the importance of the social aspects of shopping (e.g. Dennis et al., 2005; Dennis and Hilton, 2001; Dholakia, 1999; 2002a; 2002b; Lunt (2000); Shim and Eastlick, 1998; Westbrook and Black, 1985). Shopping has even been found to be central to loving relationships within the family (Miller, 1998).

Similarly, enjoyment and entertainment have been demonstrated to be important benefits of shopping, increased by a pleasant atmosphere and reflected in spending (e.g. Ang and Leong, 1997; Babin *et al.*, 1994; Donovan *et al.*, 1994; Machleit and Mantel, 2001; Smith and Sherman, 1993; Sit *et al.*, 2003; Spies *et al.*, 1997). These benefits for shoppers can link to increased sales and profits for retailers; and higher rental incomes for shopping centres. According to an overwhelming majority of studies, the link between retail atmosphere and sales is 'very strong and robust' (Turley and Milliman, 2000) with researchers also reporting enhanced mood and goal attainment in a store with a pleasant atmosphere (Spies *et al.*, 1997).

In the case of e-shopping, social influences are also important but e-retailers have difficulty in satisfying these needs (Kolesar and Galbraith 2000; Shim and associates, 2000). Rohm and Swaminathan (2003), in a study comparing a sample of e-shoppers with non-e-shoppers, found that social interaction, variety seeking and convenience were all significant motivators for e-shopping. Childers and colleagues (2001) found enjoyment to be strongly associated with

---

Box 5.3   Motives for e-shopping

- Social
- Enjoyment
- Usefulness
- Ease of use
- Convenience
- Navigation
- Knowledge and ability to make a purchase
- Influence of friends and family.

Sources: Dennis and Papamatthaiou (2003); Parsons (2002).

> **Box 5.4   Social motives for e-shopping**
> - Social experiences outside the home
> - Communications with others having a similar interest
> - Peer group attraction
> - Status and authority – raising the standing of the shopper in the eyes of friends and colleagues
> - Virtual communities
>
> *Source:* Parsons (2002).

attitude to e-shopping, particularly for examples that the authors described as 'hedonic' or pleasure-related; e.g. Amazon (www.Amazon.com) or Hot Hot Hot (sauces—www.hothothot.com) Similarly, Parsons (2002) found that social motives such as: social experiences outside home; communication with others with similar interests; membership of peer groups; and status and authority were valid for e-shopping. Social and pleasure motives, important for bricks shopping, are, despite some qualification, also significant for e-shopping.

The successful e-retailers may be those that seek to replicate or even enhance social and experiential benefits online, using techniques of web atmospherics. Kim and Forsythe (2007) investigated the hedonic usage of product virtualization technologies in online clothing shopping. The results demonstrated that hedonic motivation had a stronger positive relationship than functional motivation with the attitude toward using product virtualization technologies. The authors concluded that perceived entertainment value is a stronger determinant than is perceived usefulness.

Differences between Male and Female Shopping Styles

According to evolutionary psychologists, differences between men's and women's behaviour may be not just cultural but also instinctive, handed down from the days of hunter-gatherers on the African savannah (Buss, 1999). In Western consumer societies, gathering may have translated into comparison shopping, hunting into earning money to support the family (Dennis, 2005). Even in the United States, where

Box 5.5   Enjoyment and e-shopping

Enjoyment motives for e-shopping
- Involvement
- Not boring
- Fun for its own sake.

Enjoyment and social features of e-retailing sites
- Chat rooms
- Bulletin boards
- Customer written stories
- Product reviews
- Suggestion boxes
- Personalisation of offers
- Blogs
- Podcasts
- RSS feeds

The most popular 'enjoyment' e-shopping sites (in approximate ranked order)
- eBay (auction, www.ebay.co.uk)
- Amazon (www.amazon.co.uk)
- CD Wow (www.cd-wow.co.uk)
- Ticketmaster (show tickets, www.ticketmaster.co.uk)
- Ryanair (www.ryanair.co.uk)
- Easy Jet (www.easyjet.co.uk)
- Opodo (air tickets, www.opodo.co.uk).

Source: Updated from Dennis and Papamatthaiou, 2003

gender equality in the workplace is greater than most countries, differences in shopping styles can be clearly observed. The female style involves searching, comparing, weighing the advantages and disadvantages of alternatives, finding the best value and taking a pride in the shopping activity (Underhill, 1999). This pride is justified because on average women make a 10 percent better cost saving than men do, making women the 'better shoppers' (Dennison, 2003). Women see the activity of shopping as a satisfying experience in itself (i.e. a leisure activity). On the other hand, men see shopping as a mission and tend to go straight for what they want in a purposeful way (Underhill, 1999).

Men see shopping as being unpleasant and undesirable (Dholokia, 1999), spend less time shopping than women and generally do not take responsibility for food and clothing purchases (Miller, 1998), are less interested in clothing and fashion (Cox and Dittmar, 1995), make quick/careless decisions more commonly (Campbell, 1997), and are more independent, confident, externally motivated, competitive, and more willing to take risks especially with money (Areni and Kiecker, 1993; Prince, 1993).

The stereotypes are not 100 percent accurate, but in the UK have been found to apply to 80 percent of women and 70 percent of men (Denison, 2003). The styles have been found to be equally valid for the e-consumer (Lindquist and Kaufman-Scarborough, 2000). As with bricks shopping, the stereotype reverses when the product purchased is technical and expensive (Dholakia and Chiang, 2003).

Internet use has historically been considered as being male dominated (Liff and Shepherd, 2004; Pavitt, 1997). Longitudinal Internet studies (GVU, 1997–2000; OxIS, 2003 & 2005; Verdict, 2000–2006) show that this gender bias is weakening, and in the United States and UK there is now an approximate balance. Sixty-four percent of UK women and 71 percent of men are Internet users (Citizens Online, 2007). Given the preponderance of women in the overall population, this translates to 48 percent of Internet users being women (up from 30 percent in 1997) (Pavitt, 1997). Over half of US and UK e-shoppers are now female and women are outspending men online (Verdict, 2006). Nevertheless, there are still considerable gender differences in Internet use. For example, men spend more time on the Internet (in total, not just on e-shopping) (averaging 10.5 hours per week compared to women's nine hours per week) and view 31 percent more pages (Rice, 2004). Men spend significantly more time listening to music, being entertained and reading news (Liff and Shepherd, 2004). Conversely, reflecting bricks shopping, women spend more time e-shopping than men do (Kelkoo/Nielsen/NetRatings, 2006). Men tend to buy CDs, music downloads, DVDs, books, computer and electrical products. Men tend to be major users of games sites (eTypes, 2001), gambling and pornography. Male e-shoppers form the large majority of the most sophisticated e-Types life cycle stage

Box 5.6   Shoppers in cyberspace: are they from Venus or Mars?

Female shopping style – the gatherer
- Ritual of seeking and comparing
- Imagining and envisioning the merchandise in use
- Tally up the pros and cons
- Take (justified) pride in ability as shoppers
- The total shopping process (not just buying) is a leisure activity
- Women like to spend longer shopping than men do
- Social interaction is an important part of shopping
- Women favour sites designed for women – e.g. iVillage (www. ivillage.co.uk) – with horoscopes, health, beauty and diet
- Women are more likely to browse online, then buy instore.

Male shopping styles – the hunter
- Men are incisive, decisive and determined shoppers
- Men's excitement with shopping is at the moment of 'kill' (purchase)
- Men try to complete the shopping activity in the shortest possible time
- Men's lack of patience means they often miss the best buy
- But the stereotype reverses when the product is technical and expensive. Men do take a pride in shopping for (e.g.) cars and computers (and women are purposeful for those products)
- Men's favourite sites tend to include games, gambling and pornography
- Male e-shoppers are heavier Internet users and are more likely to shop via mobile devices and PDAs.

Sources: Dennison (2003); Dholakia (1999); Dholakia and Chiang (2003); eTypes, 2003; Lindquist et al, 2000; Lindquist and Kaufman-Scarborough, 2000; Underhill (1999).

'Wired 4 life', whereas women e-shoppers tend to be the 'Virtual virgins' (eTypes, 2001).

On the other hand, women favour clothing, footwear, lingerie and accessories (Allegra Strategies, 2006; IMRG, 2007). In light of the above research we argue that women's online purchasing behaviour is still different from men's. Perhaps reflecting the greater attention given to the selection process, US women are 30 percent more likely than men are to browse online then buy instore (Lindquist and Kaufman-Scarborough, 2000).

Case Study eTypes (www.etypes.info)

eTypes is an award winning tool for understanding online consumer behaviour. It features extensive information on how consumers behave and transact on line. eTypes has been constructed by combining demographic and lifestyle datasets from profiling company CACI with data from Forrester, the leading Internet research organisation. The system works by classifying consumers into seven groups denoting life stage, internet usage levels and twenty-three eTypes—detailing online behaviour; and five e-shopping lifestyle stages.

Box 5.7   e-shopping life cycle stages

- **Stage 1 – Virtual virgins** Only 12 percent of these Internet users have bought online, half the average. A high proportion is female. Age tends to be the youngest and oldest
- **Stage 2 – Chatters and gamers** These are avid Internet users, spending 20 percent more time online than the average. Twenty-five percent are e-shoppers (the national average). This group tend to be more worried about security than average.
- **Stage 3 – DotCom dabblers** Forty percent of these Internet users are e-shoppers. They are heavy users of entertainment and scientific sites.
- **Stage 4 – Surfing suits** These are heavy e-shoppers, but spend less time online – only 60 percent of the average. They tend to be professional and financially aware.
- **Stage 5 – Wired 4 life** The heaviest e-shoppers – 70 percent have purchased online. Many are graduates or cosmopolitan. These users tend to be in the mid-range age groups.

Source: www.etypes.info

> **Box 5.8   Components of e-retail quality**
>
> **Fulfilment/reliability:**
>
> - Accurate display and description of a product so that what customers receive is what they thought they ordered
> - Delivery of the right product within the time frame promised.
>
> **Website design:** – all elements of the consumer's experience at the website:
>
> - Navigation
> - Information search
> - Order processing
> - Personalization
> - Product selection.
>
> **Customer service:**
>
> - Responsive, helpful, willing service that responds to customer inquiries quickly
>
> **Security/privacy:**
>
> - Security of credit card payments
> - Privacy of shared information.
>
> *Source:* Wolfinbarger and Gilly (2003).

eTypes aims to tell e-retailers about the characteristics of e-shoppers and what they use the Internet for—whether it's finding holidays, buying CDs, managing their stocks and shares or just chatting. eTypes claims that this means e-retailers can get more from their e-shopper data—and a higher return on website investment (see www. webcustomers.co.uk).

In the previous section, we drew attention to the importance of shopping as a social activity. In line with the evolutionary psychology approach, these interpersonal aspects are particularly important for female shoppers (for example, see Dholakia, 1999; Elliot, 1994). Women tend to want more interpersonal contact from e-shopping than men do, preferring chat and women's sites (eTypes, 2001). 'Women want ease of navigation and sense of personalised relationship'—helped by 'community' or chat rooms (Harris, 1998). An example of the more female and 'community' oriented approach is the e-mall iVillage (referred to above) for which Tesco hosts the UK site.

e-Shopping, though, is generally poor at providing the social and experiential benefits that women want, but good for finding the best deals quickly—the male purposeful style (Dennis, 2005; Lindquist *et al.*, 2000). Male and female shopping behaviour tends to be much more similar on the web than instore, meaning that females are losing out on social and experiential benefits. According to US surveys, two-thirds of website visitors 'will not buy online until there is more human interaction' and women in particular want a 'sense of personalised relationship' (Harris, 1998; McCarthy, 2000). e-Retailers should make the buying process more personal and interactive, especially for female shoppers.

Geographical Differences in e-Consumer Behaviour

There is a distinct geographical distribution of e-shopping in the UK, with a heavy concentration in London and the Southeast. According to Kimber (2001), this is being driven by affluence and high credit card ownership. e-Shoppers in that region also are more confident about security. After London, the highest e-shopping areas are Reading, Cambridge, Bristol and Birmingham. Conversely, areas further away from London and less affluent areas tend to e-shop less and to be more concerned about security. Newcastle-on-Tyne has the lowest e-shopping level of any UK city, followed by Sheffield, York, Glasgow and Hull (eTypes 2001).

The balance of the evidence available is that a wide range of image and other attributes are important in consumer satisfaction and behaviour for e-shopping. Many attributes that are important for bricks shopping are also important for e-shopping. Some e-retailers have often paid less attention to elements such as the social and enjoyment aspects of e-shopping, but the best and most successful e-retailers are deliberately and successfully satisfying e-shoppers on motivators such as these. Emphasising the importance of addressing the overall experience of e-shopping, one survey indicated that if the worst-rated e-grocery were to improve the online experience to match the best competitor, online sales could be improved by 480 percent. For the average e-retailer, improved user experience could result in a 33 to 54 percent sales increase (Meekings *et al.*, 2003).

Case Study: Customer Service from Screwfix
(www.screwfix.com)

Screwfix's approach to customer service can be illustrated by our experience with a concrete mixer. After a few week's use, the electrical contactor start button failed, meaning the mixer would only run if the 'start' button was held in by hand. We informed Screwfix, explaining that the machine had already had some use, expecting to be offered a replacement electrical contactor. With such a large item of equipment, and the length of time it had been used, we did not realistically expect a replacement mixer. Nevertheless, the Screwfix help desk could not have been more helpful, and did authorise the replacement mixer—asking us just to pack up the old one in the original packaging and hand it over to the delivery driver who brought the new one. The problem was that the (very bulky!) packaging had been disposed of some time ago. No problem for Screwfix: 'We'll send you the new one. Unpack it over the next few days, then dismantle the old one and put it into the new packaging. We'll send another lorry to pick it up next week'.

Think Point

Why do you think Screwfix offered to replace the item, despite the heavy extra carriage requirements, when a simple replacement of the contactor would have been acceptable?

Case Study: Customer Service from McWillies
(not its real name!)

A contrasting approach to that of the previous case study can be illustrated by our customer service experience from McWillies. We used the shopbot Kelkoo to identify the best deal for a photo printer—which turned out to be from McWillies. Not only was McWillies cheapest for the printer but also there was a special offer including a free pack of photo print paper. McWillies sent an e-mail confirmation showing the price and the two items, printer and paper. The printer arrived within a few days, but without the paper. Some weeks later, despite an (unanswered) e-mail, the paper had still not arrived, so we phoned the 'customer service' line. Here is a summarised extract from the conversation:

McWillies (M): 'The paper was sent with the printer'.
Customer (C): 'But we didn't receive it'.
M: 'You must have received it because it was sent in the same box'.
C: 'There was only one box, the original packaging, and it was completely full with the printer'.
M: 'Well we sent it'.
C: 'Well we haven't received it' [and so on for a few minutes], until:
C: 'Can I speak to a supervisor'?
M: 'The supervisor's busy'.
C: 'Well, can I speak to someone at head office'?
M: 'I'll speak to head office, please hold'. [Long wait]
M: 'I've checked with head office and they say it's too late to do anything about it now'.
C: 'I would still like to speak to a supervisor'. [audible click in mid-sentence]:
M: 'Supervisor speaking. We can *prove* that we sent the paper, because we weigh all the parcels, so all we have to do is to check the weight on the docket and we'll prove that we sent it'.
C: 'That's great! What a good idea. Could you check it now, please, as it will prove that the paper wasn't in the box'.
M: '*NO!* We will not be doing that because **YOU** should've sent us an e-mail to let us know that the paper had not arrived'.
C: 'As I've already explained, we did send an e-mail'.
M: 'Well we have no record of it so the matter ends here'.
C: 'Can you check with head office before you refuse to confirm the weight of the parcel as that will prove that we didn't receive the paper'?

M: '*NO!* We can't check the weight and I'm not going to discuss this any further'.
(Line went dead).

Postscript: We still have not received the paper and have given up trying to get it.

Think Point

Why do you think McWillies suggested checking the package weights, but decided against this course of action when the customer said it was a good idea?

Case Study: Marketing Research Surveys

When we bought a new digital camera from Samsung, we had to register the software online. The registration process entailed uploading basic information on the use of the product that the supplier can use; for example, to inform us of updates or new products that may be of interest. Other suppliers use a huge lifestyle questionnaire that gives the impression of being the guarantee registration. The lifestyle data can be used for profiling, but also may be rented for a highly selectable mailing list by other companies. To comply with data protection legislation, there is an 'opt out' box that can be checked, but the 'if you don't want this service, please tick' message is sometimes in very small print almost hidden amongst many pages of conditions. Most e-shoppers just click 'accept' and never even know.

Web Atmospherics

In the 'social and experiential aspects of e-shopping' section above, it was stated that enjoyment and entertainment are important benefits of e-shopping, increased by a pleasant atmosphere and reflected in consumer spending. Many studies of the 'bricks' world have used an environmental psychology framework to demonstrate that cues in the retail 'atmosphere' or environment can affect consumers' emotions, which in turn can influence behaviour. The importance of this so-called stimulus-organism-response (S-O-R) model is that the stimulus cues can be manipulated be marketers; e.g. colour, music or aroma. The stimuli will be aimed at increasing shoppers' pleasure and arousal, which in turn should lead to more 'approach' (rather than 'avoidance') behaviour; e.g. spending. Eroglu and colleagues (2003) demonstrated that the same type of model can be applied to e-consumer behaviour—web atmospherics.

Web atmospherics refer to the sum of the cues to stimulate the senses of the online user or consumer. Graphics, visuals, audio, colour, product presentation at different levels of resolution, video and 3D displays are among the more common examples. Elements of web design that improve the attractiveness of the site or replicate the offline experience lead to satisfied customers. For example, Fasolo and colleagues (2006) found that animating the product by rotating in 3D made it preferred to the non-animated one. The creation of the virtual environment of the e-retail store includes structural design (e.g. pop-ups, 1-click checkout); media (video, audio, graphics and colour management); layout and usability (search facilities, organisation and grouping of merchandise); and sound and music. In theory, atmospherics can also include: touch (which can be simulated using a vibrating touch pad) and smell (which might be incorporated by offering to send samples).

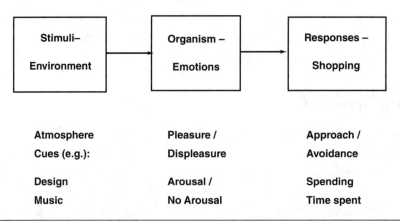

Diagram 5.1 Simplified S-O-R model of web atmospherics. *Source*: The authors, based on Eroglu et al., 2003.

Box 5.9   Website Design Features to Sell 'Look and Feel' Goods Online

Contrary to received wisdom on e-retailing, Chicksand and Knowles (2002) argue that look and feel sites, such as clothing, beauty products and furniture do have a potentially important role to play in e-retailing. In a study of 45 such e-retailers they found a clear majority did have a good design in terms of the basics: layout, navigation, information and image. In contrast, only a small minority seemed to make strong use of Web atmospherics, such as customization, colour management, technology and chat communication lines. Thus they argue that part of the reason why e-retailing of look-and-feel goods is being slow to take off may be partly due to the under-utilisation of Web atmospheric cues in these sites, rather than solely to the inherent characteristics of the products.

Chicksand and Knowles (2002) refer to a number of 'good practices' that might be relevant for 'look and feel' (and potentially any other) e-retailers to go further with their Web atmospherics. Examples using technological advances include the 'My Virtual Model' option on the Lands' End site, allowing shoppers to create virtual models of themselves online (see Diagrams 5.1 and 5.2) (www.landsend.com). Beauty product e-retailer, www.EZFace.com allows consumers to download a photo of themselves and preview make up products that will be added to the photo.

In theory, aromas can be produced through peripheral devices that can be plugged into a computer. DigiScent designed a 'personal scent synthesizer', which received code from the Web site and emits the relevant smell by blending from small ampoules of essence. This might have application for gaming (think dungeons!) but the idea has still to take off. No doubt the marketing launch was not helped by the name: iSmell.

Online colour can be improved through technology that, for example, downloads a cookie, which then reads the monitor's colour output. This issue is important because colours can be difficult to gauge when looking at a computer screen, with each monitor displaying colours differently. Retail support companies, such as E-Color (www.rosco.com), Imation (www.imation.com), Pantone (www.pantone.com) and WayTech (www.waytech.com) are targeting e-retailers selling goods such as clothing that rely on colour presentation.

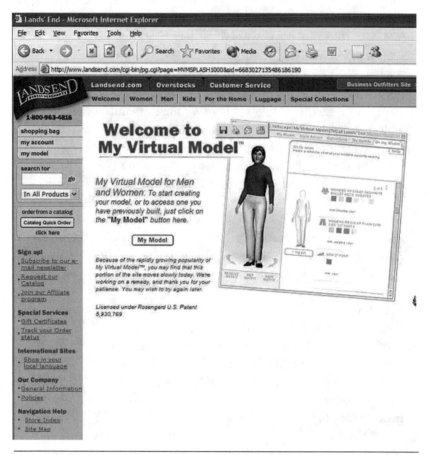

Diagram 5.2   'My Virtual Model' at clothing e-retailer Lands' End. *Source*: www.landsend.com

Towards an Integrated Model of e-Consumer Behaviour

In the sections above, we have briefly reviewed some of the main dimensions of e-consumer behaviour. This is an emerging research area. As such, most research has been based on prior classical consumer behaviour (offline) findings, often adapted by the addition of web-specific factors (Cheung *et al.*, 2005). A unified body of knowledge is yet to emerge. Nevertheless, after reviewing 355 articles on the topic, Cheung *et al.*, (2005) concluded that the Theory of Reasoned Action (TRA) and its family theories dominate. The family theories include the technology acceptance model (TAM) and the theory of planned behaviour (TPB).

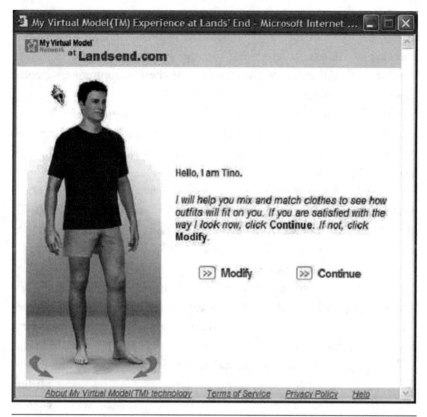

Diagram 5.3 Based on a series of online questions, the virtual model approximates the image of the Web shopper. *Source*: www.landsend.com

The basis of the TRA is that consumer behaviour is predominantly determined by intention (Fishbein and Ajzen, 1975). Intention is influenced by attitude and social factors. The dimensions of 'attitude' can be many and various but are often similar to those that we have described as 'image' above. Social factors are called 'subjective norm' in TRA and TPB. This name reflects the subjective influences to comply with norms set by others (e.g. whether our best friends think that we should make a particular purchase). As discussed in the 'social and experiential aspects of e-shopping' section above, social benefits of e-shopping, such as communications with like-minded people, can be important motivators.

TAM was originally conceived to model the adoption of information systems in the workplace (Davis, 1989) but has also been found useful as a framework for the adoption of e-commerce (Chen *et al.*, 2002). TAM identifies two specific dimensions of attitude: usefulness and ease of use. Usefulness refers to consumers' perceptions that using the Internet will enhance the outcome of their shopping experience. Ease of use concerns the degree to which e-shopping is perceived as involving a minimum of effort. Davis and colleagues (1992) have more recently added a new variable: enjoyment. Enjoyment reflects the hedonic dimension discussed in the 'Social and experiential aspects of e-shopping' section above.

TAM has been criticised for ignoring a number of influences on e-consumer behaviour. These include social ones (Chen *et al.*, 2002) and other exogenous factors (Moon and Kim, 2001). Perea y Monsuwé and colleagues (2004) therefore developed an integrated model including four exogenous factors: consumer traits; situational factors; product characteristics; and trust. Consumer traits may include, for example, age, SES and gender (as discussed in the 'Introducing e-Consumers' and 'Differences between Male and Female Shopping Styles' sections above).

In the offline world, situational factors include geographical location, which also has relevance online (see the 'Geographical Differences in e-Consumer Behaviour' section above). The most relevant equivalent factors for e-consumer behaviour are those such as convenience, ability to compare and availability, as discussed in the 'Disadvantages and Advantages of e-Shopping for Consumers'. Product characteristics refer to the extent to which products are virtual rather than physical (discussed in more detail in the 'ES (Electronic Shopping) Test' box in Chapter 10).

As mentioned in the 'Security, Privacy and Trust' section, lack of trust is one of the main reasons for not e-shopping. The characteristics of e-retail sites that lead to greater trust include, for example, safe shopping icons—discussed more fully in the 'Safe Online Shopping' box in Chapter 10.

Most studies of e-consumer behaviour have gone only as far as modelling 'intention', with few addressing actual adoption (Cheung *et al.*, 2005). Still fewer have investigated the critical issue of continuance behaviour or loyalty. Nevertheless, as mentioned in the 'Security, privacy and trust' section above, as consumers achieve more satisfactory

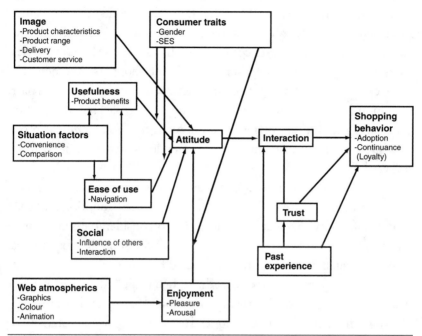

Diagram 5.4   Simplified integrated model of e-consumer behaviour. *Source*: The authors, drawing on Cheung et al. (2005) and Perea y Monsuwé et al. (2004).

e-shopping experiences, they are more likely to trust and re-patronise both e-shopping in general and specific e-retailers.

Perea y Monswé and associates (2004) have devised an overall model for 'Intention' based on the TRA, TBP and TAM framework. We have extended this by adding S-O-R (based on Eroglu and colleagues, 2003) and adoption/continuance (following Cheung *et al.*, 2005)—see Figure 5.4).

Summary

There are disadvantages and advantages of e-shopping for consumers, but retailers and shoppers are overcoming the problems and e-shopping is growing. Shopping provides not just functional goods but also real social and enjoyment benefits. Although originally thought of only in mechanistic terms, e-shopping can also provide social interaction and enjoyment. Even though in some aspects such as recreation, e-shopping trails behind bricks shopping, it is often the e-retailers that are good at satisfying these non-tangible benefits that are having most success. Although the stereotypes cannot be generalised with certainty, there are differences between the sexes in shopping styles. Men tend to be more purposeful and faster shoppers. Women take more care, and want more social interaction than men do. In the past, e-shopping has been more suited to the male style, but women are becoming heavy users of female-oriented sites. For technical products such as cars and computers, the gender stereotypes tend to be reversed.

The growth of e-shopping is still at an early stage. Security, privacy and trust concerns are still critical in e-consumers' adoption and continuance (loyalty) behaviours. There is also considerable scope for e-retailers to improve the 'web atmosphere' of the shopping experience, using cues such as colour, graphics and 3D animation.

Most theory frameworks that have been applied to e-consumer behaviour are based on the theory of reasoned action and family (paralleling offline consumer behaviour). In addition to social interaction, enjoyment, trust and atmospherics, the key variables include image, usefulness and ease of use.

Questions

Question 5.1

Why do people shop?

Question 5.1 Feedback
People shop to obtain useful benefits in terms of purchases, but also for many other reasons; for example, to enjoy the process or to socialise with others.

Question 5.2

How can the mechanistic process of e-shopping satisfy shoppers' social motives?

Question 5.2 Feedback

e-retailers' social motives can be satisfied by, for example, providing social experiences, communication with others having a similar interest, membership of virtual communities.

Question 5.3

What can e-retailers do to provide enjoyment and social benefits for e-shoppers?

Question 5.3 Feedback

e-Retails can, for example, provide chat rooms and bulletin boards; provide facilities for product reviews and suggestion boxes; personalisation of offers.

Web Links

www.nielsen-netratings.com
   Performance and viewing ratings for Internet sites and advertisers.
www.forrester.com
   Internet usage data.
www.webcustomers.co.uk
   Demographics, classifications and consumer e-shopping behaviour.
www.nma.co.uk
   New media news items.
www.emarketer.com
   e-marketing statistics and reports.

6

CUSTOMER RELATIONSHIP MARKETING

Introduction

This chapter begins by discussing the importance of building effective relationships with the various stakeholder groups both internal and external to the business. It then focuses more specifically on how e-business can assist this process in terms of managing data for personalisation and loyalty building campaigns. Finally, the chapter examines how the technology allows customers to interact with each other in order to build communities of interest or resolve particular queries, hence raising their level of trust with the business concerned.

Topics Covered in the Chapter

- Managing stakeholder relationships
- What is Customer Relationship Marketing (CRM)?
- Online CRM
- Loyalty programmes and personalisation
- Building online communities
- CRM challenges.

Learning Objectives

By the end of this chapter you should be able to:

- Discuss the relationship between internal marketing and customer relationship marketing.
- Explain the critical role of information in the implementation of effective relationship marketing strategies.

- Describe how the Internet permits relevant data to be acquired, stored, analysed and managed.
- Explain how the information derived from this data can be applied in order to build and sustain customer relationships.

Recommended Reading

Godin, S. (1999) *Permission Marketing*, New York: Simon and Schuster
Kasanoff, B. (2001) *Making It Personal: How to Profit from Personalisation without Invading Privacy*, Chichester: Wiley

Managing Stakeholder Relationships

A key role of modern marketing is that of a management mindset implemented throughout an organisation rather than confined to a particular department. This viewpoint regards marketing as a guiding management philosophy or attitude of mind that puts the customer first, and it is commonly described as a 'marketing orientation'. It is a much broader view of the role of marketing than has been envisaged in the past and it cuts across a wide range of organisational functions. Successful adaptation of a marketing orientation requires effective management of all stakeholder groups (this means people with a particular, although not necessarily the same interest in the activities of the company) such as staff, business partners, shareholders and suppliers, as well as customers.

The Internet supports the concept of the marketing orientation because it provides a powerful interactive communications medium both within the organisation (through the use of an Intranet) and externally with other key stakeholder groups (through the use of an extranet) as introduced in Chapter 1. The Internet also facilitates the gathering and management of data necessary to develop sustainable customer relationships. BT, for example, is using its intranet to develop a competencies database of employee IT skills, thereby opening up a pool of potential labour for jobs that come up and highlighting training needs.

Adopting these relationship marketing principles within the organisation is known as 'internal marketing'. The basic premise behind internal marketing is that a company's communications with its customers and other external stakeholders are unlikely to be effective unless employees within the firm are aware of the message that the firm is trying to put across (and more critically are prepared to buy into on an individual basis). It is currently fashionable to refer to employees as 'internal customers'. If all employees are clear about the company's mission, objectives and strategy then there is a much better chance that customers will get the same message. Research has shown that firms where employees understand organisational goals had considerably higher returns on capital than those where employees felt excluded or uninformed.

It has been estimated that more than 20 percent of a firm's communications are actually with itself rather than with external stakeholders, yet internal communications are rarely accorded the same degree of attention and resources as external communications. Sometimes very basic errors are made. For example, if the person responsible for mailing out corporate brochures is not told that a facility for customers to e-mail such requests to the firm has been implemented, incoming messages may well be ignored by that person in the mistaken assumption that someone else is dealing with them.

Many 'new economy' employees work in call centres that have been dubbed 'the new sweat shops' because of pressure to work as quickly as possible under electronic surveillance which monitors, for example, the number of customer e-mails responded to per hour. In these service-intensive organisations the power is in the hands of lower-level, front-line employees upon whose handling of customer services managers must depend for the achievement of organisational objectives. This means that internal marketing needs to play a critical role in ensuring that staff are well informed and motivated if a quality service is to be provided to customers. However, this is frequently not the case. It is often suggested that relationships with both staff and customers can be enhanced through induction programmes, training courses, benefits, the use of intranets or through working in cross-functional teams. However, while all these are useful, things are rarely that simple. Too often, customer care programmes are instigated as a 'quick fix', without making any changes in entrenched management behaviour, or attempting to evaluate the success of the programme implemented.

Activity 6.1

There are clearly a number of advantages to using online technologies such as e-mail and Intranet sites for internal marketing. Can you think of any disadvantages?

What Is Customer Relationship Marketing?

Having established the role of employees as a key stakeholder group in the development of effective customer service, we will now go on to examine the subject of customer relationship marketing (often referred to as CRM) in more detail.

There are many definitions of relationship marketing. For example:

> A business strategy which pro-actively builds a bias or preference for an organisation with its individual employees, channels and customers resulting in increased retention and increased performance. (Newell 2000: 182)

Relationship marketing, therefore, is based on retaining *existing* customers rather than acquiring *new* ones. For the company, relationship marketing can enhance customer retention rates. This impacts directly on profitability because it can cost much more to attract a new customer than it does to retain an existing customer. Retained customers become more profitable over time as the relationship between them and the supplier develops.

By focusing on the provision of a quality service to a customer, a company is increasing the chance that the customer will return. If that customer is subsequently treated in an individual way in accordance with what the company has learned about their preferences, then the customer is likely to take notice. If customers are so pleased with the attention and service received that they start recommending the company to others, then marketing costs begin to fall as 'word of mouth' recommendations are completely free. From the customer's perspective, developing a long term relationship with a company can also help to reduce the perceived risk associated with the purchase of goods or services.

It is not feasible, of course, for a company to try and develop a relationship with all of its customers. The key is to focus on those customers with the greatest profit potential. The Pareto Principle applies here because just 20 percent of customers may account for 80 percent of profit generation. The key is to work out which particular customers make up the lucrative 20 percent! Peppers and Rogers (2002) recommended the segmentation of customers as follows in order to focus marketing budgets on the most valuable customers:

1. Most-valuable customers (MVCs) should be encouraged to remain loyal with personal attention in order to retain their profitable business.

2. Most-growable customers (MGCs) should be encouraged to extend their currently limited contribution by buying more or related products in order that they become profitable over the longer term. A combination of online and offline personalised communications could be drawn upon to help grow this business.

3. Below-zero customers (BZCs) are not profitable and are unlikely to become so, unless significant investment in them is made. Online communication channels can be drawn upon to service such customers relatively inexpensively.

Some companies have taken this type of customer analysis much further and they have actually 'fired' unprofitable customers. Wagner (2006) in an article titled 'throttling the customer' discusses the example of DVD rental company Netflix (www.netflix.com) which deliberately gave an inferior service to its most active customers, favouring those who only used the service occasionally, and actually increased its profits as a result. Because the company charged a flat fee for unlimited DVD rentals, its most profitable customers were actually those who used the service least. Also influential in raising profits was the development of community features on the website which allowed customers to interact and post reviews. As more companies obtain detailed knowledge about the relative profitability of their various customers, such strategies of 'firing' customers could become more commonplace. The danger, of course, is that the brand image can be damaged if the affected customers object, or if other customers object on their behalf. Considerable harm can be done to the brand if complaints are aired in public forums such as blogs or chat rooms. It is also problematic if the displaced customers from one company are swept up by competitors seeking to increase their market share.

Traditionally, the majority of marketing resources have been expended on the more costly activity of new customer acquisition, without any significant effort being made to retain customers once the transaction has been completed. This can lead to disenfranchisement amongst existing customers who feel neglected and under-valued when potential customers are offered better deals. This problem frequently manifests itself in the highly competitive UK mortgage market with preferential interest rates offered to new borrowers.

Activity 6.2

Do you think that relationship marketing is really something new?

What if the customer never wished to be in a 'relationship' with the organisation in the first place? Just because an organisation has decided to change to a relationship marketing strategy, this does not mean that customers will also make the shift to the same extent, if at all. Customers may actually desire a one-way marketing relationship where they do not have to expend any effort in building and maintaining the relationship, believing that it is up to the supplying organisation if it wants to retain their custom. Price sensitive customers may simply take the benefits or savings offered from a number of firms in turn. O' Malley and Tynan (2001) observed that customers may well tolerate relationship building initiatives only for as long as it suits them because of self-interest and convenience, rather than build up the trust and commitment that the company might expect. This behaviour applies particularly to individual consumers; business to business marketing has historically relied much more heavily upon long term personal relationships.

Activity 6.3

What can companies do about customers who do not appear to offer serious long term profit potential? Should these be targeted for relationship building?

Online Customer Relationship Marketing

On the Internet, of course, it is very easy for customers to compare the offerings of different suppliers by using price comparison sites and they can switch allegiance with the click of a mouse. The main UK price comparison site is Kelkoo (www.kelkoo.co.uk) which can be used for a range of different goods. There are also a number of more specific price comparison sites; for example, DVDs (www.find-dvd.co.uk), books (http://gb.bookbutler.info) and flights (www.skyscanner.net)

Chaffey *et al.* (2006) emphasise the importance of *retaining* the customers that have been attracted to the business, and *extending* the relationship with them over time. They note the importance of understanding how customers use the technology in their purchase decision making if long term relationships are to be developed, and has developed a model summarising the tactics necessary to support customers through six stages of the buying process:

1. *Problem recognition*—At this stage the company needs to promote the website so that potential customers are aware of its potential to solve their particular problems.
2. *Information search*—Make sure that the website is displayed as prominently as possible on search engines when the prospective customer is actively researching a solution to the problem.
3. *Evaluation*—Make sure that the site is easy to navigate and contains the information that the enquirer is seeking, together with the customer service backup that will encourage them to actually purchase.

Activity 6.4

Think about a recent online purchase that you have made, or considered making. How did the company concerned help you through each of the above stages when you considered your options? What particular features of the service would encourage you to make a repeat purchase, or recommend the company to others?

4. *Decision making*—Provide a choice of channel and clear evidence of product value in order to prompt the enquirer to choose your company rather than that of a competitor.
5. *Purchase*—Ensure that the transactional facility is quick, straightforward and secure so that customers are not tempted to change their minds at this stage.
6. *Post-purchase*—Keep the customer informed about delivery schedules and the availability of customer service support if required.

Later in this chapter we will discuss the increasingly important role played by online communities in this regard, and Chapter 9 addresses the role of marketing communications in what Chaffey calls 'conversion marketing'—converting potential customers to actual customers and existing customers to repeat customers. The importance of such conversion is highlighted by Eisenburg (2005) who criticises the emphasis that many companies place on just attracting visitors to their websites, rather than focusing on converting such visitors to regular buyers by building relationships to encourage repeat purchase and word of mouth recommendations.

So-called 'CRM Solutions' can be purchased from technology vendors that purport to 'do' a company's relationship marketing. However, true relationship marketing is a company-wide process and philosophy, not a piece of technology. According to Peppers and Rogers as many as 80 percent of such CRM implementations fail to deliver. The authors blame 'inadequate vision, focus and implementation' (2004: 1) and note some common mistakes:

- *'Paving the cow path'*—Here the new CRM strategy merely automates the company's existing ineffectiveness by maintaining the same business processes.
- Buying an *'off the shelf'* solution—In this case, the buyer has to adapt the company's business processes to fit in with the standards built into the new system. Technical imperatives therefore come before customer focus.
- *Failure to translate plans that seem reasonable on paper into practical action*—For example, employees may not be trained or motivated, or legacy computer systems not properly integrated.

Peppers and Rogers (2004) also highlight how effective use of the Internet can greatly facilitate relationship marketing:

- *Using the technology to achieve mass customisation of the marketing message—and even the product itself*—Mass customisation can range from minor cosmetic choices (for example, the choice of car colour, trim and specification online) to a collaborative process facilitated by ongoing dialogue (for example, Motorola can manufacture pagers to 11 million different specifications).
- *Developing the learning relationship*—By this they mean a continuous two-way dialogue which allows the offering to be adapted to meet specific needs. It can be achieved by means of online feedback forms, analysis of queries to customer service facilities, or through use of increasingly sophisticated software that analyses customer site searching behaviour before purchase
- *Offering an incentive for the customer to engage in the dialogue*—It must also be easy and convenient for the customer to engage with the company, so lengthy registration forms are often counter-productive. The best incentive is good, free, up-to-date content.
- *Acknowledging the privacy of the customer and the other demands upon their time*—This means only communicating with customers who have requested information, and making it easy for customers to 'opt out' if they wish. It also means guaran-

teeing not to pass on customer details to other companies in the form of online mailing lists. This strategy of building customer trust is known as permission marketing and is covered in more detail in Chapter 9.

The technology company Creative Visual (www.creativevisual. com) has developed a virtual interactive assistant called a Lingubot that is capable of holding conversations with web users in real time. Lingubots can understand the context of questions, which in turn enables them to emulate human conversation in 'natural language'. The Lingubot's 'brain' comprises a knowledge base of content that is built to anticipate customer questions and respond to them based on sophisticated word and phrase pattern matching technology. The Internet bank Cahoot (www.cahoot.com) has reduced the volume of calls and e-mails it sends to customers by several hundred a day by using a Lingubot called Any Questions. It answers questions ranging from detailed product information to guiding users through the process of opening an account. Services such as this (provided they actually work!) can help to overcome a customer's natural preference for human interaction so that the technology makes a positive contribution to the development of lasting customer relationships. Cahoot believes that Any Questions has made its site more intuitive for users, engaging them in a genuine dialogue that leads to improved satisfaction and increased sales. It studies the transcripts from user conversations in order to establish where customer concerns lie, and then the website can be adapted accordingly.

As demonstrated by the Boo.com example in Chapter 1, in the early days of the Internet some firms got into a lot of trouble over these forms of technology because they were (1) unreliable, with the software in its infancy, and (2) too demanding on Internet connection speed when most people were still using dial-up access. See, for example, the screenshot of the interactive 'Ms Boo' in Diagram 6.1 which is available from the Boo.com entry on Wikipedia. At the time, few people could make use of Ms Boo because of prevailing slow Internet connections.

Now that the majority of customers have better machines, as well as broadband access, firms like Cahoot in the earlier example can adopt

Diagram 6.1   The interactive Ms Boo.

new multimedia tools such as the Lingubot to better effect than Ms Boo.

Loyalty Programmes and Personalisation

Despite the problems listed above, it does seem that relationship marketing at least has the potential to enhance customer satisfaction. Although it is easy to be cynical, a satisfied customer is more likely to be loyal than one who is not. A loyal customer base has a number of benefits to a company:

- There are higher returns from repeat sales over time.
- Increasing levels of competition means service quality may be the only differentiating factor.
- Higher costs are associated with recruiting new customers than managing existing ones (because of the need to conduct credit checks, take up references and other administrative tasks).
- It provides scope for cross-selling.
- It creates possibilities for strategic partnerships.

- Loyal customers will recommend the company to others by 'word of mouth';
- Promotional costs to acquire new business are reduced.

Loyalty programmes (also known as 'reward schemes') can be introduced to increase loyalty. For example, successful programmes have been introduced in recent years by airlines such as BA and supermarkets such as Tesco. The costs of the rewards given away can be more than offset against the additional business gained through repeat or additional purchases. For example, Tesco's club card loyalty programme now comprises over 14 million customers and special offers can be customised based upon analysis of transactional data in order to enhance the brand image and build trust. Two hundred million instore purchases per day are tracked by the programme, and over 5,000 distinct customer segments identified, each receiving personalised coupons. Tesco is now the world's third biggest retailer and has 30 percent of the UK grocery market. In April 2006 they announced that total sales had climbed more than 12 percent to £37 billion in the last year with an increase in profits of more than 20 percent to £2.03 billion.

When Tesco began selling goods online (admittedly after a shaky start when the company's computer systems were not sufficiently integrated and orders had to be re-keyed manually!) the company was a 'known quantity' in comparison with the unproven Internet 'pureplays' that were setting themselves up in competition. Additional club card points were awarded for online purchases and Tesco now dominates the home delivery market to such an extent that many competitors have accepted defeat. Safeway, for example, decided in 2001 to stop selling its goods online and concentrated instead on refurbishing and upgrading its retail outlets.

Other competitors responded with collaboration strategies to try and catch up. For example, the Nectar card is a joint customer loyalty scheme operated by Loyalty Management UK (www.loyalty.co.uk). It was launched in September 2002 with four founding sponsors: Sainsbury's, Barclaycard, Debenhams and BP. Vodafone, Adams, Ford and Threshers Group have since been added. Customer data is shared amongst the partners and customers can redeem their rewards with any of the participating companies.

Activity 6.4

Try the personalisation demonstrations on www.broadvision.com. How do such personalisation techniques allow value to be added to customers?

For case study examples from around the world of best practice in building customer loyalty, take a look at www.e-loyaltyresource.com.

Another popular method of boosting loyalty is *personalisation*. Tesco is moving in this direction with its online service which is now becoming more sophisticated in its analytical capabilities in terms of suggesting particular products or special offers that might appeal to individual customers based upon their purchase history. Personalisation software allows the name of the user to be incorporated into the web pages, any previous transaction details to be displayed and related areas of interest to be flagged. Personalised e-mail messages can be distributed to highly targeted groups of customers at a very low cost. This type of marketing is also being driven by research such as that by Cyber Atlas (www.clickz.com/stats) which established that users who configure, personalise or register on websites are more than twice as likely to buy online as those that do not. A combination of a reward scheme and personalisation can therefore be a powerful tool to drive loyalty.

Rowley (2001) notes the following methods of collecting data for personalisation:

- The customer provides information in response to a request.
- If you want to find out what motivates your customers to buy from you, just ask! Tried and tested research techniques such as questionnaires or focus groups can be administered online.
- The practice of registration where access to certain sites (or parts of sites) is only permitted to individuals who have completed an initial registration form.
- *Customers provide information about themselves during engagement in an online community*—Building relationships through

online communities is covered later in the chapter, but it is worth noting here that transcripts of community dialogues can be analysed for research information.

• *The customer provides information as a by-product of a transaction*—This can be as basic as contact telephone numbers and postal addresses, but also enables a profile of the customer's purchase choices to be built up over time. Amazon use this technique to good effect by providing recommendations of books based on analysis of order history.

• *The customer search path through the website can be tracked*—Even if an actual purchase does not take place, the server log file can be analysed to determine the sites that a user from a specific IP address has visited. This enables the attractiveness of the site to be assessed based upon where referrals are coming from.

• *The merchant uses cookies to keep track of the customer's actions*—The use of cookies to identify returning customers was also discussed in Chapter 2. One of the more benign uses of cookies lies in the personalisation of web pages so that individual customer greetings can be set up.

Rowley goes on to note that while the web allows the collection of a vast amount of data by the methods listed above, this is merely the starting point. The raw data needs then to be stored (in a *data warehouse*) and then converted into knowledge (through *data mining* techniques) before it can actually be useful for decision-making purposes. Different sources of data may also need to be integrated before they can add value. This is therefore the core of a company's marketing information system, (often referred to as MIS or MKIS). As we will discuss in Chapter 7, these difficulties are compounded when a company relies on a number of different channels (shop, mobile, PC, interactive digital television…) through which to interact with its customers.

As with relationship marketing as a whole, there has been a lot of 'hype' recently claiming that personalisation is a panacea for e-business success. This ignores the fact that in many circumstances customers are quite happy to receive a 'mass market' approach and find

Activity 6.5

Take a look at an online retailer that you have used in the past, does the degree of personalisation used by that retailer affect your intentions to return to its site at all?

any degree of personalisation an intrusive invasion of privacy. As a consumer yourself, what is your view on this?

Case Study

Hyundai cars (www.hyundai.co.uk) asked customers to contribute ideas to help develop a new model of car, the Santa Fe. Loyalty is considered by Hyundai to be vitally important to the bottom line. Twenty thousand Hyundai car owners were mailed a letter inviting them to help develop the company's first sports utility vehicle. The campaign targeted customers that it believed would be interested in the vehicle itself, as well as those who were likely to change their car within two years. The 1800 respondents were then mailed with instructions on how to offer their views which would guide the marketing strategy for the model. The mail pack was presented in a large tube, containing a covering letter, detailed questionnaire and a product guide. Also included were four collages depicting possible user groups, two sample newspaper advertisements and an invitation to 'write your own ad' headline. Customers would be able to see to what extent their responses had influenced Hyundai's thinking when they received feedback results before the vehicle's launch. The campaign met Hyundai's objectives of promoting customer loyalty as seen in the success of the overall marketing activity, which achieved a response rate of over 50 per cent.

Permission Marketing

According to Godin (1999) permission marketing is the situation in which the customer (or prospect):

- Clearly consents to having a relationship with a company.
- Is able to state clear preferences for the type, frequency and context of those communications.
- Has a high degree of control over the relationship: 'as new forms of media develop and clutter becomes ever more intense, it's the asset of permission that will generate profits for marketers'. (1999: 52)

Godin notes that by focusing only on individuals who have indicated an interest in a product, trust can be built, brand awareness can be improved and long term relationships can be developed. In contrast, he regards traditional marketing as 'interruption marketing' because people are bombarded with messages that in most cases they have no interest in and which actually stop them from doing something else (think, for example, of how annoying it is when pop up boxes cover up the screen you are trying to read).

It is important not to get too carried away with the concept of permission marketing. Ross, for example, is critical, claiming that the approach is not new: 'The large number of direct marketers who start the selling process with an ad offering information, and take it from there with a graduated programme of data collection and follow ups will wonder how it is that they have been practising permission marketing for all this time without knowing.' (2001: 14) In Chapter 9 we will discuss how e-mail can be used to develop permission-based relationships with customers.

Building Online Communities

In Chapter 4 we considered some of the new business models that are developing online. One of these was the consumer to consumer (C2C) model, upon which online communities are based. These communities have evolved considerably since the early days of news groups and chat rooms. They offer a simple means of overcoming the lack of human contact online and hence can meet consumers' social activity needs. Consequently, online communities can now represent a significant commercial opportunity.

Cisco (www.cisco.com) is a successful example of a company that has fostered customer communities and saved in excess of $550 million per year in customer support costs by letting customers help themselves to technical support information via web communities. After Cisco put their technical support function online, customers began to compete with each other to answer queries that had been posted by others.

Amazon has pioneered the process of 'collaborative filtering' whereby recommendations are made to customers on the basis of what other customers buying the same book also bought. Together with displays of unedited customer reviews, this strategy contributes towards the creation of a community of people with similar interests who will trust and act upon the recommendations of others in the group. By encouraging customers to try out other items in this way, not only are total sales increased but also their scope—customers may not otherwise have ventured outside the Top 100 books without a specific recommendation that was probably unknown to them beforehand. According to *The Economist* (2005), Amazon now makes one third of its sales from outside the top 130,000 titles.

The power of online communities is illustrated by the phenomenal growth of e-auctions, the most famous of which is eBay (www.ebay.com), which uses a Dutch auction model where the seller lists items for sale at a minimum price for a set period. The highest bidder within this time then obtains the item. According to Beynon-Davies (2004) eBay was established in the United States in 1995, became profitable within a year and secured venture capital funding in June 1997. It relied upon the loyalty of the customer base and word of mouth recommendations for increased growth. By 1999 eBay was creating communities in the UK, Canada, Australia, Japan and France. Although the average price of items sold is very low, the scale of the business is such that billions of dollars are now traded on the site. As buyers pay sellers before they receive the goods the business model is dependent on trust. Buyers rate sellers according to the level of service provided so a prospective buyer can access this data and make a judgement about whether to deal with that particular seller.

Other examples of online companies which encourage customers to rate their products and provide reviews for prospective customers include the Internet Movie Database (www.imdb.com), Last Minute for travel (www.lastminute.com) and Kelkoo for price comparisons (www.kelkoo.co.uk).

Even in the early days of the web, Hoffman and Novak noted the extent to which the online community model (based on the communication principle of 'many to many') differed from traditional marketing communications based on the principle of 'one to many':

> In this mediated model, the primary relationships are not between sender and receiver, but rather with the computer-mediated environment with which they interact. In this new model, information or content is not merely transmitted from a sender to a receiver, but instead, mediated environments are created by participants and then experienced. (1997: 50)

There are a number of different types of C2C interaction through emerging online communities. For example, they may be based on:

Purpose (www.autotrader.co.uk)

Here people with a common interest in purchasing cars can swap information on best buys, problems with particular models, garages providing high levels of customer service. etc.

Position (www.cancerresearchuk.org)

In this example for the charity Cancer Research the common ground is the medical condition, but various stakeholder groups such as patients, families, researchers and care providers can exchange relevant information perhaps related to new drugs or the existence of support networks.

Interest (www.familyfun.go.com)

Interest-based community sites bring together people with shared hobbies. There is an increasingly diverse range of such interest groups ranging from the predictable to the bizarre to the downright dangerous.

Profession (www.cim.co.uk)

Communities such as the Chartered Institute of Marketing bring together a wide range of professionals with a specialist interest in marketing.

Criticism (www.untied.com)

Untied is a vigilante site devoted to criticism of the customer service provided by United Airlines. Originally established by one disgruntled passenger, the site developed momentum as others contributed their own horror stories and the company presented a series of textbook examples of how not to handle complaints.

Another interesting example is the community site www.eggfreez-one.com which was set up by the online bank Egg for customers to comment on the services provided by the company. Some customers, however, were persistent in their criticism and the site was closed. The official reason given by Egg was that the way the site was structured did not allow for individual responses to be made to customer comments. It is easy for a cynic to believe that Egg was trying to protect its reputation here, seeing the comments on the site as a threat rather than an opportunity. What do you think?

Successful online communities must offer:

- quality content
- 'added-value' interactions
- provide efficient use of participants' time
- simple site design that can be navigated quickly
- integrated contact channels (meaning that it cannot stand alone)

Activity 6.6

Go online and try to find examples of online communities based around your own interests or your online shopping requirements. Do the online communities adopt any of the six criteria for success detailed earlier?

- minimal requirements for registering personal details.

The information posted on relevant community sites can provide companies with valuable research data. Most online communities are currently at a relatively early evolutionary stage and have yet to be subjected to serious study.

CRM Challenges

As noted above, multi-channel strategies can put severe strain on a company's data collection and analysis processes in order to get a unified view of customer activity through which to personalise its marketing campaigns. The benefits of getting it right, however, are considerable in terms of the competitive advantage that could be gained.

For example, Peppers and Rogers (2004) describe the 'unprecedented' opportunities presented by the combination of mobile technologies and one-to-one marketing strategies. They use the scenario of a travelling customer looking for a hotel room who enables her mobile to locate a convenient room at the right price. The hotel then responds with a tailored offer based upon the traveller's previously expressed needs and preferences. Services like this are just the tip of the iceberg. The authors believe that today's reliance on proprietary mobile networks will soon evolve into a more open architecture where customers can pick and choose specific features at will from many service providers, intensifying competition and stimulating further innovation in this dynamic area.

Peppers and Rogers claim that in such an environment the demands for customer information are bound to raise concerns over privacy, as discussed in Chapter 2. The authors predict the emergence of new entities called Data Aggregation Agents (DAAs) that will address the privacy issue by consolidating and controlling outside access to a customer's personal information. In order for this to work, a customer would choose a DAA when signing up for a mobile service, then register basic profile and preference information to receive customised content. Each time new services are added they can be linked to the original DAA without needing to re-supply personal data. The DAA is therefore continually learning more and more about the customer, who becomes locked in by the convenience. So for companies seeking to build customer relationships, the information held by the DAA can be drawn upon to anticipate the needs of favoured customers and hence offer customised products and services. This will increase loyalty while ensuring that marketing resources are targeted on the 'best' customers, meaning of course those deemed to offer most potential for profit.

In order for relationship marketing to be effective, companies cannot rely upon departmental solutions that address only one part of the customer account relationship. Increasingly, with the growth of online inter-organisational networks, customer communication is no longer just one customer talking to one enterprise. To provide the kind of service that improves the chance of customer loyalty, companies need to co-ordinate their partners and vendors through extranets that facilitate the sharing of information across company boundaries. The practical organisation of marketing functions and activities within such inter-firm networks may be complex. Decisions need to be taken on where responsibility lies for particular tasks, to avoid duplication and customer confusion. Open policies of information sharing mean a whole host of issues have to be addressed concerning the 'ownership' of customer data, not withstanding the technical difficulties inherent in integrating computer systems belonging to different organisations.

Case Study: Dell Computers

Dell, based in Round Rock, Texas, sells its products and services in more than 140 countries to customers ranging from major corporations, government agencies, medical and educational institutions, to small businesses and individuals. The firm employs 75,100 people from offices in over 80 different countries. It sells computers directly to customers online rather than through distributors and retailers, and was also one of the first companies to realise the potential of the Internet in building direct, one-to-one relationships with customers.

Beyond creating an online catalogue, Dell allows customers to configure PCs to fit individual requirements. All its machines are built to order, thereby increasing customer satisfaction and avoiding the need to keep an inventory of finished machines. The company also produces customised web pages for its largest corporate customers, enabling them to incorporate Dell's products directly into online procurement systems. It is also using the Internet to improve the efficiency of its own procurement, manufacturing and distribution operations. Dell's 'e-support direct' is a system for resolving customers' computer problems via the Internet. The site is divided into sections for corporate, small business and individual customers, and the language, content and layout of each part of the site is customised according to the needs of each of these customer groups.

What really distinguishes Dell.com from other sites is the sheer enormity of all the things it can do for customers. It is one of the largest websites in the world, receiving more than 2 billion page requests per quarter in 81 country sites in 28 languages and 26 currencies!

There are also more than 25,000 personalised Premier Pages for large customer accounts. Customers can configure computers in thousands of different ways, buy 40,000 different types of peripherals and software, access a massive knowledge base of customer support information, and track their order through shipping.

Dell's online support offerings extend the company's unique direct relationship with its customers. Intuitive, comprehensive and customised, these offerings include Dell Online Knowledge Base, the 'Ask Dudley' area, file library downloads and an entire suite of customised capabilities based on system service tags. Dell also has an official blog www.direct2dell.com .

By entering a systems service tag number, customers can get support information unique to their systems. Dell's Order Status system enables customers to track their orders from submission to the point of delivery. For any order, customers can see where their order is in Dell's

Activity 6.7

Having read the case study, go onto the web and have a look around the Dell site. To what extent do you agree with the analysis presented in the case study?

exclusive build-to-order process. For orders that have been shipped, customers can see detailed shipping status information.

Richard Owens, Vice President of Dell Online Worldwide, points out that the Dell.com seen by the public is only the tip of the iceberg. 'It's a pretty large tip, but beneath it is all of the business to business e-commerce transactions with our largest customers. About 70% of our online business is happening below that waterline through extranet relationships'.

Summary

In this chapter we have examined the inter-relationships between internal (staff) and external (customer and business partner) relationship building in adding value to a product or service, and considered how online marketing can support effective relationship building. The key issue is to reconcile the marketer's enhanced ability to acquire information and personalise campaigns with increasing levels of customer concern over the privacy of their data. In order to build loyalty in a climate of ever increasing customer expectations, many companies are now focusing on the challenge of integrating a range of online and offline channels to offer a seamless service to the customer regardless of the access mechanism chosen.

Questions

Question 6.1

Do you foresee any problems with the idea of involving customers in staff development?

Question 6.1 Feedback

It seems an interesting idea, but is this really a role that many customers would seek? How would staff feel about the prospect of being assessed by customers in such a way? Depending on the prevailing organisational culture, it could be perceived as an opportunity or a threat. At mobile phone company Orange (www.orange.co.uk) call centre staff welcome customer feedback on their performance because the company has won a number of awards for service quality and staff feel that customer comments are highly likely to be very positive.

Question 6.2

Implementing relationship marketing sounds very logical and straight-forward on paper. From your reading so far, why do you think so few companies get it right?

Question 6.2 Feedback

It is not easy to get a unified view of customer activity when they make contact by telephone one day, and e-mail the next. Also, many different parts of the organisation may have to work together if the customer buys a range of products and the company is structured by product range rather than by customer activity. Think, for example, of the challenge to a retail bank in obtaining an inclusive view when a single customer may have a mortgage, a branch current account, an Internet account, a pension, a loan, a business account—customers are increasingly expecting this degree of choice just in order to remain loyal. We will be discussing 'mixed mode buying' in Chapter 7.

Question 6.3

Can you think of any problems that might arise with the use of 'double opt in' policies when a company tries to develop relationships with customers?

Question 6.3 Feedback

This is an emerging paradox. There is increasing pressure on companies to grow the size of their e-mail lists, but adherence to 'double opt-in' will keep list sizes small in order to placate privacy advocates. You might well argue that it is better to have a small list of people who have a definite interest in the area, rather than a large list of people who are less committed and who may even complain when contacted. Look back to the discussion of ethical marketing and recent data protection legislation in Chapter 2 for more detail in this area.

Question 6.4

How can Dell use its website to develop effective relationships with customers?

Question 6.4 Feedback

The segmentation by customer group allows particular parts of the site to be customised to meet diverse customer needs. You might think, however, that there is a danger of the Premier Pages inducing envy and hence dissatisfaction in customers who are not singled out for such treatment. Allowing customers to customise their PCs to suit their specific requirements sets the firm apart from many of its competitors. The sheer scale of the products and services on offer sets new standards in the industry. By selling direct, Dell fosters the perception that it offers value for money to customers in comparison with competitors with expensive retail channels to support.

Question 6.5

With the increase in privacy concerns as well as spam and other unwanted e-mail, what steps can companies take to reassure customers about the safety of their personal data?

Question 6.5 Feedback

A clear privacy statement from companies is very important. This needs to be easily accessible from the company homepage, as well as easy to understand—there is little point in having a privacy statement that simply confuses customers. When users sign up to online newsletters many companies are now asking customers to acknowledge the newsletter by replying to it. This prevents anyone else from signing you up to a newsletter by inputting your e-mail address.

Feedback on Activities

Activity 6.1

One problem that can occur is employees become inundated with too much information. For example, the mobile phone retailer Phones 4U took the step of banning internal e-mail because it was taking up too much of their employees' time. It is very easy to send out reports and memos to huge mail lists within a company rather than the one or two people that actually need to read it.

Activity 6.2

Economic development in the late 20th century allowed economies of scale to speed up the exchange process. Branding replaced the need for close proximity and personal knowledge of consumers and suppliers to build trust. Relational exchange processes are still prevalent in the Far East and other countries where trust-inducing relational exchanges are ingrained within the cultural context. However, the popularity of relationship marketing has now been regained in the West with advances in information technology such as the Internet, allowing relational exchanges to be combined with the benefits of branding and thereby leveraging the advantages associated with each.

Activity 6.3

Banks face this dilemma with their loss-making current account business. They hope to cross-sell more lucrative products to these customers so that the overall customer relationship is profitable, but many customers are happy to take the free service and then shop around for other suppliers to purchase other financial products from. Banks could reduce their losses here by encouraging such customers to open online current accounts which are more cost effective than face to face services. Closing branches, however, tends to generate a high level of negative publicity. A segmentation strategy is possible whereby only selected customers are focused upon for relationship building, but this needs to be handled discreetly so that customers do not make comparisons. On the other hand, it should also be noted that powerful customers can decide to end a relationship and 'fire' suppliers, as exemplified by the UK retailer Marks & Spencer which abruptly ended its relationship with key supplier William Baird.

Activity 6.4

Look also at the 'white papers' section of the site which describes customer experiences of using Broadvision products for building customer relationships online, thereby answering the activity question. In itself this technique of making such customer testimonials available online is a good way of building trust through transparency of information, particularly if the business is brave enough to post a bad customer experience for all web viewers to see (together with an explanation of how the problem was resolved of course!)

Activity 6.5

More and more online retailers are adopting personalised options on their sites. This might be in the form of product recommendations or wish lists (www.amazon.co.uk), personalised homepages (www.ebay.co.uk) or simply greeting you by name (www.guardian.co.uk). Many people would not object to these tactics, and indeed view them positively. However, there is an argument that personalisation is an invasion of privacy, especially because cookies are used to recognise a returning customer.

Activity 6.6

There are many examples of online community available due to the popularity and growth of the Internet. It is interesting to note that while some communities are run as a business, many others are simply amateur community sites administered by people with a similar interest. For example www.dvd.reviewer.co.uk is a DVD and film fan site that is run by full time staff. However, the site deliberately keeps a 'fan' feel to it, and even uses volunteers to help run certain areas, such as the forums, and provide content. DVD reviewer has both in-house reviewers (who are not paid) as well as individual users who submit film reviews. The same principles apply on a grander scale to sites such as Wikipedia and Amazon. Amazon used to employ a team of reviewers to provide Amazon book reviews, but this task quickly became impossible and Amazon now relies on users to provide reviews of their products.

Activity 6.7

To get an idea of the sheer size of Dell.com put yourself in the position of a customer in a number of different scenarios; for example, as an individual trying to buy a basic home PC or as a business user setting up a small office network looking for advice.

Web Links

www.autotrader.co.uk
Example of an online community based on visitors' shared purpose
www.cancerresearchuk.org
Example of an online community based on servicing the diverse needs of the charity's stakeholders (i.e. patients, carers, researchers, donors, fundraisers, doctors)
www.broadvision.com
A good example (with a series of case studies) of commercial software to help personalise marketing campaigns
www.clickz.com/stats
A useful resource of Internet statistics
www.cisco.com
Classic example of an online community based around the company's technical support function.
www.dell.com
Website organised and customised around the needs of key customer groups
www.cim.co.uk
The Chartered Institute of Marketing which brings together a diverse range of companies and individuals with an interest in marketing
www.eggfreezone.com
A community site set up by Egg to canvass customer feedback
www.1to1.com
The Peppers and Rogers website with a number of personalisation case studies
www.familyfun.go.com
Example of a community site set up to meet the needs of a particular interest group
www.untied.com
A 'vigilante' site set up by customers critical of the customer service provided by United Airlines.

7
MULTI-CHANNEL MARKETING

Introduction

This chapter examines the new marketing channels made viable by developments in information technology. The key point is that the increasing scope of e-business means that a company no longer just has to consider online and offline marketing channels, but also what particular variations of online marketing should be adopted and, critically, how they can all be effectively integrated.

Topics Covered in the Chapter

- New Internet channels
  - Interactive radio
  - Mobile
  - Customer contact centres
  - Interactive digital television
- What does the future hold?
- Challenges of multi-channel marketing.

Learning Outcomes

By the end of this chapter you should be able to:

- Discuss the characteristics of the various online channels now available to marketers.
- Evaluate the internal challenges posed by multi-channel marketing strategies and explain how such issues can be addressed.

- Discuss the implications for service quality of automating channel communications.

Recommended Reading

Kirby, J. and Marsden, P. (2006) *Connected Marketing*, Oxford: Butterworth Heinemann

New Internet Channels

Recent technological developments mean that the choice for businesses is no longer merely online versus offline. Increasingly, multiple platforms need to be supported. For example, WH Smith Online (www.whsmith.co.uk) offers customers PC, mobile and digital television access to its products, as well as its established chain of retail outlets. Chaffey *et al.* (2006) note that possible benefits of such multichannel strategies include:

- Enhanced brand image
- Early mover advantage
- Learning about the technology from experience
- Customer acquisition
- Customer retention.

As noted in Chapter 2, research by the Office for National Statistics (2006) found that 43 percent of UK adults had Internet access, and of these people:

- Twenty-four percent stated that they had no need for, or no interest in, the Internet.
- Twenty four percent felt they lacked the knowledge or the confidence to use it.

These findings suggested the need for new features to attract users to existing online channels, an increased emphasis on new channels (such as iDTV and mobile) and a policy focus on access incentives and training if online channels were to become truly mainstream. Government initiatives, therefore, are now concentrated upon encouraging the provision and uptake of these new channels.

Musgrove (2006) discusses a number of examples of how the boundaries between TV and the Internet are becoming blurred, with popular shows such as *South Park* now available online as well as on the TV network. This multi-channel approach maximises the number of viewers and makes the advertisers happy. It has grown due to the success of YouTube and other video sites which have maximised the opportunities inherent in the increasing prevalence of fast broadband Internet access. Currently it is easier to make TV shows available online than it is the other way round, but Apple TV can display video streamed from sites such as YouTube on home computers.

It is important to be clear that the expression 'multi-channel' can cover a range of marketing functions. It can mean providing customers with choice when ordering or paying for goods, or when they are dealing with customer services for advice or to make a complaint, and it is these issues that we will focus on in this chapter. Companies may also promote their products and services to customers through a range of communication channels and this aspect will be considered in more detail in Chapter 9. Bear in mind also that some companies may use different channels for different marketing functions, and not necessarily offer all channels all of the time. For example, they could promote their business through online advertisements but not accept online payments.

Specific recent channel developments will now be considered in turn.

Interactive Radio

Smith and Chaffey (2005) note that there are currently two types of interactive radio:

- Digital radio allows two-way communication and is transactional. At the moment it requires a separate receiver but streaming technology is not too far off.
- Web radio is traditional radio delivered over the Internet. Once you log onto a station you can keep surfing while still listening to the radio. Quite a few radio stations are now available online (www.bbc.co.uk/radio).

Both types offer good brand building opportunities. Listeners are already used to interacting with a favourite radio station through voice or e-mail and the facility to make an instant purchase in response to an advertisement offers significant added value. On the negative side, it is still very early days for these services and audience fragmentation is likely to occur as the number of stations increases.

The Mobile Internet

As Diagram 7.1 illustrates, while ownership of mobile phones is reaching saturation point in the UK, usage of text and multimedia services continue to grow. There are actually more mobile phones than people in the UK. Of course this does not mean that every individual has a mobile, but that some people have more than one handset; for example, to distinguish between business and personal communications. Mobile communications offer considerable potential to marketers because of their unrivalled combination of:

* Instant response
* Personalised content (each customer has a unique telephone number)
* Scope for geographical location tracking.

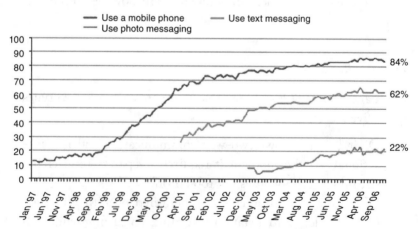

Source: eMORI Technology Tracker January 1997–September 2006 (www.mori.co.uk)

Diagram 7.1   Users of mobile communications.

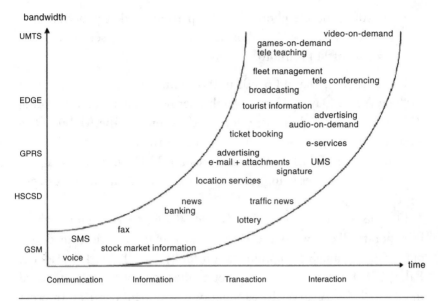

Diagram 7.2 Diffusion of mobile services (Buellingen and Woerter, 2004).

Mobile phones are rapidly evolving and becoming 'pocket portals' that provide a range of personalised services including e-mail, photo and text messaging with just one monthly bill. The much-hyped third generation of mobile communications (3G) is now gaining market share and delivers sound and images on an 'always on' basis. Diagram 7.2 illustrates how the scope of mobile services has evolved and multiplied over the past few years as the technology has matured. Insert Diagram 7.2 Diffusion of Mobile Services (Buellingen and Woerter, 2004)

SMS (text messaging) is a derivative of numeric paging technology which has been in existence for many years, updated for two-way communication. Also now widely available on modern handsets are MMS (Multi Media Message Systems) which incorporate sound and images. To illustrate the rapid growth of SMS, consider the following figures from the Mobile Data Association (www.text.it)

- In 1998, mobile phones had just 20 percent market penetration in the UK and 1 million text messages were sent in the whole year.

• In 2006, mobile phones had 85 percent market penetration in the UK and 41.8 billion text messages were sent (a daily average of 114 million).

On Christmas Day 2006, 205 million texts were sent, and the figure for New Year's Day 2007 was even higher reaching a record breaking 214 million, the highest daily total ever recorded. The Mobile Data Association has forecast that figures will continue to rise to deliver an annual total of 45 billion text messages for 2007, with an average of 3.75 billion messages being sent per month and 123 million messages per day.

On the business side, PDAs (Personal Digital Assistants) which incorporate diary, word processing and e-mail facilities are developing into a valuable communication tool. The UK market leader is Palm, which now provides Internet connection software as standard in all its PDAs. A survey by Motient (www.motient.com), an Internet communications and mobile provider, reveals that 'always-on' wireless two-way e-mail is quickly becoming a top priority requirement among PDA users. New features are emerging on a regular basis and it is clear that mobile phones and PDAs are rapidly converging. Colour screens are standard in all new devices as is the capability to display and transmit digital pictures.

There has been a lot of hype written recently about the potential of location-based technology in particular. However, current services are very basic and it is important to remember that there is some way to go before they become sufficiently reliable and useful to have a broad appeal. For example, variations on the scenario whereby a customer is called on his phone and advised of a special breakfast offer just as he walks to work past a Starbucks outlet have been heralded as the ultimate in personalised promotional campaigns. There are a number of practical difficulties though, such as customers' reluctance to be bombarded with intrusive advertising messages and the challenge of communicating effectively with the wide range of mobile devices and standards currently in use.

Keynote systems (www.keynote.com) recently launched a mobile performance measurement service to compare the services offered by all the major UK networks. It can measure delivery times, network comparisons, handset performance and geographic availability, thereby allowing content providers, networks or manufacturers to judge how successful their services have been. It also allows consumers to benchmark performance and make informed purchase decisions. In addition, for a detailed comparison of the characteristics of different mobile technologies, see Smith and Chaffey (2005).

The rate of growth of the mobile Internet has been far more rapid than that of earlier technologies. Current opportunities for marketers presented by recent mobile developments centre upon:

- The ability to interact with customers through personalised content provision and associated advertising;
- Online shopping accessibility and the ability to process transactions (m-commerce);
- Internal communications such as distribution of information to a remote workforce.

As with the growth of the PC-based Internet, it seems that communications with staff and customers are currently adding most value at this early stage, while the widespread acceptance of mobile transactions is still some way away. You must also bear in mind (as discussed with regard to online marketing strategies as a whole in Chapter 4) that not all of these applications will be relevant to all companies all of the time, and they will in most cases complement rather than replace existing channels. The key skill for marketers is to focus on the particular aspects of mobile marketing that will add value to customers in their specific industry contexts. We will now examine each of these areas in turn, drawing upon a number of examples to illustrate this important point.

Case Study: Colorzip

In most Asia Pacific countries mobile phones are used for much more than the voice and text services that dominate the UK; for example mobile TV soaps are extremely popular in Korea whereas mobile TV is barely acknowledged in the UK. In addition, mobile Internet has been in everyday use for some years. The Japanese company Colorzip provides the technology for a bar code based mobile service in use in Korea, Singapore and Japan. This proprietary system provides a service that enables the mobile phone user to download material such as video action from world cup football, a map, website, any type of digital data, by simply pointing the mobile phone at a colour zip. The source of the colour code links can be on clothing such as a 2006 World Cup T-Shirt, in magazine articles and adverts, on television and websites. Government applications in Korea include its use in museums and education establishments and it has also been used for a real-time televised public survey in a simple yes/no public opinion poll. Colorzip prompts an immediate emotional response and benefits from the instant, always on, feelings associated with using a mobile phone.

Content Provision and Advertising   3G technology offers far more scope for creative advertising than the small black-and-white text-only screens that dominated the market in the early years. Only Japan and France currently have established commercial mobile advertising in the form of banners, key word searches or sponsorship, but there are many trials underway in Europe and the United States. Mobile advertising therefore still represents a very small percentage of company promotional spend in comparison with general online advertising and more traditional media such as radio and television, but the figure is increasing. Forecasts for the size of the global mobile advertising market vary from between 2 percent and 12 percent of a company's online spend by 2011 according to Ovum (www.ovum.com).

Three models of mobile advertising are starting to emerge:

- Display advertising is targeted to the profile of the user.
- Content such as images and news from a major sporting event is sponsored by a brand which allows cheap or free delivery to the consumer.
- Relevant sponsored links are displayed through keyword searches on services such as Google Mobile.

Other technologies are also at the trial stage:

- Advertisements are displayed on 'idle screens'; for example, while a browser page is loading.

- A display advert is visible on the bottom of the screen while sending an IM, SMS or MMS message.
- 'Click to call' functionality from the mobile Internet allows the user to connect a voice call directly with a customer service representative.

Case Study: R/GA and Nokia

As showcased at the 2006 Mobile Marketing Association Awards, R/GA and Nokia raised awareness of Nokia's new Nseries high-concept line of multimedia devices by positioning the device as a multimedia computer, not merely a phone. To target Nokia's audience, R/GA created 15 different interactive posters fitted with Bluetooth technology and placed them throughout the London Underground. The posters invited users to opt in to download images of neighbourhood maps from 'Superfuture' (London's online city guide) directly to their handsets by pointing a mobile device in the direction of the poster. R/GA also made the content available to all phone models with Bluetooth capability, not only Nokia customers. This example shows that the traditionally 'static' medium of outdoor boards can now create dynamic interactions between consumers and their local area. R/GA and Nokia delivered an innovative new product launch by delivering a high value and relevant service, while at the same time helping consumers understand the more advanced functionality of their device.

Good response rates are enjoyed by advertisers in trials (perhaps due to the novelty factor!). Also, advertising based on content sponsorship or key word searches is less intrusive than the banners and pop-ups we have become used to on our PCs. The most successful campaigns have been run by companies such as the *Sun* newspaper, which has used the mobile channel to advertise competitions being run in the paper itself. In other words it is using online advertising to drive its traditional core business—which is offline newspaper sales. According to www.emailcenteruk.com (2005), mobile advertising response rates at 12 to 15 percent are much higher than those for e-mail (6–10 percent), direct mail (3 percent) and Internet banner advertisements (less than 1 percent).

Current text-based promotional campaigns can be categorised into the following types:

- Discounting, whereby an SMS is sent which includes a 'voucher' (code) for discount on an item. The recipient presents the code at the point of sale to claim the discount.
- Database development, whereby an SMS can include an embedded phone number, so that the recipient can easily call the company for more information. The individual responses are then logged.
- Added value services are provided by combining channels. For example, an estate agent may send picture messages of houses newly offered for sale to clients who have requested a particular type of property. Or an airline might text a client with details of allocated seats or changes to an itinerary.
- The provision of time-critical information by SMS, such as updates on particular share prices, traffic delays, football scores or ski conditions.

Case Study: Legion Interactive

Another winner at the 2006 Mobile Marketing Association awards was Legion Interactive, an Australian mobile marketing agency, and its client, Zodiac, an Australian marketer of pool cleaners. Zodiac wanted to increase product sales, drive warranty registration and develop ongoing customer interaction. The advertising program utilised stickers with unique codes on each product package. Consumers were required to submit the code via SMS to claim cash back or other promotional merchandise. Advertising ran in traditional media and in stores, encouraging consumers to purchase the products. All entrants were placed into a draw to win a car each week of the campaign. The campaign was a good example of how a mobile promotion could be used to generate sales and build brand awareness in a very 'traditional' and specialised market.

The key to success in all of these cases is for the marketer to operate on an 'opt in' basis, as people's tolerance of unsolicited messages (spam) falls. This means that companies should only target people who have actively agreed to receive such messages from them. To avoid giving offence, mobile advertisements must be:

- optional (meaning actively requested by users)
- personalised
- moderate in volume
- free to the recipient
- offer a means to unsubscribe.

A final application of mobile advertising is 'bluecasting'. Bluetooth is a technology which enables a message to be sent from one mobile device directly to another. Bluecasting refers to the transmission of text, video clips, audio and images to all Bluetooth-enabled phones in the vicinity of the transmitter. A successful example involved bluecasting extracts from a new Coldplay album at London railway stations: 13,000 people opted in to receive the material which was a response rate of 15 percent. The promotion was timed to take place a few days before the official launch of the album and the recipients of the video clips were prompted to listen to an interview with the band which was about to start on Radio 1.

Mobile Commerce   Mobile commerce—meaning the actual purchase of items from the mobile Internet—is currently low in volume but expected to grow rapidly over the next few years.

According to Xu and Gutierrez (2006) there are four key factors which will drive the success of m-commerce:

- Convenience—being able to access the service anywhere at any time
- Ease of use—simple and intuitive processes
- Trust—in the integrity and security of the system
- Ubiquity—access real time information regardless of location.

Forrester Research (www.forrester.com) suggests that world-wide revenues from mobile commerce could reach $100 billion by 2009. Be warned that we've heard wild projections before—in connection with the potential revenues likely to be generated by dotcoms, for example—so don't read too much into these figures. In 2000, Forrester predicted imminent huge growth in m-commerce that turned out to be significantly over-optimistic. Before getting carried away in another round of Internet euphoria, think about the recent high level of negative publicity about mobile theft, which highlights the problem of security, and the possible adverse health implications. Steps have been taken by the major market players to address these issues; for example, a common database of stolen phone numbers has been established so that the handsets can be disabled to prevent unauthorised purchases being made. Remember also that many people are still reluctant to undertake PC-based commerce, let alone transact through a mobile phone. Looking back in history, it is often the case that new technologies take considerably longer to reach mass market acceptance than early predictions suggested.

Internal Communications Business services via mobile channels are currently few and far between, but early experiments are underway with order placing, stock checking availability and order tracking to facilitate supply chain integration.

Remote workers can use wireless devices to access office systems and marketing information held on the corporate intranet. Such services are useful for logistics companies needing to keep track of their drivers' location and also to send SMS messages with reminders and alerts; for example, of schedule changes or traffic problems. Salespeople operating in the field can update customer records or request specific information automatically. Although the potential for the mobile Internet to enhance communications between staff or between staff and customers is considerable, adapting the corporate security systems to allow access through the mobile environment can be a significant headache, as can the practicalities of integrating mobile channels with existing IT systems more generally.

Case Study: Is the Future of e-Business Mobile?

In Japan, most business people have to commute everyday and will spend a good part of their working days in 'densha' or 'chikatetsu', the Japanese public transport system. As a result, mobile communication devices such as PHS (Personal Handyphone System), mobile phones and pagers have become very popular and are being supplied in a wide

Activity 7.1

In what ways do you think the usage of mobile technologies might differ across the world?

variety of models. The PHS, developed by Japan's NTT, is a lightweight portable wireless phone that can function as a cordless phone at home and as a mobile phone elsewhere. It can handle voice, fax and video signals. Users can send and receive e-mail and even develop their own web pages on tiny mobile handsets.

NTT DoCoMo, one of the most advanced companies in the telecommunication industry today, introduced the first 3G (Third Generation) mobile phone service in 2001. The 3G mobile phone service is the first step for Japan into the 'Evernet' (a Japanese term for universal access to the Internet, irrespective of place, time and equipment). The company has recently teamed up with a number of other companies (including Vodafone in the UK) to examine the next step (currently called 'super 3G'). The first stage of development is set for sometime in 2007. NTT DoCoMo is using a technology called FOMA (Freedom of Mobile Multimedia Access) which provides more freedom in terms of speed and quality than the WAP technology developed in the West. There is a demo of the FOMA technology available at http://www.nttdocomo.com/corebiz/foma/try/imotion.html

NTT DoCoMo has already begun offering its hit 'i-mode' wireless Internet service to the US market through partner AT&T Wireless, allowing US users to exchange e-mail, check stock prices and find restaurants, movies and other information from their cell phones. The mobile operator O2 teamed up with NTT DoCoMo at the end of 2004 to launch similar Internet services in the UK, Germany and Ireland. You can view their i-mode demo at http://www.o2.com/services/imode.asp

Call Centres

Service Quality   Call centre services fall into two main categories: outbound (cold calling to potential customers) and inbound (taking calls from customers with queries and problems). According to *Guardian*

Online (17 August 2004) the call centre industry continues to grow by 22 percent a year on average, making it one of the fastest growing sectors in the UK. Call centres currently employ half a million people in the UK, or 3 percent of the workforce in North England and Scotland. One hundred and sixty companies now have call centres in the Glasgow area, and business is booming because of customer dissatisfaction with services offered in foreign offices.

Cost saving is the reason behind companies pushing telephone and Internet channels. Customer relationship management company Talisma estimates that interaction with a customer face-to-face costs $300 a time, a phone conversation costs $53, an Internet chat $30, text chat $10, e-mail $3, and self-help on the Internet 10 cents. Consequently the long-term future of the telephone call centre has been questioned. However, online banking, for example, is still principally used for simple transactions, and when it comes to pensions or life insurance, customers prefer to talk to an advisor by telephone or meet face-to-face. In the UK, both Lloyds TSB and Barclays suffered from significant customer dissatisfaction and adverse publicity when branches were replaced by ATM machines in rural areas.

In these service-intensive organisations the power is in the hands of lower-level, front-line employees upon whose handling of service encounters managers must depend for the achievement of organisational objectives. Traditionally, many call centres have relied heavily on 'scripts'; staff are monitored in order to assess how tightly they comply with them. This offers the advantage of consistency of service, but at a low, inauthentic or even 'phoney' level. Customer expectations are rising; many now expect an immediate response to queries at any time of the day or night, and are unimpressed, for example, if a company's website does not display the most up-to-date product information and availability. This puts pressure on companies to ensure customer service call centres are efficiently staffed and also that their websites are easy to navigate and contain the information that the customer seeks

Multi-Channel Customer Contact Centres   Rapid technological developments mean that call centres now have the potential to become 'Customer Contact Centres'. Halifax Bank in the UK spent £90 million launching Intelligent Finance (www.if.com), which was the first organisation in Europe to offer five integrated customer communication channels; telephone agents, interactive voice response, Internet, mobile phones and e-mail.

At Capital One, a financial services company which handles more than one million calls per week, callers are automatically routed to specialist agent teams depending on the predicted nature of their call based upon past experience. A recent Datamonitor study estimated that 40 percent of all 75,000 call centres in the UK were now 'web-enabled' in order to provide multi-media customer access points. In theory, this means that a customer should be able to choose whether to 'click to talk' (speak to an employee by telephone) 'click to e-mail' (send a query and receive a response by e-mail) or 'click to chat' (interact with an employee by instant messaging).

Of critical importance in terms of perceived service quality and the building of trust in the brand is for these channels to be seamless so that a customer can switch from one to another without repeating the story. It is also important for a log to be kept of earlier conversations so that an agent is always aware of the history of the query and what stage has been reached in resolving it. It is also possible for specific customers to be flagged according to their perceived value, so that differing service levels can be applied accordingly.

Another challenge concerns the viability of V reps (automated customer service agents) which save staffing costs but rather obviously lack the human touch. This feature is common in the US, but trials by online banks in the UK have generated negative feedback and the projects have in most cases been shelved.

Finally there is the issue of managing customer expectations. After UK Building Society Nationwide upgraded its website to provide

Activity 7.2

Look up www.ananova.com and select the link called 'news bulletins' to see an example of an avatar in action. How would you feel about 'talking' to one of these characters, for example to arrange a bank loan?

more detailed information to customers, its call centre was flooded with enquiries from people who wanted further information based on the new data that had been made available. Staff became discouraged as both the quantity and level of difficulty of their work rapidly increased.

Interactive Digital Television

Digital TV offers greater choice of channels, specialist programming, supplementary information and ability to interact with programmes. It looks similar to the PC-based Internet but is delivered through the television set and can be operated using a remote control. The UK government is currently pushing for total digital television penetration, and there has been talk of switching off the analogue signal by as soon as 2010. From a standing start in 1999, market penetration in 2006 is currently around 69 percent of UK households and this is projected to rise to 95 percent by 2010, according to the Mori survey in Diagram 7.3. Leading providers include Sky Digital, Freeview and Virgin Media. One of the key drivers for this surprisingly rapid growth has been the provision of free set-top boxes by these platform providers. Services currently provided include home shopping, e-mail,

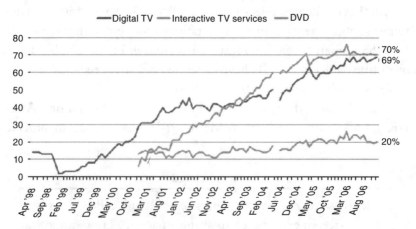

Ipsos MORI Technology Tracker April 1998 – November 2006
(www.ipso-mori.com/technology/techtracker.shtml)
Base: circa 4,000 interviews per month

Diagram 7.3   Television services in UK homes.

video, banking and travel. Interactive TV services are now used by 19 percent of the UK population (Mori, 2006).

Domino's Pizza, which is represented on satellite, cable and the Web, is one of the early success stories of iDTV. Online transactions represent 4 percent of its total business. Management credit the firm's sponsorship of *The Simpsons* as pivotal in building Domino's iDTV business. This activity has given Domino's a brand recognition figure of 98 percent in multi-channel homes.

Advertising through this mechanism is interactive as viewers can respond immediately to request further information or to sign up for a promotion. Digital TV has helped increase the fragmentation of viewers, as there are over 200 channels now available in the UK. This means that advertising can be easily targeted to tighter niche audiences; for example, through exposure on sports, cooking or health channels. Advertisers can develop their own TV channels in order to incorporate content provision and communicate with their customers less intrusively. For example, the PC version of Boots' digital health channel called Wellbeing is also automatically accessed if you type in www.boots.co.uk. Specialist digital TV channels also provide more focus for sponsorship deals.

The relationship between social class and choice of Internet access mechanism is illustrated below. In social groups AB and C1, PC-based Internet access far outweighs digital television ownership, but the ratio shifts in social groups C2 and DE, where twice as many households have digital TV as have Internet access via PC. Less than half of digital television owners have so far used interactive services such as shopping, banking, gaming or e-mail. This is because PCs have been traditionally viewed as information tools and are a logical choice for accessing the Internet and using online consumer services. The television, however, is normally viewed as an entertainment tool, and the biggest driver for digital adoption so far has been improved picture quality and a greater choice of channels, with little attention being paid by consumers to the advantages of interactive services.

Smith and Chaffey (2005) note the following advantages of iDTV to marketers:

• Direct response mass market advertising

- Highly targetable
- Move buyers through the complete buying process
- Audience engagement through interaction
- Brand building and positioning reinforcement
- Brand building through community building
- Customer service—bottle neck reduction
- Security—less risk associated with TV than websites
- Controllable—highly measurable
- Cost savings.

Some recent examples of the types of advertising delivered on iDTV include:

- *Further information*—Mecca Bingo invited viewers to 'Press Red for a free information pack'.
- *Sampling*—Brands such as Finish Dishwasher tablets, Rimmel lipsticks, and Wilkinson Sword Razors have used the sample request format.
- *Donation*—Charities such as the Red Cross, Cancer Research UK and the NSPCC have used this format. Regular donations can be made by entering account details.
- *Request a call-back*—Dial 4 a Loan and Yes Car Credit.
- *Request a test-drive*—Car brands such as Nissan Almera, Lexus and Renault.
- *Enter a competition*—The highest response rates to date have been achieved with competition offers from Rimmel, Tesco and Walt Disney.

Blogs

The use of blogs as communication tools and for search engine optimisation will be discussed in more detail in Chapter 9. Here in the multi-channel context it is relevant to note the potential of blogging to bring together the online and offline worlds by influencing a customer's purchase behaviour. The development of barcode search technology will allow the owner of a mobile phone to 'photograph' a product barcode with the phone and be presented with price comparisons for that product across a range of suppliers, with the ability

Activity 7.4

Go to www.bbc.co.uk/digital/tv/ and look at the interactive facilities listed for BBC channels. In what ways are the BBC taking advantage of this technology?

to click then through to the company website to make a purchase or read customer product reviews. Toshiba plan to release a phone with barcode technology in April 2007. The product review information can also be obtained from blogs that have discussed that particular item—and course such reviews may be positive or negative. The onus will then be on the supplier to develop its own blog and provide incentives for customers to post positive reviews, and also to ensure that these reviews are displayed prominently on Google search results so they can be easily located by prospective purchasers.

The Future

'Push' technology is the name given to a broad spectrum of products that automate the delivery of information to the user. Many websites are currently based upon 'pull' models where users seek out the information in which they are interested. In contrast, push technologies create automated communications relationships whereby products can be aimed at users who have expressed an interest and given permission to be sent targeted material. This shift in focus has significant implications for marketers which will be discussed in Chapter 12.

Although still at an early stage, the latest communication channel with potential for marketers is VOIP (Voice Over Internet Protocol). This technological development allows individuals to communicate by voice for free using the public Internet. See www.skype.com for examples of how such services can work in practice. The usage and quality of VOIP services is now increasing rapidly as broadband Internet access becomes mainstream. In the UK, British Telecom plans to migrate its whole network to VOIP by 2009. VOIP allows for the integration of voice, data and video traffic. This integration will allow companies to interact with their customers with real-time voice, data, video and other forms of multimedia.

V-commerce (short for 'voice') allows users to conduct self-service transactions alternately using the Web and the telephone. This initiative is being led by the V-Commerce Alliance which consists of a number of Internet and telecom companies. For example, a consumer would be able to make an airline reservation over the Web, and then later call a specific number to obtain departure gate or frequent flyer information. Or, before ordering a new computer online, speak to a customer service representative to check which model would be most suitable for their requirements.

Speech recognition is becoming increasingly common in US call centres, particularly in the banking and airline industries. It is also being adapted as a 'hands-free' input device for cars in Europe and Japan as the motor industry recognises that voice is the safest way for drivers to interact with in-car technologies. Nissan already sells a premium model that uses voice instruction to control audio, temperature, navigation and lighting. The new technologies promise to deliver access to information and services on a permanent basis anywhere that there is a telephone connection. In addition the spread of broadband access to the Internet in public places is fuelling the demand for instant information. What is also generating interest is the way that speech recognition is improving the quality of information services by eliminating the need for telephone queuing and badly designed menu-driven voice-mail systems.

Apart from call centres, other opportunities for telephone-based services using speech recognition include:

- self-service banking
- catalogue ordering
- weather and stock market reports
- e-mail collection
- virtual personal assistants (VPAs).

In order for the telephone and the Internet to be merged effectively, common industry standards need to be achieved so that web pages can handle voice. In July 2004 the World Wide Web Consortium (www.w3.org)—a voluntary organisation that sets international stan-

Activity 7.5

Examine the basic features of SALT (www.saltforum.org) or VoiceXML (www.voicexml.org). What possibilities might these technologies have for call centres?

dards—released Voice XML Version 2.1 for this purpose. A tutorial of Voice XML is available on www.w3.org/Voice/Guide/ and the latest developments are available from www.voicexml.org.

Consumers are often frustrated at having to deal with different service providers for each channel, thereby requiring separate billing arrangements, passwords and e-mail addresses. Consequently they will migrate to services that allow them to personalise a single service for use on multiple devices. Looking ahead, Java TV (still at a very early stage of development) will bring together television and computing technologies to enable broadcasters to deliver value added services to a range of Java-enabled devices. This means that the Internet will be rendered 'device independent' and customers will be able to switch their viewing from TV to PC or mobile—anywhere and at any time—as their circumstances dictate. However, as explained below, the organisational challenges associated with developing and integrating effective multiple channel operations should not be underestimated.

Challenges of Multi-Channel Marketing

Companies need to address a number of challenges when considering the development of multi-channel marketing strategies that allow customers to access online content from a range of devices:

Activity 7.6

Look up www.bt.com and read the reports of its VOIP trial (under the heading '21st Century Network). In what ways do you think marketers can take advantage of this technology?

- The extent to which they should invest in these relatively untried technologies, with little indication of likely customer demand or long term prospects for making money.
- The need to 'repurpose' content for each tool (Smith and Chaffey 2005). For example, trying to display a website on a WAP screen means that graphics and pictures are lost and different coding is required. The authors also note that switching between computer and digital television is problematic because websites are designed to be viewed in 'lean forward mode' from two feet away, TV in 'laid back mode' from more like eight feet away. Navigating with a mouse is also very different to navigating with a remote control.
- The unique properties of each medium in terms of the user experience delivered. For example, mobile transactions are likely to be for low value or distress purchases because the amount and quality of information that can be displayed to the customer on screen is limited. In contrast, the PC allows huge volumes of data to be searched and displayed and so is best suited to situations where the customer wants to carry out extensive research before making a purchase. Interactive television offers yet another dynamic; although still in its infancy, early usage suggests that purchases may take place in a more collaborative, impulsive and social context than through the other channels.
- Whether they should offer all their products or services across each medium (and if so, the extent to which customisation is necessary or appropriate) or 'mix and match' according to the characteristics of each channel and the specific message to be delivered.
- The need for integrated online and offline marketing campaigns. Smith and Chaffey (2005) describe how MTV asked viewers to send in SMS text messages to provide comments and vote for their favourite video. MTV then played the winning video together with the comments live. The event was promoted through offline magazines read by the target audience and the paper-based advertisement demonstrated a text message on a phone explaining how to take part.

- How to manage the necessary internal information processing that will allow the company to achieve a unified view of customer activity across all channels. For this to work, a central database is necessary to provide up to date customer details to all channel operators. Remember that customer expectations are continually rising and they may expect to use a combination of channels to effect just one single purchase.

It should be clear from this brief discussion that the technical ability to offer multi-channel access is just the starting point. Considerable investment needs to be made in the back-office computer systems and business process integration necessary to actually make it work in practice. The difficulties are even greater for small firms with limited financial resources or those with legacy computer systems that cannot be easily integrated. However, for those that succeed, the potential for combine multi-channel offerings with *personalised* content (to be discussed in Chapter 9) provides an enormous marketing opportunity.

Summary

Multi-channel marketing is a rapidly developing area offering enormous scope for creativity, brand building and competitive advantage. Mobile channels in particular can offer personalised content, transactional capabilities, targeted advertising opportunities and they also permit effective internal communications such as the distribution of information to a remote workforce.

Questions

Question 7.1

What do you think are the potential opportunities of SMS services for advertisers looking for a suitable channel through which to promote their brands?

Question 7.1 Feedback

There seems to be particular scope for companies looking to target the teenage market segment. According to NOP Research (www.nop.

co.uk) about 62 percent of children in the UK aged between 7 and 16 have mobile phones, sending on average five text messages per day. Broadcasting companies such as ITV have launched campaigns using text messages as trailers for programmes in order to reach key demographic viewing groups. The confectionery group Mars has made its advertising tune available as a free mobile ringtone delivered as a text message.

Promotional messages will only be acceptable to recipients if based upon *permission*. In other words the customer agrees to receive certain messages that are directly relevant to his or her specific interests (see Chapter 6 for a full discussion of 'permission' marketing). In addition, there are important privacy concerns about the potential for misuse of a system that can track the movements of an individual in this manner.

Question 7.2

Although the technical developments appear very exciting, to what extent do you think marketers can effectively convey brand personality through wireless media?

Question 7.2 Feedback

It is unlikely that many promotional campaigns will rely solely on mobile channels. The mobile cannot compete with the desk top in terms of display, computing power and keyboard facilities. There are no cookies to recognise passwords and personalise greetings, and if the Internet connection is broken then access cannot be resumed from where it was last used because the application will restart. Opportunities for innovation arise by combining a number of online and offline channels to develop an integrated promotional strategy. For example, car manufacturer Audi has used a combination of:

- TV for brand building
- Newspapers for providing performance data
- SMS for invitations to new model launches and test drives
- PC-based Internet for feature specification
- The established dealer network for face to face discussions with salespeople.

Each element of the campaign can therefore address a different aspect of the buying process.

Question 7.3

Why do you think the response rates to early mobile advertising campaigns were so high?

Question 7.3 Feedback
Mobile advertising is still so new that the novelty factor may well apply. In the early days of the Internet, banner advertisement 'click through' rates were high, but viewers soon learned to filter out unwanted promotions.

Question 7.4

Although many of these new channels seem very exciting, what factors do you think might constrain their rate of growth and scope?

Question 7.4 Feedback

It is easy to get carried away by the possibilities inherent in the Internet and related products. Do not forget that issues such as security and inadequacies of the existing telephone network in the face of ever increasing demand, leading to slow or interrupted access, are real problems that have yet to be fully addressed. It is also difficult to determine at this stage just how much customers will be prepared to pay.

Feedback on Activities

Activity 7.1

There are many examples that you could draw upon. For example, the potential for mobile networks is particularly high in developing countries that do not have an established wired telephone network and hence no established PC-based Internet services. In the Philippines, for example, SMS messaging has recently taken off rapidly, and mobile Internet services therefore offer huge opportunities in these emerging markets. You can read some interesting articles about recent developments at www.internetnews.com/wireless.

Activity 7.2

Avatars are popular in the US, but trials in the UK by many online banks have not been successful. Other than for very basic questions, customers preferred to speak with a real person, either face to face or by telephone. Automation of customer service in this way was felt to have a negative impact on quality, although obviously it is cheaper for the company to interact with customers in this way. Also check out www. florist2000.com which offers a compromise solution of 'real time' chat on its website, under the heading 'click for Live Help 24/7—powered by Real Person'. What do you think of this as a compromise?

Activity 7.3

BT are currently offering 'Multimedia Voice Over IP' in the UK. Voice Over IP allows for the integration of voice, data and video traffic. This integration will allow companies to interact with their customers with real-time voice, data, video and other forms of multimedia. You can view a demo of this service on BT's Global Services website: www.ignite.com.

Activity 7.4

While digital TV has actually overtaken Internet use in the UK it is still seen as an entertainment tool rather than an informational tool (according to MORI). The BBC are currently focusing on the additional services that they can offer their customers (for example, additional channels) rather than the interactive element available. However, they have started to add interactive aspects to their programming (for example, interactive quizzes for their 'Test the Nation' programmes). Check out the latest developments on www.bbc.com.

Activity 7.5

These technologies are 'multi-modal'. This enables users to interact with an application in a variety of ways. They can input information via the conventional method such as a keyboard or mouse, as well as voice. And output can be synthesised speech, audio, plain text or video. Essentially they will allow customers (and companies) a greater choice about their means of communication, as well as being much more cost effective for companies. See Ayios and Harris (2005) for a detailed discussion of the customer service potential inherent in these technologies.

Web Links

www.ukdigitalradio.com
  The latest developments in digital radio
www.howstuffworks.com
  Clear explanations of technical issues and terminology
www.w3.org
  The World Wide Web Consortium, a voluntary body responsible for developing new technical standards for the web
www.bluetooth.com
  A new technical standard that allows a range of hardware devices to communicate without physical connections
www.keynote.com
  Offers a service to measure and compare the performance of different mobile service providers
www.whsmith.co.uk
  A good example of multi-channel marketing in action
www.yankeegroup.com
  A consultancy and specialising in mobile developments
www.mysnowreport.com
  A recent example of a personalised mobile information service detailing latest snow conditions at specified resorts
www.mori.co.uk
  UK-based research into the latest e-related trends
www.text.it
  Statistics and case studies on mobile phone usage from the mobile data association.

8

ONLINE BRANDING

Introduction

This chapter examines the increasingly strategic role of branding and explains how branding can operate at a number of different levels. It then reviews the role of e-marketing both in developing new brands and reinforcing traditional ones.

Topics Covered in the Session

- The role of branding
- The broadening scope of branding
- Global v local branding
- Strategic options for online branding
- Key branding trends.

Learning Objectives

- Evaluate the broad scope of branding decisions.
- Discuss the range of online branding strategies available.
- Compare and contrast issues of 'global' versus 'local' branding.
- Discuss the emerging challenges inherent in multi-channel branding.

Recommended Reading

Holt, N. (2004) *How brands become icons: The Principles of Cultural Branding*, Boston: Harvard Business School Press
Ind, N. (2001) *Living the Brand*, London: Kogan Page
Lindstrom, M. (2001) *Clicks, Bricks and Brands*, London: Kogan Page

The Role of Branding

Kotler *et al.* provide the following rather pragmatic definition of a brand:

> A brand is a name, term, sign, symbol, design, or a combination of these which is used to identify the goods or services of one seller or group of sellers and to differentiate them from those of the competitors. (2001: 469)

Olins is rather more emotive with this description:

> Branding reaches beyond immediate commercial objectives and touches the soul. (1999: 128)

Jevons (2005) provides an interesting starting point for understanding the scope of branding. He outlines the history of meanings of 'branding' and notes that the term 'brand' is now used extensively in previously unimaginable areas, such as in relation to an individual celebrity (David Beckham) or even a whole country (Great Britain PLC).

Consumers are surrounded by brands in all walks of life, so what makes a successful brand amongst the clutter? According to Aldisert, 'Branding is not about getting your prospect to choose you over the competition; it's about getting your prospect to see you as the only solution' (1999: 36).

Large sums of money are invested each year in order to create, maintain the awareness of and the preference for a brand. Powerful brands command unwavering consumer loyalty and provide strong competitive advantage in the marketplace. Yet sometimes even the biggest promotional budgets cannot prevent a branding disaster; a good source of examples can be found in Haig (2003).

The immediate association with a brand tends to be a product name. However, treating a brand only as a name misses the main point of branding. The brand is a complex symbol, and can be applied to specific products, whole corporations or even countries. Think, for example, of the Silk Cut brand—the imagery of the crumpled and slashed silk is so strong in its own right that the company was able to circumvent UK legislation preventing cigarette advertising by merely omitting the company name and continuing to advertise.

A brand can deliver up to four levels of meaning:

1. *Attributes*—A powerful brand will be able to conjure certain product attributes in the minds of the consumer. For example, the Audi brand would suggest such attributes as 'well engineered', 'technologically advanced', 'well built', 'durable', 'high prestige', 'fast' and 'expensive'. The company might use any combination of these attributes to promote its products. In fact, Audi used its 'Vorsprung durch Technik' (progress through technology) slogan for many years.

2. *Benefits*—Customers do not buy product attributes, they buy benefits. In order to have strong brands, companies have to translate attributes into functional and emotional benefits. For example, the attribute 'durable' could translate into the benefit of not having to buy another car for many years. The attributes 'technologically advanced' and 'well built' might translate into the functional and emotional benefits of driving a safe and prestigious car.

3. *Values*—A brand also conveys something of the buyer's values. An Audi customer would value high performance, safety and prestige. The skill of the brand marketer would lie in matching the values of the targeted group of buyers with the brand benefits.

4. *Personality*—A brand also projects a certain personality. This association is often used by motivation researchers when asking, 'If this brand were a person, what personality trait would it have?' The consumers might visualise the brand as having a certain personality with which they might want to be associated. For example, an Audi car might project the personality of a young, successful executive. This brand would attract

Activity 8.1

Consider the Barclays Bank brand (www.barclays.com). How do the four levels—attributes, benefits, values, personality—demonstrate themselves with this brand?

potential buyers whose actual or desired self-image would match the brand's image.

Companies founded on strong brands are often acquired for multiples of their book value. Most successful companies have thriving brands and also a coherent, company-wide understanding of the unique benefits of their brands that makes a company worth more than the sum of its parts. From the consumer perspective, Lindstrom (2004) notes that children are becoming increasingly brand aware, and indeed in many cases they know more about the attributes of the leading brands than marketing professionals do. As this generation grows up, brand managers will find themselves dealing with increasingly sophisticated and powerful consumers.

The famous study Profit Impact of Marketing Strategy (PIMS) established that the brand with the highest market share is always more profitable. Specifically, a brand with a 40 percent market share is three times as profitable as a brand with only a 10 percent market share. See http://en.wikipedia.org/wiki/Profit_impact_of_marketing_strategy for background information about the PIMS study.

What are the world's most powerful and valuable brands? Interbrand (www.interbrand.com) a global branding consultancy, has identified 75 'billion-dollar' brands. The brand valuation calculation is based on analyses of economic earning forecasts for the world's best-known brands. At the top of the 'billion-dollar brand league' are Coca-Cola and Microsoft. The online brands featuring most prominently on this list are Google, Yahoo!, Amazon and e-Bay.

Google is ranked at number 24 in Interbrand's top 100 brands for 2006, with its brand value having increased by a massive 46 percent since 2005. Although it has built its success upon the core business of search, Google has recently branched out into an increasingly diverse

Activity 8.2

Apple is placed 39 in Interbrand's Top 100 Brands 2006. Take a look at the range of products available at www.apple.com. How have Apple managed to cement their brand through the iPod product range?

Activity 8.3

Have a look at the wide range of products now offered by Google. Do you think this has contributed to or detracted from the strength of the brand?

range of products. The mapping tool Google Earth, for example, is reported to be used in Iraq to highlight escape routes from the city in the event of bombings and destruction (*The Times*, 17 February 2007). Google terminology has become part of the English language, with the verb 'to google' (now included in the *Oxford English Dictionary*) meaning to carry out a web search. 'Google Whacking' is the pastime whereby a combination of words input into a Goggle search returns just one result, and 'Google Bombing' is the association of a particular search result with a distinctly different search term, as shown in Diagram 8.1 whereby inputting the words 'miserable failure' into a

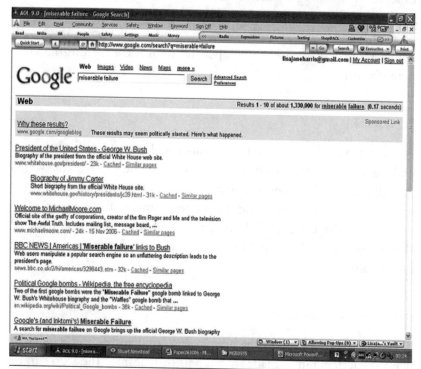

Diagram 8.1 Google bombing of George W. Bush.

Google search results in the display of the official website of George W. Bush.

The Broad Scope of Branding

Brand Name

The brand name is the part of a brand that can be spoken and which includes letters, numbers or symbols, such as Coca-Cola, VW, or Yahoo! This might be different from the legal name of the company, think for example of the use of initials such as AA or RAC or numbers such as 7-Up or 3M which have created enduring brands.

Trade Name

The trade name is the organisation's legal name, which might or might not be related to their other branded products. Some companies, such as Lever Brothers or Procter & Gamble will underplay the corporate brand, preferring to concentrate all their promotional efforts on their product brands such as Persil, Surf and Radion. Few consumers will realise that these apparently competitive brands come from the same manufacturer.

Trade Mark

A trade mark is a brand name, symbol or logo which is registered and legally protected for the owner's sole use. The 1994 Trade Marks Act allows organisations to register not only brand names and logos but also product shapes and packaging, smells and sounds. This means that the Coca-Cola bottle, the Toblerone chocolate bar and the Heinz tomato ketchup bottle are as protected as their respective brand names.

Brand Logo or Brand Mark

The logo is the element of the brand which only infrequently includes words or letters but is made of symbols or pictures. The logo can be also termed a brand mark; for example, the golden arches known the world over are the symbol of McDonalds, or the four coloured squares have come to symbolise Microsoft Windows.

Individual Brand Names

Procter and Gamble, for example, markets particular brands such as Ariel and Fairy Liquid. These brands are therefore not readily associated with the company.

Family (or Umbrella) Brand Names

These are traditionally used in FMCG markets, where brands such as Heinz or Cadbury's cover a number of products.

Co-Branding

Co-branding occurs when two different companies put their brand name on the same product. Co-branding is quite a common practice on the Internet because it is a good way for firms to build synergy through expertise and brand recognition.

An excellent example of co-branding was the barter arrangement between Yahoo! and Pepsi, where Pepsi plastered the portal's address on 1.5 million cans. In return, Yahoo! took Pepsi's already established loyalty programme 'Pepsi Stuff' online. www.PepsiStuff.com is a co-branded website, which lets consumers collect points from bottle caps. The loyalty points are redeemable for prizes ranging from electronic goods to concert tickets. Three million consumers logged on and registered on the Pepsi Stuff website providing Pepsi with detailed consumer information that would have been very difficult and expensive to obtain through market research or from focus groups. Sales rose by 5 percent during the online promotion and the cost was 20 percent of what it had been as a mail-in project. From this experience, Pepsi learned that while banner advertisements and other more traditional advertising have had some success, it is the creation of creative and interactively engaging websites like this that has given the brand the most impetus online.

Corporate Branding

Well-known companies such as Virgin that are branded in this way offer reduced risk to their customers across a diverse group of businesses. This is especially important in online transactions that can compound consumers' concerns over transaction security and privacy. Companies with an established offline reputation are more likely to engender trust online than new web-based firms.

Global v. Local Branding

Standardisation through global branding allows the organisation to maintain a consistent image and identity throughout the world. It provides economies of scale and is particularly valuable for maximising impact with the internationally mobile customer. It works best within an identified international segment and with a product of well-defined complexity. However, few brands can be regarded as genuinely global in this sense, and many companies have made some costly mistakes by ignoring the often significant cultural differences between markets around the world.

A standardised approach to marketing communications is based on the notion that consumers in various countries fall into the same socio-demographic categories with similar, if not identical, buying habits and tastes brought about by low cost cross-border travel. The same imagery, messages, product and brand positioning are used across all campaigns and all markets. Economies of scale can be achieved and global brands built as campaigns extend from one country to another.

A good example is basic office software such as Microsoft Word, which works equally well in most countries, once it has been localised for language characteristics. Other examples are soft drinks like Coca-Cola which need only minimal changes to adapt global campaigns to suit local tastes. The World of Coca-Cola museum (see www.coca-cola.com for more details) provides samples of the product from each country in which it is produced so that scope of variation in taste can be compared.

However, it is a different story for cars, which are more of a 'lifestyle' purchase. Consumer tastes in cars vary more widely between

---

Activity 8.4

Ford has a number of national websites. For example, examine the websites for the US (www.ford.com), the UK (www.ford.co.uk) and Australia (www.ford.com.au). What differences in the Ford brand can you see, simply from the main home page of these different sites?

---

countries and achieving substantial economies of scale either in product development or advertising is more difficult. Ford uses a modular approach to its branding strategies, emphasising safety in Scandinavia, performance in Italy, design in France and handling in Germany. The Ford brand may be global but the product and its supporting marketing effort is very much local.

While the Internet could be argued to support global branding because of its world-wide scope, in practice few brands have been extended across national boundaries successfully. Lindstrom (2001) notes that a global branding strategy should actually be a local plan for each component market, as he believes that applying a standard approach world-wide without considering local preferences and cultural differences is doomed to failure. Yahoo! is an example of a brand that is recognised world-wide, but the company still has had to adapt its approach by partnering with a local company with detailed knowledge of the Japanese marketplace, for example, in order to be accepted. The positioning and branding of American Express is consistent throughout the world but elements of the marketing mix such as advertising are varied to suit local conditions.

Both online and offline branding strategies need to be localised not only in terms of meaning, but also relevancy. Almost certainly the editorial content will have to be adapted in terms of products and services relevant to the population targeted and in the dialects used with the idioms and colloquialisms used locally. For example when developing a website in Spanish, it has to be made specific to Spanish speaking users in Spain, Mexico, Argentina or the South of France. Some colours such as black, white and red have different symbolic or religious meanings throughout the world. A black background can

---

Activity 8.5

Go to the gift site www.redenvelope.com. Why do you think the name is so important to this particular brand?

---

appear 'cool' and 'sophisticated' to an American audience, but black is linked to death and bad luck in Chinese culture. Purple has religious significance in Catholicism and green in the Islamic world. Customer feedback is necessary when designing promotional activities in order to avoid culturally insensitive choices.

Strategic Options for Online Branding

There are a number of key questions facing companies in respect to their choice of online branding strategy. For example:

- Should a company leverage their existing offline brands on the Internet or should new e-brands be created?
- What kind of service are they offering online? Does it enhance the offline service offering or is it something entirely new?
- Is the matter of reaching the market quickly important? In this case, it is speedier to leverage an existing brand than to launch a new one.
- Is the online strategy fraught with the risk of failure? Then it may be better to create a new online brand than to decrease the traditional brand equity by associating with a failure.

While it can be argued that a brand is a brand regardless of its environment, what's different about online branding is the way the brand's promise is executed. Migrating brands to the Internet requires adaptation to a 'bricks and mortar' strategy. One reason for this is that because the Internet encourages the growth of online communities, people expect organisations to put more emphasis on listening rather than informing. In the bricks and mortar environment, the Co-op Bank is branded as a 'socially responsible' business because of its policy of ethical investment. This emphasises the emotional value of caring, and enables stakeholders to perceive the promised experience of being in control of their savings for the good of themselves and others. The migration of the Co-op Bank to the Internet resulted in the brand undergoing changes. For example, it is branded as www.smile.co.uk and uses bright pink colouring to enable it to stand out from the more conventional approaches usually taken by banks. The site is easy to navigate and the animated smile reinforces the offline brand values of responsibility and caring, enabling a similar promise to be perceived between the offline and online brand. Another good example is the rapidly growing Australian fruit drink company Boostjuice (www. boostjuicebars.com) which makes effective use of quirky sounds and images on its website in order to focus attention on emotional aspects of the brand. A similar approach has been taken in the UK by Inno-cent (www.innocentdrinks.co.uk).

The role of online communities in developing customer loyalty was discussed in Chapter 6. Online communities can co-create brand val-ues and experience rather than just passively consume brands. Think for example of how customer to customer interaction has contrib-uted to the growth of the eBay brand. Or Weight Watchers, which through its brand promise as a slimming aid would appear to have support and accountability as two of its brand values. In the bricks and mortar environment this brand promise is delivered by regular supportive group meetings involving 'weigh-ins'. On line at (www. weightwatchers.co.uk) the brand values and brand promise remain similar, but the brand enactment is changed. In terms of guided eating, subscribers have access to a database which assigns points against different types of food to facilitate diet tracking. Online reci-pes are provided and members are encouraged to compile their own progress charts. A menu planner is available together with a shop-ping list tool which prints the items that need to be purchased. There is also a 'panic button' which provides support if a member is seri-ously tempted to eat forbidden food. Each individual can personalise the site through a choice of inspirational icons and a trophy cabinet displays stars for weight loss. If it is difficult for a member to attend the regular group weigh-in meetings, support is provided through a dedicated chat room, thereby replicating the community of weekly meetings. Moderators watch out for any wrong advice that is offered in the chat room.

Alternative online branding strategies have been summarised by Willcocks *et al.* (2000) as follows:

Brand Reinforcement

Many well-established companies are using the Internet as an additional channel to reinforce brand awareness rather than focus on transactional e-commerce capabilities. Migrating existing brand names from the real world into the virtual one is the simplest and most common approach. The best chances of success are those companies with strong, established brands, such as for example, BMW. The company's mission was to make its site 'drive and feel like a BMW' by offering users the opportunity to experience the brand. Since 2000, BMW has allowed its customers to build their own dream cars online and even to hear the sound of its M-series engine in the Z3 Roadster (www.bmw.com). The success of this campaign posed a dilemma for BMW on how far it should go towards selling through the Internet. Traditionally, the company has tended to prefer the face-to-face interaction and bonding offered by the potential customer's visit to a BMW dealership. BMW also commissioned two sets of short films with well known directors and actors, then made the films (which all featured BMW cars) available through their website (see www.bmwfilms.com)

Richard Branson's Virgin Group (www.virgin.com) spans 170 businesses, from airlines and railroads to music stores, financial services and even bridal wear. Branson believes that the Virgin name, known for its hip, consumer-friendly image, translates well to the web. 'Virgin.com isn't a company, it's a brand' says a Virgin director who is overseeing the company's e-commerce activities. The red-and-white Virgin logo is a big attraction for potential partners too. Following in the footsteps of Easyjet, the logo and the website address has been splashed on everything from shopping bags in the Virgin Megastores to the sides of trains, tails of planes and hot air balloons, saving a fortune on advertising. The latest venture is Virgin Galactica which is exploring the possibilities for space tourism.

Online Brand Creation

Some companies, particularly in the financial services sector, have established new online brands rather than use the Internet to reinforce existing brands. Examples include Egg (www.egg.com) which is owned by the Prudential and, as described above, Smile (www.smile.co.uk) which is owned by the Co-op Bank. Egg has been particularly successful in attracting customers and enjoys high levels of brand awareness, but the attractive rates of interest that it offers to savers and the high level of advertising expenditure have resulted in a perilous financial position. The bank hopes to achieve greater profitability by cross selling more lucrative products to its savings account customers. Establishing new brands for online activity offers traditional banks— often with a rather staid image—the opportunity to 'start again' and develop a more modern style to appeal to new customer segments online.

However, one drawback is the increasingly high cost of establishing an online brand as the marketplace gets ever more crowded, and another is the increasing tendency for customers to expect a choice of channels, and not be forced to conduct all their banking online. Consequently, it is rumoured that Egg is now looking to set up a physical branch network. It has also been suggested that in the early days of the Internet, the strategy of brand creation was a 'safety net' so that if the online venture failed, the established brand would not suffer by association with it!

Brand Follower

Brand followers copy successful 'early adopters' of online marketing. The high degree of visibility online means that this strategy is increasingly easy to achieve, as innovations can be easily copied. Many traditional booksellers have attempted to follow Amazon's approach to online trading, and while this might be a 'low risk' strategy it sends a clear signal to the market that the company is just a 'me too'. This means that such companies are not really committed to Internet channels if they make no attempt to distinguish their offering from that of their competitors.

Brand Repositioning

Developing an Internet presence can be a timely opportunity to reposition the brand. The courier company UPS (www.ups.com) took advantage of Internet technology to add value to its brand by including a tracking service so that customers could tell whereabouts their package was in the delivery schedule at any time. Such new features enabled the company to reposition itself in the marketplace as an information provider rather than as a courier company.

Key Trends in Branding

In the late 1990s, online brands evolved with amazing speed. Yahoo! took just five years to become a global brand whereas Coca-Cola had taken fifty. Now that the online market has matured, the degree of clutter means that brands find it harder to stand out from the crowd. In addition, the anonymity of the Internet medium means that companies have to assert their brand identity more strongly online. Many leading organisations are still grappling with the challenge of translating their brands to the online context, but branding strategy is constantly evolving and growing in sophistication.

The Focus of Brand Trust Is Shifting from Products to People and Processes

To focus on product excellence is not enough if the overall package is let down by poor customer service. Many product characteristics are easy to copy, so what is often the only differentiator between companies is the value added to the brand image by the people and processes behind the product.

Brands No Longer Close the Sale

Customers are increasingly expecting a complete 'package' and not just a 'one off' product. For example, if a customer has decided to buy a new car, it is not just the vehicle itself but the service elements that come with it that form a critical part of the purchase decision, such as regular servicing, courtesy cars, insurance and finance packages.

Brands Are Now Strategic Management Tools

As the scope of branding becomes increasingly broad and encompasses not only the product and associated services but the entire corporate ethos in many cases, then branding becomes ever more strategic and central to business success.

Companies Are Making Increasing Use of Viral Marketing

The low budget horror movie, *The Blair Witch Project* owed its world-wide success to a vast volume of 'word of mouth' recommendations passed around Internet chat rooms. Hotmail account holders were sent an advertising message that was attached to the bottom of every e-mail. e-Newsletters offer an opportunity to raise brand awareness and generate goodwill through dissemination of useful free content, and many contain the plea to 'forward to a friend'. We will return to this topic in Chapter 9.

Growth of Online Communities

As noted in Chapter 6, brand-building features such as community groups provided on the website allow customers to interact and share information with others, which helps in building up a degree of trust that can partly compensate for the absence of an established retail presence and then result in increased revenues. For a good example see the book reviews posted on Amazon, or the seller ratings on eBay.

It should be noted, however, that such facilities can also be used by disgruntled customers to humiliate a brand publicly, and the way in which a company responds to such complaints can make it a laughing stock if the task is handled badly. Special sites have also sprung up to allow customers to vent their frustrations, and the protest site www. untied.com provides detailed information about shortcomings and brings together a number of customers who have had bad experiences with the US carrier United Airlines.

Brand Convergence Across Multiple Channels

Creating a strong brand both online and offline is far more than the 'look and feel' of the web home page, the logo or the new brochure. The very essence of a strong brand philosophy is the way in which the staff serve customers—a key part of creating 'brand convergence'. Whether the customers are online or offline, the organisation must ensure consistency of all 'customer touch points' to create a single, comprehensive and memorable brand. This involves significant management and staff training, motivation and constant follow-up. Striking the right balance between online and offline delivery systems to satisfy and grow customers' relationships and maintain the uniqueness of the brand has to be the key to success.

A convergent brand strategy has to address some or all of the following issues:

- Which are the channels that the customers find best suited for delivery of each service through branch, telephone or online?
- Are the marketing strategic plans adequate to support integrated delivery through all the channels?
- Are the staff motivated and appropriately trained because a 'convergent brand' will have an impact on all areas of the organisation?

Ensuring integration of high-touch/high-tech delivery channels, creating a consistent, differentiated brand and maintaining acceptable operating costs per customer will be essential for survival. Offering customers relevant services and building a strong brand image in this way is vital for future success.

Case Study: Polo

In the post-dotcom era, one of the most important lessons learned by the survivors is that it takes more than a flashy website to succeed. It depends on a good business plan, promotion, focused customer service and an efficient distribution system. It also helps to be connected to a strong and trusted brand. When famous designer Ralph Lauren decided to launch his Polo brand on the Internet (www.polo.com) he joined forces with NBC, NBC.com and Value Vision Fulfilment services. Each of the partners brought their own speciality to the venture. Ralph Lauren supplies the product and the name recognition, NBC provides promotion on its networks and the Internet and Value Vision handles distribution and customer service. The new venture went from birth to fulfilment in nine months and distributes a wide range of products, including clothing for men, women and children, as well as Ralph Lauren's home collection. The state-of-the-art distribution centre was designed with versatility in mind, down to the last detail. Even the packaging design has a strong emphasis on customer care and branding.

An efficient returns system is an important component to any dotcom. Polo.com is recognising that the returns process is an extension of its customer care. Only about 10 percent of all ordered items are actually returned. This is about half the average industry percentage for clothing based distributors. It is also less than Polo.com originally expected.

Summary

In this chapter we have emphasised the increasingly broad scope of branding which can encompass whole corporations or even partnerships as well as specific products. The Internet poses a number of branding challenges; for example, the extent to which an offline brand can be translated to the online environment, or whether it is best to develop new online brands. As discussed in Chapter 7, the increasing tendency for companies to offer multi-channel options to their customers highlights the need for consistency of branding and integration of business processes across a range of online and offline channels, in order to provide a uniform and seamless customer experience.

Questions

Question 8.1

What advantages do 'traditional' offline brands have in terms of e-business over relatively new online brands such as Amazon and Yahoo!?

Question 8.1 Feedback

As a trusted brand name in the mind of the consumer, traditional businesses may not be very exciting in their online 'persona' but have the advantage of security and familiarity, especially if the customer is not familiar with new technologies. This factor has resulted in many established high street banks developing websites which replicate their offline 'look and feel' in order to reassure customers of their credentials. Another good example is the supermarket Tesco, the subject of a detailed brand building case study by Rowley (2005).

Question 8.2

Using an example of your choice, discuss the ways in which companies are now reinforcing their traditional brands online.

Question 8.2 Feedback

Many 'old economy' companies are reinforcing their brands online because they want to shape the perception of their stakeholders. There is also mounting pressure for some industries, such as chemicals, to be more transparent in terms of corporate behaviour. Some of these companies are now using corporate branding on the Internet as a communication vehicle. Powerful traditional companies such as BMW use online brand reinforcement in order to increase their competitive advantage. BMW is pursuing a 'brand focus' online whose mission is to make its site 'drive and feel' like a BMW. The company is ranked 15 in the 2006 Interbrand list of Top 100 global brands. Another good example of online brand reinforcement discussed earlier in this chapter is the Australian company Boostjuice.

Question 8.3

What types of small firm have been particularly successful at raising their brand profile online?

Question 8.3 Feedback
Speciality firms that have traditionally operated within a localised niche market have made good use of the Internet to raise the profile of their brands, in some cases generating orders from around the world in the process. For example, checkout www.amplebosom.com a small firm with a catchy name that now sells underwear all around the world from a Yorkshire pig farm.

Question 8.4

What challenges does the creation of a consistent brand image across multiple channels pose for companies?

Question 8.4 Feedback
There is a practical issue about the need for logos, strap lines and promotional messages to be consistent regardless of the channel that the customer chooses to use. Internal communication needs to be effective so that, for example, a special deal can be offered to customers across a range of channels. There is also the issue of service quality, which is an increasingly important aspect of the brand image. Does the customer have the same quality of experience whether interaction takes place by telephone, website or retail store? Look back to Chapter 7 which discussed a number of examples of successful multi-channel marketing.

Feedback on Activities

Activity 8.1

The Barclays' online brand has established (or at least, is trying to establish) itself as having attributes such as 'knowledgeable' 'safe', 'serious' and 'secure'. As a result of this security, for example, customers do not have to worry about their money, as they know it is in good hands. The Barclays brand places considerable emphasis on the customers and their requirements. It wants to be a brand that you can trust. This needs particular emphasis due to the scepticism with which many offline customers view the security of online transactions.

More recently, television advertising has tried to build on this image, keeping key aspects such as safety and security, but adding additional elements. For example, their slogan 'fluent in finance' highlights their international connections and their ability to cater to all their customers' finance needs.

Activity 8.2

While Apple Macintosh computers are becoming more and more popular thanks largely to innovative designs, it is the digital music market that has put the Apple brand back in the limelight recently. As you can see from the Apple homepage the iPod family have given a considerable boost to the brand. It is not only the innovative design and advertising that have caused these to sell out almost immediately in the UK, Apple have also pushed their iTunes software, allowing music fans to download digital music through their website far more cheaply than any other service was initially offering them. Thus, Apple gain both customers for their hardware but also their music download business. The digital music market is something that companies such as Sony have been reluctant to get into as there is a concern that it would cannibalise their offline music business. However, as a result of the success of companies such as Apple, Sony were forced to reconsider their strategy.

It is worth noting that as a result of the brand popularity Apple has also received a great deal of free press in the media.

Activity 8.3

The Interbrand ratings indicate continued strong growth in the Google brand. The core search product is so dominant and reliable that it gives credibility to the other products by association, i.e. Google Checkout, Gmail, Google Maps, Google Earth, etc.

It could be argued that recent developments move away the business away from the famous Google focus on search, but the various products are innovative and largely free to users and they have so far been well received. Google's purchase of YouTube brings another very prominent online brand into the fold.

Activity 8.4

While the Ford logo on these websites might be the same, the products themselves are designed for the individual countries. Certainly, each site has certain similarities—they all, for example, have store locators available from the main page. However, each site is set out independently of the global network. The US Ford site pushes the overall Ford Motor Company and its associated brands (including Ford itself). The UK and the Australian sites promote the Ford brand in particular—the small hatchback in the UK, and the off-road in Australia.

Activity 8.5

Initially, RedEnvelope was called 911gifts.com. In the earlier days of the Internet the URL of a company was often seen as a way to show what a company was about. A dotcom also usually had the 'dotcom' in the company title. However, this led to a number of generic dotcom ideas. Traditionally red envelopes are used throughout Asia for gifts. However, it is not just in Asia that the use of an envelope could be seen as a gift. The red colour is equally popular with men and women. In Europe two of the largest gift giving periods (Christmas and Valentine's Day) are associated with the colour red. The RedEnvelope brand was designed to appeal to a truly international audience.

Web Links

www.bmw.com
   A good example of a site that reinforces the traditional offline brand image.
www.egg.com
   The online banking brand of the Prudential.
www.interbrand.com
   A branding consultancy that has developed a league table of global brand valuations. The site contains a wealth of information about online branding issues, including a free newsletter.

www.open24.gr

The site established by Eurobank EFG in partnership with other brand retailers to offer an information, services and shopping experience that combines both online and express branch operations.

www.pepsistuff.com

A site set up as a result of an alliance between Pepsi and Yahoo! which allowed each company to add value to customers by combining their key competencies.

www.polo.com

A venture by Ralph Lauren to take a traditional brand online that combines the expertise of a number of key organisations working in partnership.

www.smile.co.uk

The online banking arm of the Co-op bank.

www.virgin.com

A good example of a corporate brand that incorporates a diverse product range.

www.visa.com

A good example of a company that has invested a considerable proportion of its promotional budget on building brand awareness online.

9

ONLINE MARKETING
COMMUNICATIONS

Introduction

This chapter builds on the customer relationship marketing strategies discussed in Chapter 6. It covers the operational detail of online customer communications. A company's website has to be effectively promoted in order to stand out from the crowd, encourage visitors and convert them into regular purchasers. Simply having a website is not enough to be seen amongst some 30 million commercial sites, a figure that is growing rapidly. Companies without extensive marketing budgets to spend on promotion will need to look for creative ways of attracting and retaining business.

Topics Covered in the Chapter

- History of marketing communications
- Communicating with the online consumer
- Online communication tools:
  - Search engines
  - Co-branding
  - Affiliate programmes
  - Viral marketing
  - Advertisements on websites
  - E-mail
  - Blogs
- Integrating online and offline marketing communications
- Measuring campaign effectiveness.

Learning Objectives

By the end of this chapter you should be able to:

- Discuss the purpose of marketing communications.
- Explain the relationship between online consumer behaviour and effective marketing communications.
- Describe the range of tools available for online communications.
- Explain the importance of effective integration of online and offline communications.

Recommended Reading

Battelle, J. (2006) *The Search: How Google and Its Rivals Rewrote the Rules of Business and Transformed Our Culture*, Boston: John Brearley
Chaffey, D. (2006) *Total E-mail Marketing*, 2nd edn, Oxford: Butterworth Heinemann
Wright, J. (2006) *Blog Marketing*, New York: McGraw-Hill

History of Marketing Communications

Before the 1880s the dominant function of advertising was to provide consumers with information. Content was print-based and very few adverts had a brand or slogan. In the early 20th century advertising started to become more visual; it featured slogans and encouraged consumers to buy specific brands. This trend developed further with the introduction of radio advertisements in the 1930s and was endorsed by TV advertising in the 1950s, allowing greater emphasis on the visual element.

The early 1990s saw the first business applications of the Internet. The first online advertisement back in 1994 was provided by Hotwired for the telecommunications company AT&T, and it generated a 10 percent response rate. The online advertising industry has grown immensely since the mid-1990s. Now there are more than 50 online advertising agencies within the UK alone. Technological advancements have dramatically changed the look of online advertisements since the early days, and the current options are considered later on in this chapter. For more historical detail see www.digitalhistory.uh.edu.

In general terms, the principles upon which marketing communications are based (regardless of the particular medium used) can be summarised by the AIDA model which charts how a viewer progresses through various stages on route to purchase:

Attention—Grabbing the attention of the viewers, readers or users is vital if the advert is to get noticed. Attention can be attained through appropriate positioning and by the size and shape of the advert.

Interest—Gaining attention is one thing, however to insert the advertising message deeper into the consumer's mind an advert must have the ability to retain interest. Although interest varies according to every individual, it can be prompted through the provision of creative and relevant content.

Desire and Conviction—Both these actions go hand in hand; consumers need to be enticed to develop a 'need' for a product or service. In order to transform the desire into a conviction, customer testimonials, details of product benefits or celebrity endorsements might be drawn upon.

Action—Coupons or free samples can be used to encourage this final step where the customer makes a positive response and actually buys the product.

Different types of promotional message, whether online or offline may well be necessary at each of these stages.

The standard model of how marketing communications work, which was developed by Schramm (1955), can be adapted to help understand the effectiveness of online marketing:

Encoding—The design and development of the promotional message, which could be the website itself or the content of an e-mail.

Noise—This impacts upon the quality of the message that is transmitted. In an online context it might be slow download times or an excess of irrelevant content on a website.

Decoding—The way in which the message is interpreted by the recipient, which could be heavily influenced by whether it is perceived as spam or not.

Activity 9.1

Grabbing the attention of the user is a key step in the AIDA model. Read Nielsen's article on making web advertisements work (www.useit.com/alertbox/20030505.html). What are the relevant points for gaining attention online?

The figures in Table 9.1 illustrate the astonishing rise in online expenditure within the UK alone. Jupiter research (www.jupiterre-search.com) forecasts a further 35 percent increase in 2006. Within the UK there was a 27 percent increase in the number of banner ads served between November 2003 and November 2004.

Chaffey et al. (2006) describes eight key changes in communication characteristics as marketers move from traditional to new media:

1. *From push to pull*—Traditional media such as TV and radio are known as 'push' media which reflects the dominant flow of information from company to customer; but the Internet is an example of 'pull' media, where customers actively seek out the information they require from the website.
2. *From monologue to dialogue*—The Internet allows two-way interaction between company and customer through which information can be gathered and relationships developed over time.
3. *From 'one-to-many' to 'one-to-one'*—Instead of the same pro-motional message being sent to all customers, communi-

Table 9.1 Expenditure on Marketing Communications (UK)

£ MILLIONS	2004	2005
TV	4653	4820
Radio	606	579
Print	8742	8589
Cinema	192	188
Outdoor	986	1043
Online	825	1366

Source: www.adassoc.org.uk

cations can be tailored so that individual segments or even individual customers receive a customised message.

4. *From 'one-to-many' to 'many-to-many' communications*—The growth of customer to customer communities was discussed in Chapter 6. Online discussion groups can provided valuable added value such as product endorsements from fellow customers, but also allow rapid circulation of bad publicity which can be damaging to the brand.

5. *From 'lean-back' to 'lean forward'*—Websites can be described as 'lean-forward' media because while studying a website visitors tend to give it their undivided attention. The drawback is that if customers cannot easily find what they are looking for they will go elsewhere.

6. *New media change the nature of standard communication tools*—For example, in terms of the way advertisements are absorbed by recipients and paid for by advertisers, or the degree of targeting and personalisation that can be achieved with a promotional message.

7. *Increase in communications intermediaries*—This would include new models such as portals, search engines and specific online communities, as well as traditional channels such as newspapers and magazines which have migrated online.

8. *Integration*—The most effective marketing communication campaigns do not focus solely upon new media, but rather upon integrating the old and the new in creative ways. We will look at some specific examples of this later in this chapter.

Communicating with the Online Consumer

Interaction

Online advertising has a huge advantage over traditional methods in terms of encouraging consumers to progress through the AIDA stages, and that is *interaction*. Users are provided with instant information regarding products and services via a click of the mouse; they can then raise queries, compare the offer with that of other suppliers or buy instantaneously. Consumers have a considerable degree of control in comparison with more traditional means of advertising where users tend to be passive and adverts are pushed at them. As noted in Chapter 7, customers increasingly expect access to a range of communication channels with the company just in order to effect a single purchase (mixed mode buying).

Permission

We discussed permission marketing in Chapter 6. The use of permission-based e-mail to communicate with customers is a massive growth area in online marketing. By focusing only on individuals who have indicated an interest in the business and given permission for further information to be sent to them, brand awareness and trust can be developed.

A practical problem in terms of managing permission-based e-mail marketing campaigns is that the definition of what actually constitutes 'permission' can change over time. Just because a customer agreed to participate at one instance, does not necessarily mean they will still be interested a few weeks later. The Data Protection Act is regularly updated to protect consumers from unwanted messages; see www.ico. gov.uk for full details.

There are a number of ways in which customer permission can be established, outlined here in increasing order of thoroughness:

1. 'Opt-out' mailing lists assume permission by forcing people to take action to remove themselves from future mailings. An individual may be automatically added to the mailing list if they register at a website and fail to notice the 'tick here if you do not want to receive future communications' box. This practice is now illegal in the UK for B2C marketing due to recent updates in the Data Protection Act.

2. 'Opt-in' lists require a box to be ticked saying, 'Yes, please send me future communications'. However, the problem here is that people can sign others up for these services because there is no check as to the ownership of the e-mail address entered. 'Opt-in' communications are now a basic requirement for compliance with the Data Protection Act. Custom-

ers must also be given the facility to update their details; for example, to opt out if they change their minds.

3. 'Double opt-in' still means 'yes please' but then an e-mail is sent back requesting the customer to say 'yes please' again before their name is actually added to the list.

4. The final category of 'double opt-in' is becoming increasingly common in a business climate where people are less and less tolerant of spam—the process of bombarding customers with unsolicited promotional messages without seeking their permission. The privacy issues surrounding spam were discussed in Chapter 2. Internet Service Providers (ISPs) employ draconian 'anti-spam' filters to protect their customers from unwanted messages, and this means that many genuine e-mails are also undelivered if the sender is not recognised by the system. The onus is now on the recipient to individually flag such items as 'wanted' in order for them to get through the filters.

Other problems that are developing with e-mail as a means of customer communication are the sheer volume of messages that many people receive on a daily basis, which means that even messages that they have requested may be regarded as annoying and intrusive if they just add to the general clutter. Finally, e-mail has now been so often associated with the transmission of viruses that messages which are not recognised may well be regarded as suspicious. As we will discuss in Chapter 12, e-mail is a 'push' means of communication which, because of these problems, is increasingly under threat from 'pull' techniques whereby customers actively select only what they want to receive (and filter everything else out) using technologies such as RSS.

We will now move on to consider the various ways in which companies can communicate with current and prospective customers online.

Online Communication Tools

Search Engines

Harnessing the power of search engines to enable a business to stand out from its competitors is becoming increasingly central to effective online marketing. Clearly if a prospective customer knows the exact web address they can find the business directly, but attention also needs to be paid to attracting visitors to the site who have searched for a relevant keyword. According to www.statmarket.com, 14 percent of site visitors find it via search engines, 21 percent by following links from another site and 65 percent by direct navigation.

There are two distinct aspects of search to consider, 'natural' (or 'organic') search and sponsored search (or 'pay per click'). The objective of natural search is for the site to be displayed as prominently as possible in a user's search results for the key words of the business. If a user is searching for a product or service using a search engine such as Google, it is likely that they will only consider results that are displayed on the first page when selected key words are entered, and the higher in the list a company is displayed then the greater the chance that it will be chosen by the user. Research in 2004 by Atlas DMT (www.atlassolutions.com) found that position 4 obtained 40 percent of the clicks obtained by position 1, and position 10 only attracted 10 percent of the links. It is important, therefore, for a business to optimise its search engine rankings if it wants to attract more visitors to its website.

Search engines use 'link popularity' in locating and ranking sites. This term refers to both the number of other sites linking to the measured site and especially the importance and relevance of the linking sites. Improving link popularity raises a site in search engine rankings. Specialist companies now exist offering registration and ongoing optimisation of rankings as the process becomes ever more complex. Two very useful and comprehensive guides are www.searchengineguide. com and www.searchenginewatch.com, both of which offer regular updates on the latest developments via e-mail newsletter. www.battel-lemedia.com also provides a useful blog with up-to-date commentary on developments in search technology.

Registration with Google can easily be obtained by visiting www. google.com/adurl/ and submitting the URL of the business. Once registered, the 'only' cost to the marketer is that of time invested in raising the profile of the site. To do so, the marketer might choose to:

- Include the best key words in the webpage titles and inbound links to the site.

- Request inbound links from highly ranked websites.
- Request links from non-commercial sites which are favoured by Google.
- Create an 'autosignature' in all blogs, e-mails and articles that link back to the site, which allows the reader to click directly back to the website.

Link building means that the business has to make its brand visible on a range of complementary websites that will include a link back to the site. This process can be automatic (for example, by using an auto-signature as described above) or it can be achieved by providing useful content such as free articles, or by building relationships and working in partnership with other organisations.

Additionally, a business can pay a search engine for a link to its website to be displayed as a 'sponsored link'. This 'pay per click' (PPC) service as developed by Google Adwords (www.adwords.google.com) offers highly targeted advertising because a charge is only incurred by the business if a user clicks on the link. It enables the business to bid for words and drive traffic to the site, setting a maximum fee in accordance with budget restrictions. The measurement tools offered by Google Adwords allow popular keywords to be defined and these can then be fed back into natural search strategies.

One of the major success stories of the Internet is that of the search engine Google. Although the business is barely nine years old its terminology has already pervaded the English language, as we now talk of 'googling' a search term or 'doing a google' on a piece of research. More than 250 million searches are performed on Google every day. The technology used by Google to carry out searches is more sophisticated than that of its rivals, meaning that the search results obtained tend to be more accurate. However, what has really set Google apart

---

Activity 9.2

Take a look at the Google Adwords website (https://adwords. google.com/). In particular read some of the case studies or 'success stories' that are linked towards the bottom of the page. What do you think makes Google Adwords so popular?

is its focus on sponsored search rather than banner advertisements on the search screen as other major search engines have done. This business model assumes that a user who is inputting particular search terms to Google will at least be interested in viewing advertisements from companies who have specified these same key words to describe their business offering. If a company wants its website to be displayed at the top of a list of Google sponsored search results in response to particular keywords, then it will be paying a very large sum of money to Google for every user that 'clicks through'. Competition to be at the top of the list means that the price of staying there can constantly be bid upwards.

You can read more about the history of Google at www.google. com/corporate/history and about how the technology works at www. google.com/technology/index.htm.

Activity 9.3

Take a look at the Google technology page (http://www.google. co.uk/technology/index.html)—how does the PageRank function work and why is it important?

Co-Branding

Co-branding refers to an arrangement in which companies display each other's content on their websites or carry out joint promotions. There need to be appropriate synergies generated by such recipro-cal arrangements in order for both companies to benefit. Examples include the budget airline www.ryanair.com and the car rental com-pany www.hertz.com whereby both companies provide customers with related, but not competing, services. Joint promotions are offered to customers both online and offline.

Affiliate Programmes

Affiliates earn a commission when a visitor to their site clicks the link to the major player and then makes a purchase. Amazon has several hundred thousand affiliates (called 'Associates') who each display a banner advertisement for Amazon on their websites so that a user can click straight through to the relevant part of the Amazon website in order to purchase related books. See http://associates.amazon.co.uk for more information.

Viral Marketing

Viral marketing was introduced in Chapter 8 in the context of raising brand awareness. The term was originally defined as 'network-enhanced word of mouth'. Marketers have long believed that people who hear about a product or service from a trusted source are more likely to buy it than those who heard about it in other ways. Viral marketing is a communication strategy that uses ideas, slogans, catch phrases and icons to transmit a message about a product as widely as possible. Like viruses, such strategies take advantage of rapid multiplication to explode the message as widely as possible. The message is initially focused upon opinion leaders and early adopters, in the expectation that they will pass it on and lead by example, encouraging others to try out the product. A common use of viral marketing is when e-mail is used to transmit a promotional message to key customers in the expectation that each recipient will pass the message on to a number of others. This harnesses the network effect of the Internet to ensure that a large number of people see the message within a short period of time, and can be regarded as 'word of mouse'—the online equivalent of 'word of mouth'—by customer advocates. Examples of viral campaigns can be found (and passed on further!) at www.viralbank.com.

People can now 'spread the word' and share information virally via peer to peer communications such as online communities, blogs and e-mail referrals. From the company's point of view, this is very cheap promotion provided that the messages are positive. For example, allowing customers to post product reviews on the company website can backfire spectacularly if their opinions are in fact negative.

Businesses that wish to make use of this cost-effective communications mechanism need to take care not to break the law. According to the Privacy and Electronic Communications Regulations 2003, a company which encourages the recipient of an e-mail to pass it on to somebody else should tell its customers only to forward e-mails to people that they are certain would be happy to receive them. The danger is that such messages might be perceived as spam. See www. icompli.co.uk for more details.

An influential book by Malcolm Gladwell, called *The Tipping Point* (2000) describes the domino effect of viral messages which can drive product diffusion through to mass-market adoption once a 'critical mass' of referrals are made. Gladwell emphasises that the value of the referral depends on an individual's degree of influence, not just a willingness to be an early adopter. This means that the quality of a referral is more important than the quantity. For example, individuals that the marketer should focus upon include:

- 'Connectors'—people who are social hubs in peer networks— to showcase new products and 'kickstart' demand.
- Public opinion leaders who 'punch above their weight' online by generating 'buzz' about brands.

Kirby and Marston (2006) refer to these people as 'e-fluentials', and together they make up some 10% of the online population. One e-fluential shares an experience with an average of 14 people, thereby shaping the opinions and attitudes of the online community. They are dynamic web users who regularly forward news to others, correspond with companies by e-mail, post to bulletin boards and write or contribute to blogs. Company websites should harness these enthusiasts by providing a forum such as a blog for e-fluentials to more easily spread a viral message about their products or services. See www.efluentials.com for more information.

Mazda has made effective use of viral marketing to raise brand awareness and boost demand for the Mazda B-Series pick-up, by making the vehicle a cheeky status symbol. The campaign provides culture-driving, online influencers with exclusive entertainment content to interact with and pass on to their contacts. Online viewers can then hotlink to a Mazda web page to watch other entertaining Mazda viral films, view product information, order a brochure, request a test drive or locate their nearest Mazda dealer. You will find more examples of viral marketing in the 'e-mail' section later in this chapter.

Online Advertising

Online advertising can be compared to the more traditional billboard which is used to grab attention in the 'real' world. Banner advertisements similarly point viewers to websites, but unlike the billboard they are interactive and their success can be measured. The standard banner size is 468x60 cm and there has been a recent addition; the super-sized banner. There are also formats available such as skyscraper (12×600 cm) and buttons (120×60 cm). The Interactive Advertising Bureau (www.iabuk.net) has a useful presentation for free download which provides examples of these different types of online advertising. It also showcases best practice with an Awards micro-site (www.creativeshowcase.net) that features demonstrations of the prize-winning advertisements.

There have been many changes over time in the way that online advertisements are presented, partly because the technology has become more sophisticated and also because more people have broadband access allowing faster download times. Most forms of web advertising are now presented in an animated rather than a static format and increasingly they offer interactivity as well. For example, an airline banner advertisement might allow users to type in their required destination in order to display special fares, or a bank banner might allow a user to calculate the monthly repayments on a special mortgage offer by inputting the amount they wished to borrow.

'Pop-up' advertisements can be extremely annoying to website users, and indeed many ISPs offer free software which blocks unwanted pop-up messages. Research by Dynamic Logic (December 2004) suggested that interstitials (which are displayed between loading pages) are less intrusive than superstitials (which are displayed in an extra pop-up window that the user has to close). This research also discovered that online adverts that featured audio or video achieved greater brand impact than other more basic advertising formats. As the technology matures, more and more creative 'media rich' advertisements are being developed. According to Jupiter Research, 11 percent of online advertising spending is now reserved for video, and media rich formats are expected to account for 56 percent of expenditure by 2009 (www.jupiterresearch.com).

Due to the novelty factor, response rates for media rich advertisements are reasonably high, although the click through rate for the original static banners has fallen over time as users learn to automatically filter them out when viewing a site. Advertisers pay the host website per number of viewers or per number of click throughs to their site. There seems to be evidence to suggest that online advertising is effective even when users do not click on the advertisements, as they help to increase purchase intent because of a subconscious increase in brand awareness which then only manifests at a later stage of the AIDA model.

There are three key locations for banner advertisements:

1. Portals sites such as Yahoo! where a banner may either be placed on the home page for all viewers to see or generated automatically in response to relevant key words specified by particular users. In 2004 the Ford Motor Company promoted a new truck with banner advertisements on the home pages of the leading portal sites AOL, MSN and Yahoo! for just one 24-hour period. In total 50 million web surfers saw the advertisements and at one stage the company was receiving click throughs at a rate of 3000 per second. Sales increased by 6 percent, and Ford now routinely spends 10 percent of its promotional budget online. The cost of this single campaign was approximately $300,000 per portal site used and so it should be clear that such coverage is only financially viable for the biggest brands.

2. Special interest sites that are complementary to the product or service that is being advertised. For example the useful marketing resource, 'What's New in Marketing?' (www.wnim. com) carries advertisements for the Chartered Institute of Marketing qualifications.

3. Advertising networks such as DoubleClick (www.doubleclick.com). The company was founded in 1996 and operated in the Internet banner and pop-up advertisement business space, with global headquarters in New York City and, at its peak, 37 offices around the world. DoubleClick is able to target potential customers on behalf of its advertising clients by

gathering information about Internet users' software, Internet addresses and browsing habits. It acts as a facilitator between companies that want to advertise to specific types of users and users who may be interested in receiving such advertising. It does this by matching an Internet address to a database of domain names and business types, and obtaining information about a user's operating system by reading the hardware and software configurations revealed by the browser program.

When a user visits one of the websites participating in Double-Click's network, the server assigns the user an ID number. The information gathered from subsequent visits is stored in a cookie. The cookie contains information on the customer's buying and browsing habits as well as the ID number. DoubleClick then uses the data to refine advertising campaigns by selecting a client's advertisement that appears most relevant to the user's identified profile. Adverse publicity about the privacy issues raised by the DoubleClick business model and consequent lawsuits have resulted in difficult times for this erstwhile favourite of the 'new economy', and it was sold to Hellman and Friedman in 2005.

A recent trend with online advertising is to commission user-generated content. *Time Magazine* captured the zeitgeist by voting its 2006 'Person of the Year' as 'You'— meaning the consumer. This award was based on the massive growth and influence through the year of compelling brand communications created online by consumers, mostly displayed prominently on the hugely successful video sharing site YouTube.

Nike created the Nike Chain on www.nike.com to unite football lovers around the world. The video begins with Brazilian player

Activity 9.4

How do you feel about companies such as DoubleClick tracking your online movements? Take a look at DoubleClick's privacy policy at http://www.doubleclick.com/us/about_doubleclick/privacy/—do you think this will help to soothe privacy concerns?

Ronaldinho, who is sponsored by Nike, kicking a ball across the screen from left to right. A chain of separate video clips submitted by users showing off their football skills then appear to carry on the ball's trajectory as started by Ronaldinho. Each day visitors to the Nike website can view the latest submissions, vote for their favourite and 'mix and match' the clips so that the ball seems to flow seamlessly from one clip to the next. Needless to say, a large number of 'spoof' versions can now be viewed on YouTube.

In addition to exercises like this which focus on raising brand awareness, some companies are now using the interactivity of the Internet to process ideas for new product development. The idea is to increase consumer engagement and loyalty by involving them in this way. Volvo has promoted its new C30 car with a TV advertisement requesting viewers to 'tell us what you think' on the company's website (www.volvo.com) where they can view a series of video clips featuring the car. The danger with this approach is that the viewer's response cannot be controlled, as Chevrolet found when green activists hijacked the company's invitation for users to piece together images and texts to create an advertisement for a new SUV on its website. The activists emphasised the environmental damage caused by such vehicles, a tactic which was clearly not anticipated by Chevrolet when they came up with the idea of inviting people to contribute to the design of advertisement in this very transparent way. The challenge remains for a company to give power to the consumer in such a way that will not risk this type of embarrassment on a global scale; because as noted in the Nike example, spoof video clips tend to end up on YouTube.

According to the Interactive Advertising Bureau (www.iabuk.org, February 2006), YouTube has announced plans to share advertising revenue with the creators of the most popular video clips that are displayed on its site. The company intends to use 'audio fingerprinting' to ensure that only genuine copyright holders will benefit from the scheme. Currently YouTube has 80 percent of the online video market, but only a very limited revenue stream. The danger of course is that its millions of users could be put off if significant commercial activity encroaches on the site. Care will need to be taken not to make the advertising messages too intrusive if members of the user community are to accept it. It does, however, present significant opportunity for marketers to target 'hard to access' demographic groups, and may also inspire consumers to be even more inventive if there are significant sums of money on offer for the best content.

E-Mail

According to emarketer (www.emarketer.com in August 2006) e-mail still comprises the most common usage of the Internet, with 99 percent of Internet users claiming to be regular users, despite the growth of spam and 'phishing' (fraudulent messages claiming to come from your bank asking you for password details). Research company Gartner (www.gartner.com) estimates that 57 million U.S. adults received a 'phishing' attack e-mail within the past year. More than half of those who responded to Gartner were also victims of identity theft. Nearly 11 million online adults—about 19 percent of those attacked—have clicked on the link in a phishing attack e-mail. 1.78 million Americans, or 3 percent of those attacked, remember giving out sensitive financial or personal information, such as credit card numbers or billing addresses, by filling in a form on a spoof website. Gartner believes that at least a million more individuals may have fallen for such schemes without realising it. Direct losses from identity theft fraud against phishing attack victims, including new-account, checking account and credit card account fraud, cost U.S. banks and credit card issuers about $1.2 billion in 2006.

Gartner also found that nearly 70 percent of online consumers said that recent security incidents have affected their trust in e-mail from companies or individuals they don't know personally. More than 85 percent of these delete a suspect e-mail without opening it. Forty-six percent of respondents said that concerns about theft of information, data breaches or Internet-based attacks had affected their purchasing payment, online transaction or e-mail behaviour. Online commerce (including online banking, online payments and online shopping) is suffering the highest toll. AOL blocks about 75 percent of the two billion e-mails it receives each day in order to protect its customers from spam.

In Chapter 12 we will discuss how customer 'pull' techniques, whereby requested information is carefully filtered, are threatening the effectiveness of 'push' techniques such as e-mail, even when 'opt in' regulations are adhered to. However, e-mail is far from dead as a marketing tool and it remains a cheap and quick method of customer communication if it is effectively managed. According to a survey by Peppers and Rogers (2005), interactive marketers expected e-mail effectiveness to increase over the next three years.

There are two main aspects to e-mail marketing communications:

- Outbound messages to customers, which can be regarded as an electronic form of direct marketing;
- The management of inbound enquiries from customers.

Outbound messages can be in the form of e-mail newsletters which may also include appropriate paid-for advertising in the form of links to the advertiser's website. For a good example see www.wilsonweb. com. This strategy was discussed in Chapter 6 in the context of building customer relationships.

The basic principles of managing an outbound e-mail marketing campaign can be listed sequentially as follows:

- Acquire e-mail addresses (with customer permission!).
- Target appropriate audience for e-mail marketing campaign.
- Develop content and personalisation of message.
- Execute and administer campaign (in co-ordination with other channels).
- Respond to customer replies (in co-ordination with other channels).
- Maintain and 'clean' e-mail lists.
- Track and measure campaign performance.

In 2004, US corporations spent $1.8 billion with over 200 e-mail 'solution' providers to support their e-mail marketing programmes. In addition, for every dollar spent externally, two dollars was spent on internal support such as:

- campaign management
- permission policy management
- database development
- systems integration.

So you can see that buying the necessary technology to conduct e-mail marketing campaigns is merely the starting point. The costs become much greater when the challenges of managing the entire process effectively are factored in. For example, consider the cross-functional journey of an e-mail relationship:

- A customer may register on a company's website, perhaps to receive useful content such as a free white paper.
- The registration and permission information will then be stored in a centralised marketing database.
- The e-mail address might be selected for a forthcoming promotional campaign.
- In response to this promotional e-mail, the customer may (a) telephone the call centre to place an order, or perhaps (b) telephone to complain about receiving unsolicited e-mails (if the permission has not been recorded correctly!).
- Ideally, the call will be passed on to sales to arrange a sales visit, or to customer services to issue an apology, but in practice many organisations have not integrated their online and offline operations sufficiently for this process to be smooth, or indeed to happen at all.

Companies need to be well prepared if they are to deal effectively with e-mail messages received from customers. It can be cost effective if automation is not taken to extreme—the budget airline EasyJet (www.easyjet.com) has been criticised in the past for forcing customers to interact via standardised e-mail enquiry forms rather than provide a (more expensive of course) telephone-based support service. In response, EasyJet set up the following sequential 'Contact Us' options on its website:

1. An extensive and searchable list of frequently asked questions (FAQs) deal with routine enquiries automatically.
2. Standardised e-mail enquiries whereby the customer completes a particular online form that matches their specific enquiry and which is then routed to a specific team within EasyJet.

Activity 9.5

Take a look at the Easyjet customer services pages on www.easy-jet.com. How difficult is it to find solutions to particular issues or problems? If you think of a particular problem that you might have as a customer, how many clicks does it take to find the solution?

3. Customer Services for an individual response. EasyJet undertake to reply to an e-mail enquiry within 20 days, which does not appear overly generous.
4. Finally telephone numbers are provided 'if you are still stuck'.

Peppers and Rogers (2006) have derived what they call the 'Five new rules of 1to1 e-mail marketing' that are necessary for success in today's multi-channel world that now also includes blogs, podcasts, RSS and instant messaging. They note that the basic rules of e-mail communication, as described above, are now simply the basic starting point to 'stay in the game' and are insufficient in themselves to 'stand out from the crowd' given the sheer volume of e-mail that now exists. The rules are:

1. *Build your reputation, not your list*—This means focusing on quality rather than quantity of contacts, making it easy for people to unsubscribe and adhering to 'double opt in' policies as described in Chapter 6.
2. *Micro-segment promotional e-mails*—A travel company, for example, might customise a message just for 'people who skied in Austria in March' and have several hundred versions tailored to specific customer segments.
3. *Use e-mail to enhance the customer experience*—For example, only promote a product to those customers who have not yet purchased it, or exclude people who have already made a purchase from a subsequent promotional offer. Instead, give them an offer on a related product to add value.

4. *Get creative*—Broadband connection and higher spec PCs allow more people to appreciate a rich media of audio, still images and video. Combining channels (as discussed in Chapter 7) but including 'click to talk' or 'click to instant message' buttons can encourage customer interaction and engagement.

5. *Consider the cost of non-responders*—For example, if 2 percent of your customers have responded to a promotional e-mail, how are the remaining 98 percent feeling? Are they just not interested, or perhaps they are annoyed at what they perceived as spam?

The screenshot from *Times Online* in Diagram 9.1 incorporates a number of the customer communication features that we have discussed in this chapter. Viewers are able to interact with the map of the world and focus on an area of interest, where they have the option to access travel stories relating to the selected region. The stories are all generated by users and include a combination of text and photographs. Viewers can submit their own stories or comment on the stories that they read. This gives the material an air of authenticity that a travel brochure cannot match. The site includes a facility to share specific stories with others by forwarding them via e-mail. It is also possible

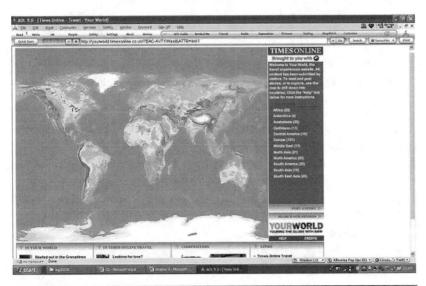

Diagram 9.1 Times/BMW online advertising campaign.

Activity 9.6

Check out the Times/BMW 'Your World' website at http://
yourworld.timesonline.co.uk. In what ways do you think this
represents a 'new' form of advertising? Does it make you more
inclined to find out more about the companies involved?

to access related content that has been published in the travel section of the Times newspaper. The site has been set up in partnership
with BMW under the strapline 'touring the world with BMW' and
there are links to information about European Festivals and the Three
Peaks Challenge, with accompanying video clips showcasing BMW
cars in exotic locations that are also available as podcasts.

In this chapter we have briefly mentioned some Web 2.0 tools that
are still at an early stage of development, for example blogs, podcasts
and RSS feeds. These new tools will be discussed in more detail in
Chapter 12.

Integrating Online and Offline Marketing Communications

Integration of marketing communications has been defined by Kotler
as follows:

> the concept under which a company carefully integrates and co-ordi-
> nates its many communication channels to deliver a clear, consistent
> message about the organisation and its products. (2005: 47)

Chaffey *et al.* (2006) summarise the characteristics of integrated
communications in terms of the 4Cs:

- *Coherence*—Different communications are logically
  connected.
- *Consistency*—Multiple messages support and reinforce, and
  are not contradictory.
- *Continuity*—Communications are connected and consistent
  through time.
- *Complementary*—The whole is greater than the sum of the
  parts.

A simple way of integrating marketing communications is through the provision of 'callback' facilities. If a customer wishes to discuss a possible purchase with a company representative before making an online purchase, then by clicking the callback button on the company's website they can arrange a call from the company at a time to suit them. Of course the company will need to ensure that call centre staff are available to make such calls, particularly if a large volume of calls might be expected at once in response to a particular sales promotion.

Offline promotional methods should not be forgotten when planning a campaign. Creative use of the website address in more traditional media can spark initial interest and help drive visitors to a website. Gibson (2004) describes how online advertising has become an integral part of the overall marketing communications mix for a number of major brands. For example, many car manufacturers draw upon online advertising to launch new models, usually displaying a sophisticated advertisement incorporating both video and sound in conjunction with an opportunity for the viewer to sign up for a test drive. At the 2004 Super Bowl, Mitsubishi Motors bought a 30-second advertisement encouraging viewers to visits its website and view a video of a Mitsubishi car in crash tests with a competing Toyota. Eleven million people visited the site over the next six hours to watch the video and check out the new model. This was significant because research has shown that car purchasers spend an average of five hours researching cars online before visiting a showroom.

Measuring the Effectiveness of Online Communications

Traditional methods of testing the effectiveness of advertisements can also be applied online. For example, levels of brand awareness can be tested both before and after an online promotional campaign and the results compared.

If a company uses a specific web address that is unique to one particular advertisement, then all viewers of the site must have responded to the URL quoted there. A variation of this measurement technique is to publish a specific phone number on the promotional message so that the total numbers of calls that are generated by the advertisement can be calculated. The return on advertising spend can then be established if the total sales revenue resulting from these customer interactions is compared with the amount spent on the original advertisements.

Companies such as Webtrends (www.webtrends.com) provide software for measuring online campaign performance, search engine marketing, website conversion and customer retention.

The website includes options for free trials of the software, details of awards won by the business, customer case studies of successful advertising campaigns and free white papers.

Chaffey *et al.* (2006) summarises a number of methods for evaluating the success of a promotional campaign:

1. Calculate the number of unique visitors to the site through software such as www.hitwise.com.
2. Measure the percentage of unique visitors who actually interact with the site; for example, by registering to receive free white papers.
3. 'Cost per click' is the amount that the company has to pay to a search engine for each referral; for example, through Google Adwords
4. Calculate return on investment by dividing the profit or revenue generated by the total amount spent on the advertising campaign.
5. Branding metrics which compare awareness before and after a promotional campaign.
6. Lifetime value is a measure which takes into account the revenue obtained versus the ongoing costs of keeping a customer over an extended period of time.

Ensuring that the right message is sent to the right customers can be facilitated by using a new technology called behavioural targeting, and a number of behavioural targeting infrastructure and software companies help advertisers to find potential customers whose web-surfing patterns and behaviour indicate a willingness to be receptive to customized offerings for their products and services. These programmes do not upset privacy advocates by accumulating personal data, but they use cookies to focus on user behaviour. For example, by establishing which website the visitor comes from, how much time

Activity 9.7

While some research has indicated that users are now getting used to online advertising and therefore automatically filtering these adverts out, there is much evidence to suggest that some forms of online advertising irritate users more than others. Take a look at Nielsen's recent paper on the subject at http://www. useit.com/alertbox/20041206.html.

Do you agree with the findings described here? Are there any types of online advertisement that you do not find intrusive?

is spent reading particular parts of the site and which advertisements are clicked on, the visitor's preferences for advertising content can be inferred with increasing accuracy. Imedia Connection has a number of case studies on its website www.imediaconnection.com.

Summary

In this chapter we have discussed how a company's website has to be effectively promoted in order to stand out from the crowd, encourage visitors and convert them into regular purchasers. A number of innovative online advertising techniques are now available and for best results online and offline marketing campaigns need to be effectively integrated. Companies without extensive marketing budgets to spend on promotion can make use of low-cost techniques such as viral marketing or search engine optimisation in order to attract and retain business.

Questions

Question 9.1

What advantages does online advertising offer over more traditional methods?

Question 9.1 Feedback

Online advertising offers scope for interaction with customers, the ability to target key customer groups and directly measure the impact of individual advertisements. It also provides opportunities for creative integration of online and offline campaigns.

Question 9.2

Why have click through rates on banner advertisements improved over the past couple of years?

Question 9.2 Feedback

The technology behind banner advertisements has matured and so provides increasing scope for animation, sound and interactivity to engage the viewer. As more Internet users upgrade their computers and migrate to fast broadband connections that can download content quickly, opportunities are provided to incorporate video clips into advertisements more widely. It could be argued that the novelty factor of these innovations will soon wear off, because in the early days of the Internet even static banner advertisements attracted the curiosity of viewers.

Question 9.3

Why is permission such a key aspect of effective online customer communications?

Question 9.3 Feedback

Companies which take care to engage only with customers who have actively given their permission (and sustained this permission over time) will reap rewards in terms of customer trust and loyalty, even if the total number of customer contacts is reduced. It can be argued that what is lost in terms of quantity is gained in terms of quality. Consumers are increasingly intolerant of spam but research indicates that people are receptive to a reasonable amount of relevant advertising in exchange for such benefits as quality service or useful free content from a website.

Question 9.4

Why do you think web advertising expenditure has increased so much recently?

Question 9.4 Feedback
One important point to note is that companies want to reach as many potential customers as possible. As noted earlier in the book, the number of Internet users is rapidly increasing in the UK, as well as in the US. By adopting web advertising, companies are not only reaching a great population of potential customers, they may well also reach customers that they would not reach through other means. The growth of broadband access allows greater creativity of online advertising; for example, video clips can now be easily viewed over even the most basic broadband connection.

Feedback on Activities

Activity 9.1

The response made by the recipient to the message received, which might be direct or via a visit to the company website. As Nielsen states, accept that web design is interaction design, understand hypertext, and, most importantly, understand the psychology of the viewer.

Activity 9.2

One of the aspects of the Adwords service that makes it so successful is that it can be tailored to almost any organisation very easily. It is not designed to be used exclusively by large multinational corporations, but can be used by any organisation that wants some form of online business, regardless of their size. Small firms can easily cap the costs involved, as well as view effectiveness reports generated by the Adwords service. The key words that are found to work well for a business in terms of attracting clicks from potential customers can also be built into the site to enhance its position in 'natural search' results.

Activity 9.3

Essentially, PageRank involves rating a website's importance via the number of other web pages that link to it. So the more sites that are linked into another site, the higher that site will feature in a Google search for specific associated keywords. Unfortunately search engines are also susceptible to a form of spam. 'Spamdexing' or 'search engine spamming' involves altering the webpage code of a file so that it appears higher than it should do in the list of results (as discussed in Chapter 2). If this deception is discovered, the website is likely to be blacklisted by Google so that it will not feature at all in search results.

Activity 9.4

DoubleClick's privacy policy is both easy to access (one click from the main home page) and well set out. Its layout means that the policy is easy to understand and not overwhelming. DoubleClick has also helped its cause by associating with external validation organisations such as Trust-e (www.truste.com).

Activity 9.5

While the online help pages do cover some basic problems, they are listed in such as way that makes the solutions difficult to locate. If a customer cannot find a solution online, a phone number and e-mail address for customer services is provided. However, the language used is such that many potential customers may be put off from bothering, possibly going to a competitor instead.

This is in direct opposition to the customer services options of firms such as Tesco. The Tesco website (www.tesco.com) does have online help pages, but if you want to actually contact them, you cannot do so electronically; the only options are by phone or post. While the lack of an e-mail option may be a problem, the phone numbers are categorised for different issues, and the language used encourages, rather than discourages, customers from using this service.

Activity 9.6

Your answers to this activity will be based upon your own views.

Activity 9.7

There are a number of factors that put users off. Top of the list are:

- pops-up in front of your window
- slow loading times
- trying to trick the user into clicking on advertising.

Research by Orange (www.orange.co.uk/mediapack/research) provides another dimension to this debate by plotting the impact of different forms of online advertisement on a graph against the degree of intrusion that users associate with each type. The types of advertisement which found most favour with users were skyscrapers (tall thin rectangles down the side of the page) and mastheads (page headings). The most unpopular advertisements were pop-ups.

Web Links

www.jupiterresearch.com
> A useful source of research into the growth of e-business.

www.linkpopularity.com
> A measure of the number of websites linking to a particular site. The greater the number, the higher the search engine ranking is likely to be.

www.searchenginewatch.com
> A comprehensive guide to how search engines work.

www.searchengineguide.com
> A useful guide to how search engines work, with emphasis on the smaller business.

www.viralbank.com
> Examples of viral marketing campaigns.

www.iabuk.net
> The Internet Advertising Bureau brings together research into online marketing effectiveness and includes useful free material.

www.adassoc.org.uk
> The Advertising Association promotes and protects the rights and responsibilities of players within the advertising industry. Website has useful statistics and white papers.

www.revolutionmagazine.com

Keep up to date with developments in online marketing.

www.marketing-online.co.uk

Extensive resource on all aspects of online marketing communications.

www.creativeshowcase.net

Award winning demonstrations of creative online advertising hosted by the Internet Advertising Bureau.

www.webtrends.com

Award winning software for measuring the effectiveness of online advertising campaigns.

www.battellemedia.com

A useful blog detailing the latest developments in search marketing.

10

E-RETAILING

From 'Clicks' to 'Clicks and Bricks'?

Introduction

This chapter examines e-retailing; i.e. the final stage of the distribution chain when the benefits are transferred to consumers. It considers the role of e-retailers in satisfying consumers and the factors contributing to their success.

Topics Covered in the Chapter

- What is e-retail?
- Disadvantages of e-retailing for retailers
- Advantages of e-retailing for retailers
- Is the product suitable for e-retailing?
- Strategic options for retailers
- Success factors in e-retail
- Growth prospects for e-retailing
- Multi-channel retailing
- The e-retail mix.

Learning Objectives

After completing this chapter you will have an understanding of:

- What e-retail is, advantages and disadvantages for retailers.
- The success factors for e-retail (and the no-nos).
- The e-retailing strategic options for retailers.
- The growing importance of multi-channel retailing.

- The tools and techniques of e-retailing—the e-retail mix.

Recommended Reading

de Kare-Silver, M. (2001) *e-Shock: The New Rules*, Basingstoke: Palgrave
Dennis, C., Fenech, T. and Merrilees, W. (2004) *e-Retailing*, London: Routledge
Tiernan, B., (2000) *E-tailing*, Chicago: Dearborn

What is e-Retail?

e-Retail is the sale of goods and services via the Internet or other electronic channels, for personal or household use by consumers. This formal definition encompasses all the activities of business to consumer (B2C). Since 2001, e-retailing has been steadily growing, particularly for the 'top seven' products which account for three-quarters of all European sales: books, music, groceries, software, hardware, travel and clothes.

Disadvantages of e-Retailing for Retailers

Retailers have been slow to take up e-retailing. Research from Barclaycard Business indicated that 69 percent of bricks retailers do not trade online and are missing out on the current fast growth in e-shopping. Twenty-three percent of retailers cited cost of setting up as a reason for not going online and 13 percent said that they did not have the know-how. Bill Thomson, commercial Director of Barclaycard Business commented 'Many retailers perceive setting up online as a costly exercise. In fact, the opposite is true. Starting to trade online can be extremely quick and cost effective; a move that can deliver new business which will quickly repay any initial costs (*Retail Bulletin*, 2006). Set-up costs can start from as little as £20,000 for a small site, although they can rise to £500,000 for a large operation. Older businesses are more conservative about e-retailing, with the Barclaycard survey finding only 24 percent of business 10 years old online, vs. 36 percent of businesses set up within the last 2 or 3 years (*Retail Bulletin*, 2006).

Box 10.1   Disadvantages of e-retailing for retailers

- May lack know-how and technology
- Substantial set-up, investment and ongoing costs
- Complex logistics of fulfilment
- e-Selling less powerful than face-to-face – uptake slow for goods selected by taste or smell
- Less impulse purchases
- Legal problems
- Less role for traditional high street retail expertise
- Pressure on margins and prices in-store.
- After-sales care difficulties.

Legal problems can also inhibit retailers from e-retailing. For example, if purchaser and supplier are in different countries, there may be conflict between the laws of the two countries. A further disadvantage is that e-selling is less powerful than face-to-face selling (it is easier to say 'no' to a computer). This viewpoint is linked to a concern of traditional high street retailers that e-retailing offers a diminished role for their expertise. For example, there are obvious difficulties with products sold by 'atmosphere'—touch, feel, smell—and impulse purchases. In addition, consumers have a perception of lower prices online. This puts pressure on margins for e-retailing, and can lead to shoppers expecting consistent low prices in store. Finally, after care can be difficult, especially if the shopper is overseas.

Advantages of e-Retailing for Retailers

On the other hand, there are a number of advantages for retailers. Firstly, location is unimportant. According to some textbooks, adapting an old saying, the three most important elements in retail are 'location, location and location'. The best high street locations are therefore expensive. The e-retailer, though, can sell equally well to anywhere in the country and even overseas. Secondly, size does not matter—small e-retailers can compete on equal terms to large ones, and reach a larger audience than the high street—and be open 24 hours a day. For example, the independent, northern UK-based Botham's of Whitby has been a pioneer of e-retailing and become one of the best-known UK case studies.

Mini-Case Study: Bothams of Whitby (www.botham.co.uk)

This family-run craft bakery in the ancient port of Whitby on the North Yorkshire (UK) coast is a benchmark of best practice and an e-retailing pioneer. Products are from original recipes, using the 'finest ingredients, skilfully combined to produce biscuits, plum bread and cakes of the highest standard'. The site is packed with interesting information about the products with frequently updated interest content such as 'meet the family' and 'kids pages'. The independent, local business has built a reputation for UK and world-wide delivery of hampers and cakes.

There are many other advantages to e-retailing. The socio-demographic profile of e-shoppers is attractive to many retailers, with higher-than-average education, employment and disposable income levels. In theory at least, online selling saves on the wages of face-to-face salespeople and the costs of premises. The savings may be less than expected though because there are still costs in Internet customer contact and packaging and delivery can be more expensive to

Box 10.2 Advantages of e-retailing for retailers

- Location is unimportant
- Size does not matter
- Saves on the wages and premises costs
- Reach a larger audience
- Higher disposable income profile than average
- Accepts orders 24-hours a day
- More opportunities for CRM, micro-marketing, cross- and up-selling
- If we don't, our competitors will.

provide. Perhaps a more substantial advantage is the ease with which e-retailing integrates with Customer Relationship Management (CRM) and micro-marketing systems—identifying and treating the customer as an individual. This, together with the easier provision of product information, leads to greater opportunities for cross-selling and selling-up. Finally, the late entrants into e-retailing are largely being driven by 'if we don't, our competitors will'.

In the early days of the Web, some retailers were put off e-retailing by what they perceived as consumer resistance. According to the Oxford Internet Survey, 61 percent of UK homes are now connected to the Internet and 74 percent of the occupants of those homes shop online, so shopper resistance is fading (OxIS, 2005).

Is the Product Suitable for e-Retailing?

How important is e-retailing for various classes of products? Which high street retailers are going to be most affected by the growth of e-shopping? Can some products be sold just as effectively by e-retail as by conventional retail? Are some products unsuitable for e-retailing? Michael de Kare-Silver has developed the e-shopping (ES) test aimed at estimating the proportion of the target customers who will be likely to buy the product online. Its author claims that the approach can be applied to any product or service in any industry sector. The test consists of three dimensions: (1) product characteristics; (2) familiarity and confidence; (3) consumer attributes. Products with 'likely high ES potential-scoring' include basic grocery, household and clothing, plus drinks, financial services, travel, hotels and books (de Kare-Silver, 2001).

Strategic Options for Retailers

If a retailer's products or services have a potential for e-retailing, what courses of action are available? de Kare-Silver lists 10 options which can be arranged on a scale from 'no e-retail operations' to 'switch fully', in order of increasing e-shopping responsiveness, paralleled with increasing commitment to e-retailing.

Box 10.3   The ES (electronic shopping) test

The ES test has been designed to quantify the likely e-retailing potential of a product. The 3-step test considers:

1. Product characteristics. The more virtual a product's appeal, the higher the score, the more physical, the lower. The main appeal can be scored from 'intellect' scoring 10 at the 'virtual' end of the scale, through 'sight', and 'sound', down to 'smell', 'taste' and 'touch' scoring 0 at the physical end.
2. Familiarity and confidence. This dimension is measured by considering previous use, satisfactory use and branding or reputation, again on a 0-10 scale.
3. Consumer attributes. Consumers' attitudes can outweigh the first two steps, so this factor is accordingly weighted higher, with a 0-30 scale. The essential test is the percentage of the target consumers responsive to e-retail offers. Are the target consumers mainly 'habit-bound die-hards' and 'social' shoppers, unresponsive to e-retail? Or are there a high proportion of e-responsive 'convenience' shoppers? The scale runs from 0 (no e-responsive shoppers) to 30 (90% e-responsive).

Sample products with likely high ES potential scores

PRODUCT	1. PRODUCT CHARACTERISTICS (0–10)	2. FAMILIARITY AND CONFIDENCE (0–10)	3. CONSUMER ATTRIBUTES (0–30)	TOTAL
Basic grocery	4	8	15	27
Basic household	8	8	15	31
Basic clothing	4	7	8	19
Drinks	4	8	15	27
Financial services e.g. car insurance	10	5	8	23
Travel	10	6	15	31
Hotels	7	6	15	31
Books	8	7	23	38

The evaluation should be repeated regularly to track trends. Any score over 20 represents substantial e-shopping potential.

Source: Adapted from de Kare Silver (2001).

Box 10.4   Ten strategic options for retailers – in order of increasing commitment to e-retailing

- No e-retail operations
- Information only
- Export
- Incorporate into existing business
- Add another channel
- Set up a separate business
- Pursue all fronts
- Mixed system
- Best of both worlds
- e-retail only

Source: Adapted from de Kare Silver (2001).

No e-Retail Operations

This is the defensive option, based on revitalising the 'experience' and 'social' aspects of shopping as in towns and shopping centres. Consumers, though, expect every organisation to have at least an information website and an e-mail address.

Information Only

Reluctance to tackle the disadvantages of e-retailing leads some well-known high street retailers (for example Monsoon www.monsoon. co.uk) to use the Internet purely as a marketing communication channel rather than for online sales.

Export

This approach is aimed at protecting the business of the high street stores whilst widening the potential customer base with the e-channels. de Kare-Silver cites the example of bookseller Blackwells (bookshop.blackwell.co.uk) which has 82 outlets in university towns and campuses across the UK, but their listing of 1 million specialist and academic titles is now available world-wide on the Web.

Incorporate Into Existing Business

This option seeks to protect the existing stores by using an 'order and collect' system. By coming to the store to collect the order, the shopper is more likely to think of extra purchases or to pick up impulse buys. Sainsburys (www.jsainsbury.com) has implemented this system but has not gained the popularity of market leader Tesco. Sainsbury's home delivery service is much more popular than its 'order and collect'.

Add Another Channel

Retailers such as Next (market leader in online clothing sales, according to retail researcher Verdict), use e-retailing as an extra route to reach more of their target customers.

Mini-Case Study: Next (www.next.co.uk)

Next is a top name in high street fashion, and since 1987 has built a successful mail order business, Next Directory. The expertise in order handling, fulfilment and customer care has proved invaluable, taking the business to the Number 1 spot in UK clothing e-retailing. The entire Next Directory is available online, including formalwear, casual wear, accessories, shoes, swimwear, lingerie, men's and children's wear. To shop online you have to set up an account which can take a day or two to arrange. There is a small charge for next-day delivery and a courier picks up returns free.

Set Up a Separate Business

The idea of the separate business is to offer competitive e-shopping benefits without alienating the existing customers for the high street operation, who probably pay higher prices. The separately-branded direct operation has been popular for financial services—for example, Abbey National's e-bank 'Cahoot' (www.cahoot.co.uk).

Pursue All Fronts

This is the National Westminster Bank multi-channel system, based on making every possible channel open to the customer: high street branches, direct mail, ATMs, phone, interactive TV and Internet (www.natwest.co.uk).

Mixed System

This approach recognises that strong brands are essential to successful e-retailing. Brand strength is showcased in flagship stores in major cities; for example, Virgin Megastore (www.virginmega.com).

Best of Both Worlds

Is it possible to retain all the high street operations whilst at the same time being state-of-the-art in e-retailing? This is probably only practicable for a clear market leader in a sector, and represents a high-investment strategy, making it more difficult for competitors to catch up—the Tesco approach.

e-Retail Only

Few retailers are brave enough to close all high street outlets and operate only virtual shops. Dixons (UK electricals retailer) pulled out of all 190 high street branches to become an online-only brand (www.dixons.co.uk) in 2006—but the high street stores were re-branded and continued operation as 'Currys.digital' (Dixons bought Currys in 1984). Pre-dotcom crash, a number of e-retail only operations were developed (see Boo.com in Chapter 1), the best known and most successful being Amazon.com. Only those operations high in e-shopping potential, such as travel, and with the backing of substantial budgets to build the brand (e.g. www.Lastminute.com), are likely to be leaders with Internet-only operations.

Success Factors in e-Retail

According to research company Forrester (www.forrester.com), two-thirds of e-shopping transactions are aborted after the shopper has already placed goods in the shopping basket, and 9 out of 10 buyers do not make a repeat purchase. e-Retailers need to make the purchasing process reliable, easy to use and efficient, removing the reasons for abandoning purchases. Help (virtual or human but customers like human to be available as a last resort) needs to be available to sort out problems—at least by e-mail, but preferably also with a phone option. Forty-one percent of Internet users would be more likely to buy if human interaction was available (www.forrester.com). A software device such as HyPhone from Byzantium allows 'phone-through' without dropping the Internet connection (www.byzantium.com) although the need for this service is diminishing as most Internet users now have a broadband connection that does not monopolise the telephone line.

A US survey correlated website characteristics with customer satisfaction. The conclusion was that success followed the content. A further important discriminator between high and low customer satisfaction was the 'chat' aspect (Feinberg, 2001). Other US studies have found that the strongest predictor of consumers' intention to e-shop was 'hedonic'—that is, the pure enjoyment of the experience (Childers *et al.*, 2001; Dholakia and Uusitalo 2001). The importance of the enjoyment and human communication aspects is borne out by, for example, eBay (auction site—www.ebay.com and www.ebay.co.uk) which, if considered to be an e-retailer, is the largest one in the UK.

Growth and Prospects for e-Retailing

The rise in online shopping is far outstripping that of the high street to reach £11 billion by 2007 (IMRG 2007; Verdict, 2006). Books, movies and software, high on 'factual search' are natural for e-retailing and were the early growth categories (Shim *et al.*, 2001) but less obvious sectors such as groceries are also increasing (Verdict, 2006), with clothing being one of the fastest growing categories with an annual growth rate of 64 percent (IMRG, 2007). Most growth is at

Box 10.5 Dos and don'ts of e-retailing

Don'ts

- Save your best page till last
- Use too many graphics (long download)
- Fill each page, leaving no 'white space'
- Use too much narrative and long-winded wording
- Have too many sequential click-through pages

Dos

- Make it easy to buy ('3 clicks') *
- Provide good service and aftercare *
- Provide membership incentives *
- Human communication, chat rooms and bulletin boards *
- Make e-shopping an enjoyable experience – especially for female shoppers. Design the 'web atmosphere' for enjoyable shopping - video, audio, graphics and virtual store layout. *
- Open with a strong introduction – great home page
- Design creative visual images
- Create a company image that makes your web site stand out
- Avoid a clustered visual image (too many banners, too much information
- Reinforce brand image and build brand strength
- Use short, concise phrases
- Vividly describe product benefits
- Offer speed-navigation to known points
- Build in customer interactivity
- Provide expert information
- Update displays regularly
- Price competitively
- Provide loyalty incentives
- Include testimonials from satisfied customers and, if possible, well-known personalities
- Offer a clear guarantee

Sources: Adapted from Tiernan (2001), except points marked * – various sources

expense of existing channels (approximately half diverted from catalogues, half from high street). Currently, e-shopping is growing at 35
percent per year as compared to around zero growth for bricks retailing (IMRG, 2007).

The UK market leaders in their sectors are Amazon (books, plus
CDs, DVDs, electronics and more), Tesco (groceries plus a wide
range of non-food items), Dell (computers) and Next (clothing). The
main service is travel, and the main virtual product is sex (mainly
downloaded videos but contact sites are a huge source of advertising
revenue)—often absent from published statistics, but accounting for
around 10 percent of all e-retailing.

Think Point

If people can e-shop easily, why should anyone use the high street?

Mini-Case Study: Amazon (www.amazon.co.uk)

US-based Amazon is well known as the world's biggest e-retailer of
books, head-to-head with Barnes and Noble for the title of the World's
Largest Bookstore, even though Amazon only sells online. From a
start-up in 1995, sales have grown to $13 billion and the company has
three million customers—but reported its first profit only in 2002.
Other products include CDs and videos. The UK site was formed
in 1998 by the takeover of Bookpages, and is now Amazon's biggest market outside the US. Amazon.co.uk followed the US parent's
example of using heavy (non-electronic) advertising to promote brand
awareness. Traffic to the site is encouraged using the affiliate system.
For example, popular search engines such as Altavista offer links to
books related to the keywords. The site is user-friendly, enabling e-
shoppers to quickly find books by title, author or subject. You can find
your title in seconds from a few keywords. Synopses and contents lists
are provided, along with a list of other relevant books. Amazon keeps
a record of customers' preferences and advises when new books likely
to be of interest are published. One of the main selling propositions
is a discount of up to 40 percent, but such deep discounting made it

hard for the company to reach profitability. Amazon is renowned for customer service, security and fast delivery.

Mini-Case Study: Dell (www.dell.com)

Dell have been pioneers in telemarketing and direct selling since the late 1980s, demonstrating that a complex product like a computer could be sold without face-to-face contact. Much of the success has been due to investment in staff training and customer service systems: 'We will use our employees to deliver the personal touch that many customers desire—you do not need physical contact to do that'. The company was one of the first e-retailers and is the market leader world-wide for computer hardware. Dell does not use high street stores, but remains dual channel, telesales and Internet.

Source: Adapted from de Kare Silver (2001).

Mini-Case Study: Marks and Spencer (www.marksandspencer.com)

Marks and Spencer were once well known as the most successful retailer in Europe. After a period in the doldrums, the company's high street operation is regaining its sparkle and the e-retail site is a model of good practice. It is easy to navigate with a good selection of clothing and underwear, plus home furnishings, gifts and flowers—but not food. Two-day delivery is free at the time of writing. Returns can be made either to an M&S store or with the post-paid label provided.

Source: Adapted from Sunday Times Doors 'Webwatch' site test.

Mini-Case Study: Boots (www.wellbeing.com)

Boots's new site is packed full of health and nutrition information content and also better stocked than most high-street Boots, with 10,000 products available. You can track your order progress online and there is currently no charge for deliveries (except for a charge for Saturday delivery). Returns can be posted back free.

Source: Adapted from Sunday Times Doors 'Webwatch' site test.

Think Point

The traditional slogan for the (UK telephone directory) Yellow Pages was 'Let your fingers do the walking'—use the phone to save trudging round the shops. Now, to solve a problem we tend to turn first to the Web: 'Let your fingers do the clicking'. Why should retailers pay to advertise in paper directories if consumers hardly use them?

Think Point

With a Boots on every high street, why shop at Boots online store?

Multi-Channel Retailing

According to Forrester Research, multi-channel shoppers spend 50 percent more than single channel shoppers and also spend on more expensive items such as televisions and computers. Nevertheless, studies by Gartner indicate that that multi-channel shoppers are less loyal than single channel ones (Kittle, 2007). Thus, e-retailers can easily lose high-spending multi-channel shoppers whenever customer service is standards falter (Lucas, 2007). For example, a survey by Zoomerang and Affluent found that 41 percent of shoppers were less likely to visit a retailer's bricks store after a frustrating experience on that store's e-store. Fifty-nine percent said that a frustrating experience hurt the image of the retailer (*Internet Retailer*, 2007).

Multi-channel retailers often want to persuade online shoppers to visit the bricks store where the strength of face-to-face selling can be used to trade shoppers up to more expensive items or sell on extras. The reverse sometimes applies, with a smaller bricks store branch advising customers to go to the website to access the full range.

Think Point

Interactive digital TV enables e-shopping without a PC, potentially doubling the e-shopper customer base. Could this development spell the end for the high street retailers most vulnerable to e-retail competition?

The e-Retail Mix

The blend of tools and techniques that e-retailers use to provide value for customers is sometimes called the e-retail mix (Lazer and Kelly, 1961). In a parallel to the well-known '4Ps' of the 'Marketing Mix' (McCarthy, 1960), the e-retail mix can act as a useful framework for e-retailers' strategies and tactics aimed at providing satisfaction and adding value for customers. Dennis and colleagues (2004) introduced the 'Sale the 7Cs' e-retail mix based on Lauterborn's (1990) '4Cs', which are claimed to be more customer orientated than the '4Ps'. 'Sale the 7Cs' is a simple, easy to remember aid for e-retailers to structure decision making of the elements of their offers to customers that are essential to success.

The Marketing Mix adapted for e-Retailing

The 4Cs are: Convenience for the customer ('Place' in the 4Ps); Customer value and benefits (Product); Cost to the customer (Price); and Communication (Promotion). As discussed in Chapter 6, reflecting the emphasis of 'new' marketing on long-term relationships with customers, we include customer relationships within the umbrella of the 'communication' C.

C1 Convenience for the Customer 'Place' (from the 4Ps), rather than implying managements' methods of placing products where they want them to be, can be thought of as 'Convenience for the customer', recognising the customers' choices for buying in ways convenient to them. For the bricks retailer, 'Place' incorporates what can be the most critical decisions concerning 'location', reflecting shoppers' preferences for short travel journeys, easy access, parking and so on. For the e-retailer, this is also important, as many customers prefer a multi-channel approach (as discussed in Chapter 7): browse on the Web, buy instore or *vice versa*—or buy on the Web and return to the store for a refund! This perhaps goes some way towards explaining the success of high street and multi-channel retailers in e-retail, compared to the dot-com 'pureplays'. Physical location can also be important for the e-retailer as many customers prefer to buy from, or are more

BOX 10.6   Sale the 7Cs – the (E-)Retail Mix

C1 Convenience for the customer ('Place' from the 4Ps)
- Physical location
- Multi-channel options: browse the web, buy instore or vice versa – or buy on the web, return to the store for a refund
- Virtual location and ease of finding the website: registration with search engines, location in e-malls and links from associates
- Website design: connectivity; navigation; 'shelf' space allocation and ease of purchase.
- Layout: 'free-flow'; 'grid'; or 'free-grid'

C2 Customer value and benefits ('Product')
- Satisfactions wanted by customers
- Solutions to problems or good feelings
- Specify (sometimes design) products reflecting closeness to the customer and benefits that customers want
- Selecting the range of products offered for sale – assembled for target markets from diverse sources
- Wide and/or deep range – where the 'clicks' e-retailer can score relative to the 'bricks' retailer
- Content: describing a compelling offer of products clearly in customer value and benefits terms
- Customisation of products to match the wants of customer segments as closely as possible

C3 Cost to the customer ('Price')
- The real cost that customers will pay including transport, carriage and taxes
- Costs of Internet telephone access
- Customers' perceptions that prices should be cheaper online than instore

C4 Communication and customer relationships ('Promotion')
   Communication is a two-way process also involving feedback from customers to suppliers, including:
- Marketing research surveys
- Public relations (PR)
- Direct mail
- E-mail

- Internet
- Offline advertising such as magazines and 'click here' sections of newspapers
- Online methods include banner ads and pop-ups (often incentivised); paid-for listings in search engines and directories; and affiliate programmes
- Atmospherics and Web atmospherics: visual (décor, colour management, video clips, 3D), olfactory (perfume and samples), touch (smooth and cool or soft and cuddly – communicated by visuals or samples) and oral (music). (but need to avoid long download times – 'click here for broadband').

Customer relationships
- Social networks
- Marketing database and loyalty schemes
- The e-retailer can enhance product value using Customer Relationship Management (CRM) and data mining to tailor products specifically to individual customers.

C5 Computing and category management issues
- Supplying the products that customers want, in the right sizes and quantities, at the right time and in the right place
- Efficient supply chains with computer network links between suppliers and retailers
- Minimising stocks and speed of response: QR or ECR
- Co-operation between suppliers and (e-)retailers aiming to improve the efficiency of satisfying customers whilst minimising stocks and costs. On the larger scale, this is 'Category Management' (CM), the retailer/supplier process of managing categories as strategic business units
- Efficient logistics systems are an important component of Customer care and service

C6 Customer franchise
- Image, trust and branding – long-term investment in quality, corporate communications and Customer care and service
- Safeguards including fraud protection and dispute resolution
- Safe shopping icons, e.g. Which? Webtrader

(continued)

BOX 10.6   Continued

C7 Customer care and service
- Creating assortments at competitive prices in an accessible format
- Fast and reliable deliveries at times convenient to the shopper
- Availability of help; return and refund facilities
- Click-through telephone help, bulletin boards and chat rooms make the experience more interactive and add community
- Addressing customer concerns, particularly for credit card security, e.g. displaying the 'padlock' secure site logo.

Source: Adapted from Dennis et al., 2004.

likely to trust, an e-retailer based at least in the same country, where carriage costs and maybe taxes are cheaper.

'Location' for the e-retailer also means virtual location and the ease of finding the website. This entails registration with search engines, location in e-malls and links from associates.

Convenience also includes key aspects of website design such as navigation, layout and ease of purchase. For the 'bricks' retailer, convenience decisions include shelf space allocation and layout. The equivalent in 'clicks' e-retail is site design and page layout. For example, whether layout follows the 'free-flow' or 'grid' type of layout, or indeed a combination such as 'free-grid' (Vrechopoulos, 2004; see Dennis *et al.*, 2004 for more on e-store layout and design and all elements of the e-retail mix).

C2 Customer Value and Benefits   'Product', rather than being something that a company has to sell, can be thought of as a 'Customer value and benefits'—meaning the bundle of service and satisfactions wanted by customers. People do not buy 'products' as such, but rather solutions to problems or good feelings. Retailers and e-retailers now specify (and sometimes design) products to a much greater extent than previously, reflecting closeness to the customer and appreciation of benefits that customers want in terms of choice, style, uniqueness, and so on. An essential task of retail and e-retail is selecting the range of products offered for sale—assembled for target markets from diverse sources. The wide and deep range that can be offered is one of the areas where the 'clicks' e-retailer can score relative to the 'bricks' retailer. The lowest price does not always result in the highest sales, as many shoppers may value aspects such as style, design and fashion, for example.

When buying online, customers are far less likely to request help than they are in the store. Rather, e-shoppers who need help in understanding a product are more likely to abandon the transaction and find an alternative supplier or even buy through a different channel. e-businesses, therefore, need to be particularly careful about describing products clearly in customer value and benefits terms.

C3 Cost to the Customer 'Price' may be what companies decide to charge for their products, but 'cost to the customer' represents the real cost that customers will pay, including, for example, in the case of bricks retail, their own transport costs. For clicks e-retail, there are also the costs of carriage and perhaps taxes to be added to the quoted prices. High carriage charges may be one reason for the high rate of carts abandoned at the checkout. Customers also need to consider the possible costs of Internet access. They often have a perception that prices should be lower online than instore, and this can cause problems when customers buying via other channels realise that they are paying more than online customers. If a customer who has looked up what they want online, then telephones the company to order, he or she can be irritated to learn that the extra discounts are not available when ordering by phone.

C4 Communication and Customer Relationships 'Communication' is equivalent to the final 'P' in the 4Ps: 'Promotion'. Promotion suggests ways in which companies persuade people to buy, whereas communication is a two-way process also involving feedback from customers to suppliers. Reflecting an increasing control of elements of the retail mix by retailers rather than manufacturers, retailers spend more on advertising than manufacturers do (assisted by advertising allowances from manufacturers). Retailers are closer to the customer than are manufacturers and have more access to customer feedback.

As discussed in Chapter 9, communication is not just advertising, though, but all the ways in which retailers communicate with their customers, including, for example, marketing research surveys, public relations (PR), direct mail, e-mail, Internet, marketing database and loyalty schemes. Successful e-retailers often use offline advertising such as magazines and 'click here' sections of newspapers integrated with online marketing communications. Online methods include banner ads and pop-ups (often incentivised); paid-for listings in search engines and directories; and affiliate programmes. Successful e-retailers need communication media are to be integrated in order to reinforce a consistent, positive perception (see 'Customer Franchise' below).

In addition to solving problems (see the 'Customer Value and Benefits' section above), there is another reason for customers buying products—to get good feelings. This is a particularly difficult area for e-retailers. The 'bricks' retail store and the face-to-face sales person are often much better at identifying and satisfying customers' emotional needs and wants. The physical store uses atmospherics in the attempt to change mood and give shoppers a pleasant emotional experience when buying. Emotional cues may include visual (decor), olfactory (perfume), touch (smooth and cool or soft and cuddly) and aural (music).

e-retailers can create a 'Web atmosphere' using, for example, music and visuals such as 3D displays and downloadable video clips. Such enhancements must always be a compromise, on account of the need to avoid long download times. One way of tackling the problem is to provide a 'click here for low bandwidth version' button.

Customer relationships are an area that successful bricks retailers such as Tesco (www.tesco.co.uk) have used to gain a major lead over competitors. In the 'Communication' section above, the importance of the emotional aspects of selling was mentioned. The sales representative selling face-to-face in the 'bricks' retail store can use verbal and non-verbal (body language) communication to build personal relationships with customers, enhancing the emotional value of products. In trying to replicate the physical buying experience, the e-retailer is at a disadvantage. On the other hand, with transaction data ready-digitised, the e-retailer is well placed to enhance product value using Customer Relationship Management (CRM) techniques. For example, data mining can be used to build a picture of products most likely to be wanted by individual customers. Products tailored specifically can be offered pro-actively. Amazon (www.amazon.co.uk) for instance, uses a collaborative filtering system to match new books, DVDs or music to existing customers likely to be interested in them.

Three More Cs in the e-Retail Mix   When the marketing mix is extended to suit the needs of e-retailers, other dimensions such as brand image and logistics need to be incorporated (McGoldrick, 2002). Simplifying previous versions of the retail mix, Dennis and associates (2004) added three more 'Cs', in a parallel with the 7Cs or 8Cs of e-shopping experience (Kearney, 2000 and Jones *et al.*, 2001 respectively). These are: Computing and Category management issues; Customer franchise; and Customer Care and service.

C5 Computing and Category Management Issues   The success of retailers has been founded on supplying the products that customers want, in the right sizes and quantities, at the right time and in the right place. A proliferation of products has come with the growth in consumer choice. e-Supermarkets, for example, carry 20,000 plus branded products and e-department stores from 100,000 even up to 1 million or more. Efficient control of this degree of complexity needs effective computer and logistics systems.

Retail logistics have been changing rapidly over recent decades. Firstly, the growth of retailer power has involved major retailers taking more control of their supply chains. The involvement of wholesalers has been reduced, tending to give way to contract logistics (under retailer control). At the same time, supply chains have become more efficient with Internet links between suppliers and retailers. Increasingly, retailers such as Tesco are allowing Internet access to their suppliers for real time Electronic Point-of-Sale (EPoS) data. Trusted supplier partners can thus respond more quickly to changes in customer demand.

Co-operation between suppliers and retailers has been key to improving the efficiency of satisfying customers whilst minimising stocks and costs. On the larger scale, this co-operative process is known as 'Category Management' (CM), the retailer/supplier process of satisfying consumers by managing categories as strategic business units.

High efficiency of the computer-controlled logistics systems is largely behind the success of bricks and clicks retailers such as Tesco. Ironically, deficiencies in this area have been a major factor in the failure of a number of pureplay dotcoms that have concentrated on advertising and promotion at the expense of other areas of the e-retail mix (see Boo.com in chapter 1). One exception is Amazon, which is founded on efficient logistics systems with excellent customer care and service. In the UK, Amazon is using its logistics expertise to carry out distribution services on contract for bricks retailers such as WH Smith (www.whsmith.co.uk).

C6 Customer Franchise   e-Retailers attempt to develop positive profiles or images in the marketplace. The most successful 'bricks' retailers have invested heavily in quality, customer care and service in order to raise their standing in the assessments of customers. Some authors refer to the accumulated value of image, trust and branding as the retailer's 'customer franchise'. Customer franchise might be seen as stemming from communications and customer care, but we consider that e-retail image is so central to business success that it merits a separate category. Many bricks retailers have high quality brands with clear personalities backed by long-term corporate promotion. These strong brands give bricks and clicks retailers a head start over pure-play dotcoms. Lack of trust has been one of main factors inhibiting the growth of e-retail. As McGoldrick (2002) pointed out, with greater choice, consumers choose the brands that they trust. Start-up brands must work hard on trust. For example, one of the few pure-plays to prosper, the auction site eBay (www.ebay.co.uk) includes five levels of safeguards including fraud protection and dispute resolution.

C7 Customer Care and Service   For the e-retailer, good service means, for example, reasonably fast and reliable deliveries at times convenient to the shopper; availability of telephone help; return and refund facilities. These are aspects on which the early e-retailers have been lamentably poor, with the big majority of e-shoppers still having a sorry tale to tell.

For the bricks retailer, even in self-service settings, store personnel play a crucial role in forming retail images and patronage intentions. The e-retailer is at a disadvantage, but elements such as click-through telephone help, bulletin boards and chat rooms can help to make the e-shopping experience more interactive. In general, the successful e-retailer sets out to make shopping more enjoyable, more convenient or less worrying for the customers.

When buying high priced items and those with a high 'personal' content such as cars, shoppers particularly value personal service. Retailers such as Virgin (www.virgin.co.uk) attempt to overcome this drawback with a pop-up window with a telephone number to reach a sales consultant, and the working hours in which they are available.

The computing, category management, supply chain and delivery systems are areas in which early e-retailers, particularly pure-play dot-coms, were sadly lacking; and this affected trust, image, and customer care and service. The stronger brands with greater customer franchise have higher sales and potentially higher profit; for example, Tesco (www.tesco.com) and Next (www.next.co.uk). It is often the already strongly branded bricks retailers with established computer and supply chain systems, who are making the running in e-retailing. Notable exceptions include Amazon (www.Amazon.co.uk) and Dell (www.dell.com), both well-known for efficient systems, quality, service, communications and interaction.

Case Study: Tesco (www.tesco.com)

Tesco is Britain's biggest grocery retailer and has been active in tele-sales (at pilot locations) since 1996. The initial telesales pilot, at Ealing, West London, was developed from the home delivery service to less mobile consumers, subcontracted from the Local Authority. This low-tech operation was developed into the pilot for e-retailing—built on the proven delivery system and hand-picking from the shelves of the grocery stores. Tesco still use this tried and reliable system for groceries in preference to a heavy investment in warehouse picking

Box 10.7   Safe Online Shopping

Security fears have always been a major factor tending to put people off shopping online. But as the Internet becomes a more familiar part of our everyday lives, most of us are overcoming our fears and finding that e-shopping is safe and convenient. Even so, things can still go wrong occasionally; especially if shoppers neglect to take simple precautions, leaving themselves open to crimes like identity theft and credit card fraud. Chip-and-pin cards have gone a long way towards reducing card fraud in-store but this may be simply moving the fraudsters online. First, it's essential to ensure that your computer is protected by firewall anti-spyware and anti-virus software. Otherwise, fraudsters may be able to infect your computer with bugs that can track everything that you key in and look at, including passwords and credit card details. I suggest only dealing with websites that you know you can trust. If you're unlucky enough to encounter a problem when dealing with Tesco, John Lewis, Marks & Spencer or any of the major household names, it's reasonable to expect them to bend over backwards to try to come to the rescue. On the other hand, if the supplier could be a private individual or is a company that you've never heard of, then think carefully before buying. Retailers should ask for the 3-digit security number from the back of the card, in order to help make it more likely that the buyer has the card and not just acquired the card number from a transaction record. But would you give those details to someone that you didn't know that you'd met in the street? If the person that you give it to is a fraudster, they might try to use your card for their own purchases. Of course, retailers should only deliver goods bought on your card to your address but if the fraudulent purchase is for, say, online gambling, you could lose a small fortune.

Major credit cards are implementing encrypted passwords which, like the pin in chip-and-pin, are never seen by the retailers. But when you're dealing with a retailer you might be transferred to the credit card site, so you need to be sure that the site is genuine as you will have to confirm account details! Why not go directly to the credit card site now and sign up, e.g.:

www.visaeurope.com/verified
www.mastercard.co.uk/securecode

Here's a few tips for safe online shopping:

- Only deal with suppliers that you know and trust. It's very rare for fraudsters to hack into secure sites, so your details should be safe. Be sure to keep a record of the transaction, including telephone number and postal address. If the site doesn't have these, you might decide not to touch it (and don't rely on a PO Box number)! Many blue-chip sites will have the logos 'ISIS' (Internet Shopping is Safe) and 'IDIS' (Internet Delivery is safe). If there's a problem with them, the Interactive Media in Retail Group (trade association) can arbitrate (www.imrg.org). You can also look for the logos 'Secured by Thawt' and the credit card secure access 'Verifed by Visa' & 'MasterCard Secure Access'. Click on any of these logos to verify that the site is genuine. Alternatively, shop through an 'online mall' that claims to list only secure sites, e.g.: www.topoftheshops.co.uk
- Make sure that you've seen the delivery times & charges; and returns & privacy policies. The supplier should keep your details private unless you give permission for them to be used (e.g. for the supplier or others to contact you with offers). But if you 'Accept' the conditions without reading them, you won't know whether you've given that permission!
- Don't give out any personal and credit card details until you come to an encrypted check-out page with an address that starts with 'https' rather than the usual 'http'. Make sure that there is a closed padlock symbol in the bottom right hand corner of the screen
- Never reply to emails that might be spam, especially if they ask you to click a link to confirm your account details as this might be a 'phishing' counterfeit site. Instead contact through telephone numbers, email addresses or websites that you know to be genuine
- Never tell anyone your password or pin. If you are unlucky enough to be a victim of credit card fraud, the credit card company might be able to detect this using profiling techniques. This could be a genuine reason that you might receive a phone call asking for your details. But don't give your details out if

(continued)

Box 10.7   Continued

they phone you! Insist on phoning them back on a number that
you know to be genuine before discussing any further
- Always pay by credit (rather than debit) card as if something
  goes wrong like the supplier goes bust or even if the goods are
  faulty or not how they were described, the credit card company
  is often liable.

Source: The authors.

centres (although non-food items such as books and electricals are
now handled from a non-store distribution centre). Customers can
purchase any of the 20,000+ grocery product lines available from the
stores, for next-day delivery for UK customers within delivery distance of a store (including 96 percent of the UK population). Sales of
non-food goods are currently growing at an astounding 50 percent
per year. A more limited product range is available for delivery world-
wide. Tesco sends shoppers three-monthly vouchers and information
on special offers by mail plus regular, tailored special offers via e-mail.
The typical shopping list is automatically stored using cookies, which
can speed up and simplify the ordering process, as the customer does
not have to go through a long order process each time. This is a big
'convenience' benefit because 80 percent of grocery shopping is replen-
ishment. Tesco follows the maxim 'make it easy for your customers to
buy', accepting orders by web, fax, telephone, home delivery or collect, and of course shop instore. You can buy books, music, clothes,
PCs and Internet service. There are regular paper mailings and special
offers, including non-food promotions such as 'The top 50 books 10
percent cheaper than Amazon'. The Tesco site links to iVillage, and
thereby addresses the need for more social interaction, particularly
for female shoppers, providing information and chat rooms. With an
e-turnover of over £500 million per year, Tesco claims to be the UK's
biggest e-retailer and the world's largest e-grocer.

Summary

e-retail is the sale of goods and services via the Internet or other electronic channels, for personal or household use by consumers. Success factors in e-retail include making it easy for consumers to buy, providing good service, making e-shopping an enjoyable experience and including human communication. The 'don'ts' include having to many graphics, too much narrative and too many click-through pages. Retailers must choose an e-retailing strategic option based on degree of commitment and responsiveness to e-shopping. Multi-channel retail (high street plus e-retail) is becoming more dominant. The well known marketing mix of 4Ps (or 4Cs) can be extended by the addition of three more Cs to make a more catchy retail mix: 'Sale the 7Cs'. The three extra Cs are particularly relevant to e-retail success:

- computing and category management issues
- customer franchise, trust, image and branding
- customer care and service.

e-Retail is growing, and the leaders are mainly those performing well on the three extra Cs.

With the technical security issues now largely resolved, consumers are steadily overcoming reservations and e-shopping is growing steadily. Market forces in action mean that the e-retailing survivors and leaders are the strong brands who are successfully addressing the customer service and fulfilment issues. Given the unstoppable progress of e-retailing, traditionalists can at least take comfort in the current e-success of the high street multi-channel retailers—one hopes preserving at least some vibrant bricks shopping alongside the growing proportion of clicks.

Questions

Question 10.1

What do you think would be disadvantages of e-retailing for an independent baker like Bothams?

Question 10.1 Feedback
The company might be put off by high set-up, investment and ongoing costs plus level of know-how and technology needed.

Question 10.2

What do you consider are the main advantages of e-retailing for a small independent baker like Bothams?

Question 10.2 Feedback
Location is unimportant; size does not matter; and reaches a larger audience.

Question 10.3

Why do you think Abbey National's e-bank is separately branded as 'Cahoot'?

Question 10.3 Feedback
High street customers might consider they were being unfairly treated if e-customers of the same bank received a better deal.

Question 10.4

Which of these companies' products would you expect to be most and least suitable for e-retailing: Bothams, Next, Amazon, Marks and Spencer, Boots, Tesco?

Question 10.4 Feedback
According to de Kare Silver's ES test, the most suitable should be Amazon followed by Tesco—both high on consumer attributes, having a high proportion of e-responsive convenience shoppers; with Amazon rated higher on product characteristics, i.e. more virtual appeal of the product. Least suitable would be Next and Marks and Spencer, both low on consumer attributes, having a high proportion of social and comparison shoppers.

Web Links

Adapted from the Virgin Internet Shopping Guide

www.amazon.co.uk
> Busy, friendly and informative; the market leader for books plus music and much more

www.petsdirect.co.uk
> Masses of goodies for pets

www.sendit.com
> The top choice for videos and CDs

www.dell.co.uk
> Market leader for computer sales

www.fao.com
> Fantastic range of thousands of toys

www.landsend.com
> Simple, cotton clothes in a clean and airy site

www.softwareparadise.com
> Wide range of software

www.tesco.com
> Top grocery supermarket online as well as instore

www.unbeatable.co.uk
> Great prices on electrical goods

www.wallpaperstore.com
> Huge range of wallpaper styles

www.winecellar.co.uk
> Good range of wines.

Price-Comparison Sites

These sites allow comparison of the prices of the same item from different e-retailers.

www.buy.co.uk
> Finds the cheapest electricity, gas or other utility—plus a directory of e-shops

www.ComputerPrices.co.uk
> Finds the cheapest computer kit in the UK

www.priceline.com
> Creates a market or reverse auction. Enter the price you want to pay for a range of services such as air travel and car hire. The system searches for suppliers willing to sell at that price.

Directories of UK Shops

www.british-shopping.com
www.enterprisecity.co.uk
www.ishop.co.uk
www.shopguide.co.uk
www.shoppingcity.co.uk

11

E-MARKETING PLANNING

Introduction

The chapter begins with a review of the necessary steps in effective e-marketing planning. It goes on to examine the increasing importance of the Internet to marketing strategies, with particular emphasis upon the need to integrate offline and online marketing activities into a coherent and logical plan. The organisational implications of these developments are then considered in terms of the need for appropriate leadership, resourcing and change management.

Topics Covered in the Chapter

- The marketing planning process
  - Conducting a marketing audit
  - Setting SMART objectives
  - Segmentation and choice of strategy
  - Implementing the chosen strategy through the marketing mix
  - Applying suitable metrics to evaluate success
- Internet marketing plans
- Organisational implications of online marketing.

Learning Objectives

By the end of this chapter you should be able to:

- Critically evaluate the effectiveness of the planning cycle for online marketing operations.
- Demonstrate how an online marketing plan is constructed by:

- Carrying out a marketing audit
- Setting SMART objectives
- Segmentation and choice of strategy
- Implementing the chosen strategy through the marketing mix
- Applying suitable metrics to evaluate success
- Explain the implications of e-marketing for organisational structures and internal business processes.

Recommended Reading

Kanter, R. M. (2001) *Evolve!: Succeeding in the digital culture of tomorrow*, Boston: Harvard Business School Press

The Marketing Planning Process

A marketing plan is an operational planning device detailing both the initial development and implementation of the chosen strategy and how the associated marketing activities can be integrated in order to meet the stated objectives.

It is important not to confuse the planning *document* (see example later in this chapter) with the planning *process*, which is illustrated in Diagram 11.1.

The principles of marketing planning apply just as much to online marketing as they do to more traditional marketing activities. Planning forces a proactive approach which involves:

- Defining objectives
- Assessing the operating environment
- Reviewing alternatives
- Selecting the best approach based upon effective matching of skills and resources with identified market opportunities
- Evaluating progress towards meeting the defined objectives.

Only by setting realistic objectives and assessing whether they have been achieved can a firm evaluate the contribution its online marketing is making, and then use this information to guide the choice of future strategy and its implementation. In this chapter we will be

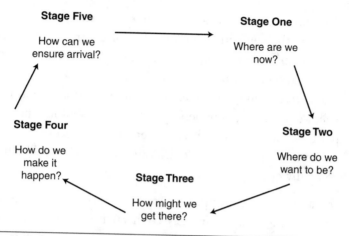

Diagram 11.1 The marketing planning process.

focusing on outline plans, but a model guiding the planning process in extensive detail has been developed by McDonald (2004) if you wish to examine this topic in more depth.

As illustrated in Diagram 11.1, the planning cycle can be represented as follows:

- Stage 1 (the marketing audit) addresses the question 'Where are we now'?
- Stage 2 (setting objectives) addresses the question 'Where do we want to be'?
- Stage 3 (segmentation and choice of strategy) addresses the question 'Which is the best way of getting there'?
- Stage 4 (implementation of strategy though the marketing mix) addresses the question 'How do we make it happen'?
- Stage 5 (evaluation and control of strategy) addresses the question 'How can we ensure arrival'?

Having completed Stage 5, the cycle then begins all over again from the new starting point! We will now examine each of the stages in turn.

Planning Cycle Stage 1—Marketing Audit

The marketing audit comprises research and analysis of the internal and external environment as follows:

- The internal audit reviews existing marketing activities and assesses their effectiveness in terms of contribution to revenue, brand enhancement, customer service, customer retention, market share or sales leads.
- The external audit considers the micro-environmental influences (customers, suppliers, partners, distributors and competitors) and macro-environmental influences (political, economic, social, technological and legal) within which the company operates.

From a company's perspective, the various components of the micro-environment are intimately connected with the operations of its business, but the macro-environment is one step removed. This means that a company has some degree of control over the micro-environmental influences, but cannot directly influence the 'bigger picture' of the macro-environment, which would include such issues as interest rate changes, new legislation and so on. By conducting a marketing audit, the company can at least monitor and be aware of the implications of likely changes in the macro-environment, even if it cannot directly control them.

Competitor Analysis An important part of the audit is competitor analysis, where the goal is to undertake a benchmarking exercise by identifying the company's chief competitors, analysing their individual marketing strategies, and hence seeing where to position the company for maximum advantage. The first step is to identify the major players in the market. The Yahoo! Directory (www.yahoo.com) provides a comprehensive categorisation of many business sectors. You can often see which companies get the most traffic by checking the Media Metrix 500 (www.comscore.com).

The second step is to study the top competitors carefully; you can learn a lot from the material posted on their websites. Look for:

- Scope of products or services offered
- Distribution system for products
- The scope of guarantees, policies and other customer service procedures
- The overall look, feel, and functionality of the website

Activity 11.1

Select two directly competing organisations and compare their websites using the above criteria. What features in particular give one company an advantage over the other in your view, and why?

- Sophistication of the payment system
- The degree of personalisation offered
- Advertising campaigns and offers
- Strengths and weaknesses from the customer's point of view
- The statement of vision or purpose
- Areas where the competitor holds a market advantage
- Vulnerabilities or gaps in what is offered.

Customer Analysis   Wilson, in www.wilsonweb.com provides the following framework that can be used to analyse customers and their changing needs (see Table 11.1).

SWOT Analysis   The analysis of the internal and external environment can be pulled together by means of a **SWOT analysis** (see examples later in the chapter).

S = strengths
W = weaknesses
O = opportunities
T = threats

This exercise allows the marketer to compare and match a company's internal strengths and weaknesses with the opportunities and threats identified in the external environment. It can therefore facilitate the

Activity 11.2

What can a company learn through segmenting its customer base by lifestyle?

Table 11.1   Customer Analysis

GEOGRAPHIC	Are they grouped regionally, nationally, globally?
CULTURAL AND ETHNIC	What languages do they prefer to do business in? Does ethnicity affect their tastes or buying behaviours?
ECONOMIC CONDITIONS, INCOME AND/OR PURCHASING POWER	What is the average household income or purchasing power of your customers? What are the economic conditions they face as individuals? As an industry?
POWER	What is the level of decision-making ability and job title of your typical customer groups?
SIZE OF COMPANY	What company size are you best able to serve? Do you determine this best by annual revenue or number of employees?
VALUES, ATTITUDES, BELIEFS	What are the predominant values that your customers have in common? What is their attitude toward your kind of product or service?
KNOWLEDGE AND AWARENESS	How much knowledge do your customers have about your product or service, about your industry? How much education is needed? How much brand building advertising do you need to make your pool of customers aware of what you offer?
LIFESTYLE	How many lifestyle characteristics can you name about your purchasers?.
BUYING PATTERNS	There is a growing body of information on how consumers of different ages and demographic groups shop on the Web. This is vital information for a marketing plan
MEDIA USED	How do your targeted customers learn? What do they read? What magazines do they subscribe to? What are their favourite websites?

choice of the most appropriate strategy for achieving the stated objectives through definitive and focused action. Speed of action is particularly important for plans which include a significant element of online activity, because competitive advantage tends to be short-lived

Activity 11.3

Go to www.amazon.co.uk and then draw up a list of features (strengths, weaknesses, opportunities and threats) to produce a SWOT analysis.

with competitors easily monitoring each other's online activities as described in the previous section on competitor analysis.

Marketing Planning Stage 2—Setting SMART Objectives

Without quantifiable objectives, strategies take place in a vacuum because the degree of success cannot be measured. The popular SMART mnemonic can be usefully applied to the objective setting process:

Specific   Objectives must be focused.
Measurable   Objectives need to be quantified to aid measurement of success.
Achievable   Objectives must be realistic, in other words compatible with the skills and resources of the organisation.
Relevant   Objectives should relate to core business activities.
Timed   Achievement of objectives channelled within realistic deadlines.

An example of a SMART objective could be to raise the contribution of online sales as a percentage of total sales from 10 percent to 15 percent over the next year. Other possibilities might include:

- Increasing retention of customers by 5 percent over the next six months
- Providing a response to customers' e-mail queries within 24 hours
- Reducing promotional costs by 20 percent within the next quarter

Activity 11.4

Examine the websites of a few organisations with which you are familiar. Can you work out which of the above objectives are being pursued from the content, style and language that is used?

Communication of SMART objectives ensures that all staff are aware of the targets set. Progress made towards achieving the objectives can be assessed at regular intervals so that changes can be made if necessary.

Chaffey (2006) notes that there are five key e-marketing objectives which he summarises as 'the 5 Ss':

Sell—Use the website to increase sales.

Serve—Add value to customers; for example, by swift response to queries made by e-mail.

Speak—Create a dialogue with customers by listening and responding to their feedback; for example, by monitoring online discussion boards.

Save—Use the website to reduce costs, which in turn allows discounts to be offered to customers in order to increase market share.

Sizzle—Use the online medium to reinforce brand values (see Session 6 for more detail in this area)

Marketing Planning Stage 3—Segmentation and Formulation of Appropriate Strategies

The next step is to *segment* customers into specific categories. This process requires considerable market research and careful analysis, but it enables much more focused marketing efforts. The marketing plan should contain a paragraph explaining how customers are segmented, indicating which products or services are most suitable for each segment. Different marketing strategies might be required for each market segment if their needs are diverse. Depending upon the characteristics of the various market segments, more or less emphasis upon online marketing may be appropriate in each case. No channel strategy should *force* customers online, but instead offer appropriate *choice*. A flexible strategy will add to costs but maintain the focus on specific customer needs. In practice, budgetary constraints and the company's attitude to risk will probably mean that a compromise has to be reached with regard to the extent of channel choice offered. This topic was addressed in Chapter 7.

Once the segmentation exercise is complete, the next task is to *target* resources on the segments deemed to offer most potential. It is unlikely that a firm would be able to meet the needs of a diverse range of customer groups, and once again the audit results can be used to select and prioritise the segments the firm is best placed to focus upon.

Positioning is the process of designing an appropriate image and value so that customers within the target segments understand what the company stands for. It also refers to the firm's location in the market in relation to its competitors. Through competitor analysis the firm can identify where gaps lie that it may be well-equipped to exploit through careful positioning.

The most important factor governing strategic direction will be the extent of the financial and psychological support given by the senior management team. Without such a commitment, new developments will lack direction and appropriate resourcing. Following the planning approach can help firms to take a long term view, by forcing them to think about matching their competencies with identified market opportunities, how to build upon their initial commitments over time, and how they will go about evaluating success.

Which of the alternative strategies should be chosen? If the audit has been conducted thoroughly, the best 'fit' between internal strengths and external opportunities should be apparent. But the decision can rarely be taken in isolation of often constraining organisational factors, such as a desire to maintain the status quo, the funds available and the commitment to change from senior management. If significant change is required to existing business practices, then critical roles may also be played by 'project champions' in driving effective implementation.

Activity 11.5

Have a look at how IBM segments its markets (www.ibm. com/businesscenter)

Why do you think this is an effective way to present information on line?

Kumar (1999) suggests that a firm should decide whether the Internet will primarily *replace* or *complement* other channels to market. In the former scenario, it is important that sufficient investment is made in the necessary infrastructure to achieve this. It is a critical decision because it forces the firm to think about whether the Internet is just another channel to market, or whether it will fundamentally change the way that the firm interacts with its customers. He suggests that replacement is most likely to happen when:

- Customer access to the Internet is high.
- The Internet offers a better value proposition than other media.
- The product can be standardised, and ideally also delivered over the Internet.

The attitude of the senior management team will be critical in establishing the degree of commitment to online strategies and hence the choice of most appropriate strategy given the resources available. In many cases, firms are reluctant to commit to providing Internet channels to market because of a fear of 'cannibalising' their existing business. This means that they fear providing alternative channels to customers will add to costs because existing customers take advantage of the ability to switch at will between different ways of dealing with the firm, without any new business being generated by the existence of the new channel. This is undoubtedly a risk, but the alternative of not providing the channel at all may mean that customers go where the choice is provided by competitors. So while the Internet channel may not generate additional business (at least in the short term) it should at least ensure that existing customers do not defect.

Marketing Planning Stage 4—Implementation through the marketing mix

The marketing mix is a generic expression originally devised by McCarthy (1960) and it is often referred to as the '4Ps':

Product
Price

Promotion

Place.

'Product' means both tangible product and also 'service' and all the ways that an organisation adds value. Online marketers need to be particularly careful about describing products clearly in customer benefit terms because the customer cannot directly check or handle the product. 'Price' means not just the price charged, but also all aspects of pricing policy including, for example, distributor margins. 'Promotion' is not just the more specialised 'sales promotion', but also every way that a product is promoted to customers from print advertising to websites. 'Place' is not quite self-explanatory, but refers to the routes that organisations take to get the benefits of the product or service to the intended customers—channels of distribution.

Pricing decisions generate revenue, whereas the rest of the marketing mix involves costs. Pricing decisions are particularly critical because there is a customer perception that prices should be cheaper online than otherwise. In some cases, customers can make much bigger savings buying online. For instance, to buy tickets from a travel agent in the UK for the Calgary Stampede rodeo (www.calgarystampede.com) is likely to be expensive because the agent will probably only sell these as part of a package. Tickets can be booked directly via the Internet at a substantial saving.

More recent authors have added service-related elements to the mix:

- People
- Process
- Physical evidence.

'People' has two meanings in this context. Firstly, customers are people, often buying according to emotion and whim. Without these fickle customers, the business will not exist. Secondly, people make it happen. Without people to put marketing plans into operation, nothing happens. For a service, where there is no tangible product, the process of providing the service is all-important. Similarly, a service cannot be sampled. The provider needs to present evidence of the quality of the process.

Traditional channels such as the retail store are often much better than online channels at identifying and satisfying customers' emotional needs and wants. The physical store uses atmospherics in the attempt to change mood and give shoppers a pleasant emotional experience when buying. Emotional cues may include visual (decor), olfactory (perfume), touch (smooth and cool or soft and cuddly) and aural (music). A sales representative has the opportunity to use verbal and non-verbal (body language) communication to build personal relationships with customers. Customer resistance to buying online can be partly broken down by the use of testimonials from satisfied customers or endorsements from celebrities. For example, Europe's largest direct sales yachting equipment company, Compass (German based, www.compass24.com) successfully launched in the UK with endorsement from Robin Knox Johnston, the famous ocean rower and yachtsman.

The 4Ps are a useful framework for designing e-marketing strategies—and have the benefit that they are clear and familiar to most managers. Successful e-businesses bring together the elements of the marketing mix into an integrated offer representing value to the customer.

Case Study: Screwfix

Screwfix (www.screwfix.com) is primarily a trade wholesale supplier, but also sells to individuals. Products include not only screws, bolts and nails, but also fixings, adhesives, tools, hardware, lighting, plumbing and cleaning products. The homepage has many examples of good practice, for example:

Register/Login—Optional registration makes ordering quicker and easier.

Special Offers—A number of good deals are always available.

Recommend a Friend—Get a reward when they order for the first time.

Open a Business Account

Express Shopping—If you have the catalogue, simply type in the quantities and catalogue number, or alternatively use *Search* to find what you want.

Activity 11.6

In what ways might the traditional marketing mix need to be adapted to the needs of an e-business?

Screwfix provides a useful example of the additional 3Ps:

People—A free phone telephone number is available 24 hours per day, plus fax and e-mail options, offering improved personal interaction.

Process—Delivery is promised within 24 hours.

Physical evidence—Testimonials on the site—'I have just received my order and felt I must congratulate you on an excellent service. Your site is well designed. The products are well laid out and the order processing excellent'.

'Your website is brilliant, the designer needs a big pat on the back. Well laid out, and to order on-line is so easy'.

Strategy implementation centres upon effective management of the marketing mix. To see the variety of ways that the mix can be employed in practice, have a look at the sample WH Smith marketing plan which is illustrated later in this chapter.

Marketing Planning Stage 5— Evaluation and Control of Strategy

Analysing the effectiveness of a site is crucial in analysing the strategy and then revising it if necessary to overcome problems. If clear, quantifiable objectives were set in Stage 2 then the evaluation process is facilitated because it can be easily established whether or not the objectives were met! In general terms, the measurement process can be summarised as follows:

1. *Goal setting*—What do we want to achieve?
2. *Performance measurement*—What is happening?
3. *Performance diagnosis*—Why is it happening?
4. *Corrective action*—What should we do about it?

Specific tangible evaluation methods that may be used include:

- Return on investment
- Operational cost reduction
- Revenue earned
- Site profitability
- Number of new customers gained
- Changes in customer satisfaction levels ascertained through market research.

Kaplan and Norton (1993) devised an integrated measurement system called the Balanced Scorecard that provides a framework with which to evaluate the success of a strategy against the objectives set. The scorecard includes:

- Customer concerns such as service quality, cost, response times
- Internal measures such as staff productivity and range of skills
- Financial measures such as revenue, profitability and costs
- Learning and growth/innovation measures such as rate of new product development, availability of staff training.

More intangible measures include:

- Corporate image enhancement through online PR
- Brand building
- Building of long term relationships with clients.

Whatever evaluation methods are used, they must be flexible enough to be adapted to the increasingly broad range of online marketing strategies that companies are pursuing. For example, if the site is not transactional then the relevance of financial measures may be limited.

It is also possible to measure site usage patterns electronically which can help with the evaluation process. Here is a summary of key techniques with some practical examples:

- Log file analysis allows companies to track visitors, site usage and evaluation. Companies such as WebTrends (www.webtrends.com) provide such a service.
- Panel data is available via Nielsen NetRatings (www.netratings.com) giving detailed monthly statistics of trends in Internet usage by country (including the UK and US) and company.

- Online questionnaires can be distributed via e-mail or on a website. Web Surveyer (www.websurveyor.com) is an example of software that can make it easier for companies to produce customised online surveys quickly with little technical knowledge.
- Online focus groups can be used to collect valuable data from the interaction and exchange of opinions between a small number of customers; see, for example, www.e-focusgroups.com
- Online mystery shopping allows companies to test every aspect of a website from customer's perspective; for example, www.edigitalresearch.com/eMysteryShopper
- Benchmarking can be used to measure the speed and performance levels of a company website in comparison with others; for example, see www.gomez.com.

So once again you can see the key role of research here in evaluating the success of the strategy implemented.

Internet Marketing Plans

An Internet Marketing Plan is an operational planning device detailing both the initial implementation of the website and associated marketing communications to achieve the aims of an Internet marketing strategy.

Case Example: Online Marketing Plan for WH Smith

Marketing Audit

The traditional high street retailer WH Smith sells more than 122 million magazines and newspapers a year from its high street stores in the UK. The company also has a presence in the US, Australia and New Zealand via Hodder Headline publications. WH Smith Plc has already established new channels to market through the Internet, digital television and WAP mobile phones. The company has a huge high street presence with 1,500 stores nation-wide. It also now has stores across the globe on major transport routes at airports and railway stations, and already has over five million members registered with a 'club card' scheme. These are already loyal WH Smith customers who have experienced the company through its stores. Moving this confidence online will be far easier than trying to generate new business online. One way to analyse WH Smith's current Internet strategy is to examine performance in terms of the Digital Marketing Cycle (Chen, 2001):

1. Visitors are *attracted* to the ISP through in-store promotions.
2. They are *engaged* by the WH Smith Portal's useful content.
3. WH Smith send fortnightly e-mails to *retain* customers.
4. Data is gathered when the customers sign up allowing the company to *learn* from its customers.
5. Either the product or the marketing effort is *customised* and tailored to one consumer at a time.

Strengths

- Well-established brand and customer base
- Club card membership
- ISP
- Customer trust and loyalty
- Links to e-intermediaries
- Warehousing
- Offline stores

Weaknesses

- Lack of integrated links between offline and online operations
- Separate departments
- e-commerce not a company-wide consideration (stores have little contact)

Opportunities

- Large offline database to bring online
- Build customer relationships and increase sales through provision of choice of integrated channels

Threats

- Cannibalisation of offline business by online competitors
- Weakening economy
- New data protection legislation

Objective

The objective is to provide a seamless service across all channels through 'my WH Smith' in order to improve customer relationships and generate additional revenue per customer. Specific objectives can be summarised as follows:

- Sign up one third of club card members to 'My WH Smith' within two years.
- Increase spend per club card customer by 15 percent within one year.

In order to build the trust necessary for Customer Relationship Marketing (CRM) to be effective, Sawhney and Zabin (2001) recommend 'presenting a seamless face to customers, regardless of what they buy, where they buy, and how they choose to interact with the firm.' Chapter 6 covers the topic of CRM in more detail.

Strategy

By providing an integrated multi-channel service WH Smith can pursue both market penetration (selling more to existing customers) and market development (attracting new customers) in terms of the traditional Ansoff model.

Implementation of Strategy through the Marketing Mix

- The initial stage is to introduce club card members to the product 'My WH Smith' (an online customer relationship marketing scheme) by sending a welcome pack containing the 'My WH Smith' CD and a new updated club card.
- The 'My WH Smith' product is free to all customers.
- Potential members will be offered a welcome pack in the firm's retail stores.

- In a seamless multi-channel environment people must be able to sign up via all possible channels (high street stores, travel stores, WAP phones, digital television, the Internet). They should only have to register once to use them all. Once a customer has signed up they will be able to use their e-mail address or WH Smith Net ID plus a password to access any channel.
- On Internet channels customers will be offered the option to store a cookie on their machine to identify them. The company should only use cookies with the customer's authorisation. The company's policy on cookies should also be detailed in the privacy statement.
- The customer can order goods from any channel. They can have goods delivered to their desired destination or arrange to collect them at their nearest store. Customer services and return facilities should be available through both online and offline channels.
- The customer should be able to maintain control of the relationship at all times. In order to achieve this they should be able to change the terms of the relationship as required.
- Personalised permission-based e-mails can be used to promote special offers and inform the customer how many club card points they have acquired.

Evaluation and Control   The success of this project will be monitored by the following values:

- 'My WH Smith'/club card ratios (reviewed monthly).
- Annual revenue contribution (reviewed bi-monthly by moving average).
- Spend per club card customer (weekly targets reviewed fortnightly).
- The targets will be set at each review and adjustments made to promotions and site structure if required in order to achieve objectives.
- Store managers will be set targets for signing up new customers.

Activity 11.7

Go to www.whsmith.co.uk. How have WH Smith encouraged potential online customers to use the site? What else could they do?

- It is also important to keep a monitor on the amount and type of customer queries received. This will allow the feedback pages to contain answers to popular questions.

Organisational Implications

For most well-established companies, developing online marketing strategies is not a matter of innovation from scratch, but of organisational change and adaptation—even corporate transformation. Kalakota and Robinson note: 'In the e-business world, companies must anticipate the need for transformation and be ready to re-examine their organisations to the core' (1999: 8).

The Internet continues to have an enormous impact on how organisations operate. It provides new opportunities for businesses of all sizes and has created an entirely new sales channel. Consequently, as Jackson and Harris (2003) note, companies have to be prepared to reorganise and restructure themselves continually, so that understanding how to effectively manage change becomes essential. Greenley *et al.* (2004) claim that traditional marketing plans do not include sufficiently robust processes for addressing change. This final section briefly examines the key principles of change management.

Barriers to Change

It is worth reporting here the recent findings of Rosabeth Moss Kanter (2001) who undertook a survey of 785 US companies to investigate the barriers to e-business change. The results are listed below in overall descending order of importance from 1 (most important) to 17 (least important). Bear in mind the point that companies more than 20 years old face fewer marketplace and technology barriers than younger ones do, but they face many more internal barriers—from decision-making uncertainty to divisional rivalries.

1. The unit does not have staff with adequate technical or web-specific skills.
2. Customers and key markets do not want to change their behaviour.
3. There are more important projects that require existing resources and time.
4. Technology and tools are inadequate, unavailable or unreliable.
5. It is hard to find the right partners to work with.
6. Suppliers are not co-operative or not ready for e-business.
7. Employees are not comfortable with change.
8. Leaders are not sure where to begin: they don't understand how to make the right choices.
9. Top executives do not personally use computers and are not personally familiar with the Internet.
10. Rivalries or conflicts between internal divisions get in the way.
11. It is hard to find the capital for new investment.
12. Managers fear a loss of status or privileged positions.
13. Employees fear loss of jobs; unions and employee groups fear loss of membership.
14. Government rules and regulations get in the way.
15. The company is successful as it is: leaders see no need for change.
16. The company had a bad previous experience with new technology.
17. It is a waste of time or money: it is not relevant to the business.

It is evident that there are a number of difficulties in implementing the intellectual, cultural and structural shifts necessary to succeed in a much more interactive business environment, which require a diverse range of management skills.

Integrating Technologies

One of the first challenges companies face when attempting to develop online channels is to consider how such a strategy will impact upon their traditional bricks and mortar organisation. Developing a clicks and mortar operation may result in a more virtual form of organisation where traditional ways of working are mixed with electronic communications. It is here that a company encounters its first problem, which is usually one of technology. The particular difficulty relates to the attempt to evolve 'legacy' systems (i.e. the technical infrastructure that has accumulated to support the business over time) to an infrastructure that will support e-business. Few businesses find themselves in the position where they can 'throw away' the old and introduce new, customised computer systems. Legacy systems often perform essential activities upon which daily business processes depend.

While start-up companies can leapfrog these problems, established ones face some difficult challenges. Effective e-business solutions demand integrated front and back end systems, a process which may demand close co-operation between two groups (or even sub-cultures) within the organisation. System integration means that when customers place orders and purchase goods online, the stock control and financial systems should also speak the same language and carry out their part of the transactions. The problem is that many such back end systems are unlikely to be based on open Internet protocols and may even have been custom-built. Nonetheless, such systems may be critical to a company's business, and include such details as bank account data and stock rotation information. Replacing or upgrading such systems also takes time, which may impact adversely upon the marketing planning process.

Resistance to Change

There are a number of reasons why both managers and staff may be unwilling to accept organisational change:

- Stability and security are threatened.
- Coping strategies and comfort zones are affected.
- The uncertainty of change creates anxiety.
- Imposed change reduces perceived autonomy and control.
- Job content is changed and new skills demanded.
- Authority structures and reporting lines are altered.
- Work groups and other relationships are disrupted.

- Established routines and practices are abandoned.
- An individual's power and authority is threatened.

Involving employees fully means that they become responsible for the success of the change, becoming 'owners' of the change process.

Another critical point to make is that organisations are bound to encounter complications in asking individuals to make changes that they are incapable of implementing. Adequate investments in training and development programmes are therefore essential, particularly, for example, if new skills in web design are required. If individuals do not possess the skills and capability necessary to introduced planned changes, the likelihood of success is significantly reduced.

Dell Computers, for instance (www.dell.com) brings customers into the product planning and manufacturing processes, with all employees encouraged to have contact with customers. Through effective collaboration across boundaries, ideas can be shared about product designs and value propositions. The result is faster and more customer-focused product and service innovation. To produce the capacity for this, considerable attention must be placed on organisational structures, processes, skills and culture—elements that may need a radical overhaul in established companies.

The Role of the Change Agent

Boddy and Buchanan (1992) emphasised the importance of having an appropriate 'change agent' or 'project champion' in the successful implementation of change. The change agent should be someone who is committed to the success of the project and prepared to 'go the extra mile' in order to motivate, bully or cajole other participants as

---

Activity 11.8

Dell sell directly to customers through the website www.dell.co.uk. This direct model allows Dell to build every computer system around the customer. How does the way in which the business is organised support its online marketing activities?

required. There is a diverse range of skills associated with performing this role, for example:

- Influencing
- Negotiating
- Selling
- Inspiring
- Commanding respect
- Political
- Magic and miracle working!

You can see that it is a tall order for any one individual to have all of these skills, and some will be more important than others at different stages of the project. In practice, therefore, there may be more than one change agent required.

It should now be clear that over and above the technological matters, major organisational change issues may need to be recognised and addressed for online marketing solutions to be realised successfully. This is because of the need to redesign business processes and structures, change organisational culture, demonstrate effective leadership, overcome employee resistance and engage in the necessary education and training. Internal marketing between individual departments plays an important communication role in many of these issues.

Summary

In this chapter we have examined the process of online marketing planning and the construction of online marketing plans. Effective change management is critical if the implementation of new online marketing activity is to be successful, yet this topic is rarely given the attention that it deserves.

Questions

Question 11.1

Why do you think some organisations may be reluctant to undertake formal e-marketing planning?

Question 11.1 Feedback

Staff may be hostile and resistant to making the changes that they anticipate will be deemed necessary. The planning process may lack high level support, or be regarded as just a 'one-off' activity. If internal communications are poor, then it will be difficult to acquire the necessary information for planning to be effective. Another common reason for avoiding planning is because of the rapid changes taking place in this area, which quickly render plans obsolete.

Question 11.2

Why is setting SMART objectives so important to the marketing plan?

Question 11.2 Feedback

Setting SMART (Specific, Measurable, Achievable, Relevant and Timed objectives) is an essential element in the second stage of the marketing plan. The remaining stages all hinge on realising these objectives, and if they are not, the plan will fail.

Question 11.3

The additional '3Ps' were devised for an extended marketing mix for services. Why are they also useful for an e-business selling tangible products?

Question 11.3 Feedback

'Service' is becoming an increasingly essential element of any business's success. In addition, customers may be more suspicious of the less tangible e-business than they are of an established bricks business. An emphasis on the real people aspects and presenting physical evidence of reliability can help overcome this customer resistance. Getting the process right is also essential to build customer confidence.

Question 11.4

Do you think it is possible to be too focused upon change management?

Question 11.4 Feedback

We are told that 'the only constant is change' but it is possible to be too enthusiastic, and embrace change for its own sake, even if the status quo is still valid. Some firms appear to feel they need to change their strategies each week in order to remain competitive—is this too extreme in today's environment? What do you think?

Feedback on Activities

Activity 11.1

It is unlikely that any two competing websites will be identical in their style and scope, although bear in mind that new ideas can be very quickly copied online. Examining new service offerings from the Internet market leaders such as Amazon (B2C) or Cisco (B2B) can also give valuable insight into the latest possibilities.

Activity 11.2

Lifestyle segmentation allows sub-groups of customers to be targeted with specific marketing messages. Have a look at the CACI website (www.caci.com). The firm has developed the fascinating ACORN system of 43 closely targeted lifestyle profiles that can be tied to specific postal codes for highly targeted promotional campaigns.

Activity 11.3

Strengths
- Strong, well established brand
- One click purchase
- Customer trust and loyalty
- Range of goods
- Wish list option

- Wedding lists
- Website personalisation (for example, purchase recommendations)
- Affiliation programme.

Weaknesses

- Lack of online/offline integration
- 'Clutter' on site.

Opportunities
- New product ranges (for example, electronics, jewellery).
- New service ranges (for example, Amazon Marketplace, Amazon MasterCard and DVD rental)
- Build customer relationships via joint ventures with offline businesses such as photo printing with Photobox.

Threats
- Ease of price comparison online
- New entrants
- Internet regulation
- Cannibalisation of new Amazon goods by Amazon Marketplace (new and used goods auction).

Ideally your SWOT analysis should *rank* each feature according to importance. This means that what you consider to be the most significant strength is displayed first in the list, followed by the second most significant strength.

Activity 11.4

Obviously not all of these objectives will be relevant to every online business. The marketing audit should identity the most important areas for the organisation to focus upon, based upon assessment of key business strengths and perceived market opportunities. If you check out www.easyjet.com, for example, there is a clear focus throughout on cost reduction by encouraging customers to interact with the company online. The savings generated are then translated into low prices.

Activity 11.5

You can see that IBM interacts with each of its separate classes of customer differently. Within each category are products particularly designed for that customer segment, with the layout, language and emphasis of each part of the site customised accordingly.

Activity 11.6

This can be illustrated, for example, by outlining aspects of the 4Ps of the marketing mix of the office supplies company, Quill (www.quillcorp.com).

Place—Customers are offered the convenience of easy ordering—not just online but with expert personal assistance readily available by telephone. A particular benefit is the UPS order tracker so that customers can track the delivery status of their order.

Product—Quill offers a wide range of office and computer supplies, furniture and speciality products. The main selling point is the very wide range available from stock—almost everything imaginable for the office. This is a 'hypermarket' type approach, offering customers far more choice than would be expected from most traditional suppliers.

Price—Competitive, discount prices can be offered. Low price levels are sustainable because of the e-efficiency of the business, and also the economies of scale arising from successfully selling large volumes.

Promotion—Quill is promoted by a wide range of integrated marketing communications of which an affiliate programme and e-newsletter are central.

Activity 11.7

From the WH Smith homepage the user is immediately presented with a number of options. Online offers have been given a lot of priority on the page across a range of their products. However, there are some more subtle enticements as well. There are some important direct links from the homepage to reassure users:

- 'Free delivery to store' option
- Register for club card—to gain immediate benefit
- Browse by product or go to specific special offer
- 'Store search' option.

Surprisingly, they have not placed a direct link to their privacy and security statement, which should be given priority in order to reassure users as to the safety of using the WH Smith site. These statements are, however, available in the 'help' section.

Activity 11.8

Not only does Dell's direct model allow every system to be built around the customer, their use of Internet technology allows customers to review, configure, price and purchase a system all through the website. Once purchased, the order can be paid for and tracked online. This allows Dell to build on the customer relationship by knowing what customers want to buy, and it means that the company does not have to rely heavily on inventory. At support.dell.com customers can see information about their exact system, once again cementing the relationship. There is also a customer forum—Dell Talk—where customers have formed an online community. Dell also use the Internet technology to build relationships with their supply chain. Their site https://valuechain.dell.com/ allows suppliers to check inventory, product quality and status.

Web Links

www.webtrends.com
    Log file analysis which allows companies to track visitors, site usage and evaluation.
www.netratings.com
    Panel data is available via Nielson NetRatings giving detailed monthly statistics of trends in Internet usage by country (including the UK and US).

www.websurveyor.com

Websurveyor is an example of software that can make it easier for companies to produce customised online surveys quickly with little technical knowledge.

www.e-focusgroups.com

Online focus groups can be used to collect valuable data from the interaction and exchange of opinions between a small number of customers.

www.edigitalresearch.com/eMysteryShopper

Online mystery shopping allows companies to test every aspect of a website from the customer's perspective.

www.gomez.com

Benchmarking which can be used to measure the speed and performance levels of a company website in comparison with others.

www.yahoo.com

Contains the Yahoo! Directory which provides a comprehensive categorisation of many business sectors.

www.comscore.com

Includes the Media Metrix 500 which compares the volume of traffic visiting a range of websites as an aid to competitor analysis.

www.wilsonweb.com

Detailed guidance on the preparation of marketing plans, although aimed at a US audience.

www.marketingteacher.com

A useful student resource with examples of marketing plans for a range of industry sectors and business priorities.

www.ibm.com

A good example of a site which is segmented according to the needs of key customer groups.

12
THE FUTURE OF
E-MARKETING

Introduction

In this final chapter we discuss recent developments which can be described under the general heading of 'Web 2.0'. They present significant opportunities and threats for online marketers. We then examine what lessons may be gleaned from the past to help understand the present and hence illuminate the role of new technologies into the future. We conclude with some case studies which demonstrate how new technologies have the potential to transform entire industry structures and that the 'winners' will be those players who actively embrace change and are not afraid to challenge traditional business assumptions.

Topics Covered in the Chapter

- Maximising the opportunities of Web 2.0:
  - RSS
  - Blogs
  - Podcasts
  - Online networking
- Where are we now? Successes and failures.
- What does the future hold?

Learning Objectives

By the end of this chapter you should be able to:

- Discuss the ways in which lessons learned from the past can be applied to e-marketing operations.

- Evaluate examples of recent technological developments and consider their likely impact on the future of e-marketing.
- Apply your learning from throughout this book to contemporary examples of technological change.

Recommended Reading

Surowiecki, J. (2005) *The Wisdom of Crowds*, London: Abacus
Wright, J. (2006) *BLOG Marketing*, New York: McGraw-Hill

Maximising the Opportunities of Web 2.0

There are a number of fundamental insights and technologies that allow businesses to take advantage of the tools of what has become known as 'Web 2.0' to make themselves appear larger, more competent and more important than their peers (and maybe than they really are). For example, many social networks are now being formed and carried out wholly in cyberspace, making geographical location far less important for effective networking than before, and providing easy, fast and low-cost methods of maintaining new contacts on a world-wide basis.

The characteristics that Web 2.0 tools share are open access, a focus on micro-content rather than whole websites, and a reliance on users to provide content. The underpinning rationale is that the collective intelligence of a group of enthusiasts helps to ensure high quality through peer review and the consequent reiteration of edits and updates. The classic example of a Web 2.0 website is Wikipedia (www.wikipedia.org) which allows users to edit each entry, thereby creating an open editing and review structure. Sites such as YouTube (www.youtube.com) allow users to rate the videos they watch and add selected items to their 'favourites' so that, in theory at least, the high quality items are flagged up for the benefit of other viewers. The section highlighted in red in Diagram 12.1 demonstrates that this spoof Apple iPhone commercial on YouTube has been viewed 2,485,759 times, attracted 1,173 comments and been placed 7,584 times into viewers' favourite videos. It has also been rated on average four stars out of a maximum of five by its viewers.

Diagram 12.1   The rating system on YouTube.

We will now examine a number of Web 2.0 developments in turn.

RSS (Really Simple Syndication)

As discussed in Chapter 9, e-mail marketing increasingly has to cope with the resentment of individuals against intrusive marketing, and the rising tide of legislation against unsolicited marketing that applies in both European and US jurisdictions. While people can easily throw unwanted junk mail away it is more difficult to avoid insistent e-mails or telephone calls. The tools available are unsatisfactory—there is plenty of anecdotal evidence of perfectly respectable e-mails being caught in company spam filters and not delivered, and the defences against intrusive telephone calls are largely all or nothing. So, rather than risk their messages being perceived as spam, early adopter companies are looking at ways that enable their story to be picked up *only* by people who are interested in what they have to offer or say.

One of the key tools for achieving this is the RSS feed (see the RSS logo in Diagram 12.2) which essentially takes the form of a headline and a body of text. An RSS feed is a stream of updated information

Diagram 12.2 The RSS button.

sourced from a blog or website, which lets an RSS reader know that an update has happened. RSS readers are now available in all the major Internet browsers and search engines such as Google, Yahoo!, AOL and MSN. When the RSS reader sees an update (for which it is constantly scanning), it takes the headline, or the headline and some of the content, or the headline and *all* of the content and displays it. Once the feed is set up, there is a direct, permanent, updated connection to a source of content. It means that people can choose to stay in touch with anyone who interests them and who is making relevant communication available to them.

So if a prospective customer finds useful content and the website displays the RSS button, it can be clicked to set up a newsfeed so that future communications from that site can be received automatically as soon as they are posted to it.

Diagram 12.3 shows an example of a personalised Google home page complete with a series of RSS feeds. The most recent results are displayed first so that the page provides a snapshot of current events across all of the author's areas of interest. It is also possible to set up several pages under different tabs in order to segregate material, for example between business and social information.

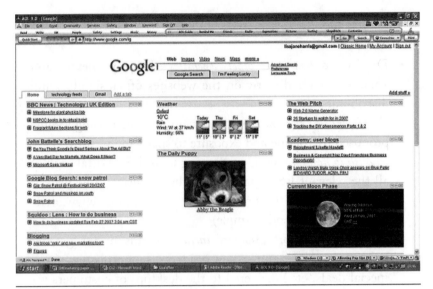

Diagram 12.3   Personalised Google home page.

From the point of view of the marketer, the crucial task is to move the company mindset from collecting potential customers' e-mail addresses and then following up with e-mails and e-zines, to encouraging prospective customers to sign up to a blog via an RSS feed. Subscribers will then be automatically notified of anything that the marketer may choose to post—about events that are being run, free downloads, workshops, new products, relevant observations and worthwhile links that they will find interesting. The key to making a success of this marketing communications strategy is as follows:

1. Interesting content—regularly refreshed.
2. The back-up mechanisms available to turn other people's interest into money.
3. Make sure that you create as many links as you can to appear as widely as you can and encourage referral.

These are the initial steps on moving from a 'push' to a 'pull' marketing regime. Obviously it cannot work in isolation and needs to be backed up by offline techniques like postcards, PR and online advertising as well as whatever face-to-face marketing fits the business model.

The following list describes some early uses of RSS feeds for marketing purposes:

- *Display content on other websites*—Display news and announcements directly on the websites of subsidiaries and distributors.
- *An alternative to e-mail*—A channel that is increasingly compromised by volume and exposure to spam and viruses.
- *Publish to news feeds*—Contributing to an RSS Portal enables all the relevant RSS channels for that industry to be viewed in one location in front of a relevant audience (see www.oreillynet.com for a good example)
- *Provide content for customers' intranets*—this means getting information (for example, new products, support issues, news, special deals, etc.) delivered to the desktops of customers via their intranets.
- *Create customised channels*—customising content can be a costly and difficult business. RSS allows individuals themselves to customise the data they receive.

Activity 12.1

Set up a RSS feed for yourself if you have not done so before. A good place to start is the BBC website (www.bbc.co.uk) which has feeds available in a wide range of subject areas and provides a tutorial explaining how to subscribe to something that interests you.

Blogs

We are living in a well-informed, flexible and interconnected society in which people are active market participants. Consumers are tired of the old style of impersonal one-way marketing; tired of the distraction of unwanted marketing messages (Godin, 2001). Today people are part of global social networks and prefer to rely on each other to gather information and exchange experiences. They no longer depend on companies to provide them with information. Into the future, marketing will increasingly be based on building a relationship with the customer and engaging him in a dialogue, which creates a two- or multi-way communication.

One tool with massive potential in this change is the blog (also called a weblog), which is an interactive participatory form of online media. It is a frequently updated website where articles or content are written in an informal, conversational style and published in reverse-chronological order with a date and time stamp associated with that particular entry.

Businesses have to get involved in the world-wide information community (McKinnon, 2004) and use blogs to speak to current and potential customers. But blogs are more than just another new communication tool; companies need to understand the social rules of the blog in order to effectively approach customers.

Features of Blogs

Most blogging software provides the following features which are highlighted in Diagram 12.4:

1. A post (article) with a date and time stamp that indicates when the post has been written. At the bottom of the post a link to the 'comment' section, a link called 'trackback' and a link called 'permalink' can be found. A reader can comment on a post by clicking on the comment link. This feature promotes 'democratic self-expression and networking' (Kahn and Kellner 2004: 91). The trackback link shows if a reader of a blog has posted an article on his blog and added a link to the blog he is reading. This technology allows conversations to be followed that have started on one blog and have spread onto another blog. Each post gets a unique URL, called a permalink. This allows a permanent link to a specific blog post that will not change over time.

2. Each blog post can be categorised, which makes it easier for the reader to retrieve articles of interest.

3. As noted in the previous section, one can 'subscribe' to a blog with the help of syndication formats like RSS and Atom. These so-called feed aggregators allow the reader to receive

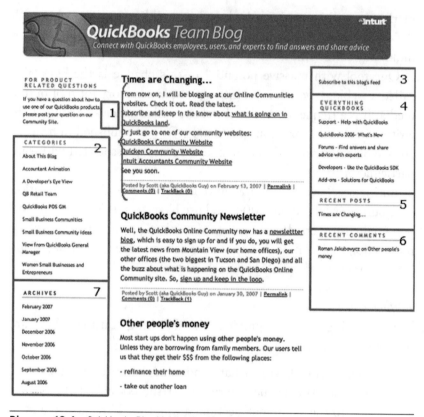

Diagram 12.4   Quickbooks Blog highlighting blog features.

posts from different blogs and web pages, without having to access each one in turn. As soon as a page has been updated, the reader gets a notification.

4. Links to other pages (e.g. website).

5. Links to recent posts.

6. Links to comments.

Older articles are archived by date. Some blogs allow archiving of posts by author or alphabetically.

Additional functions, such as a search function for the blog, an 'about' page and podcasts can be found on blogs. Links to other blogs or web pages can be found either in the blogrolls or directly in a post itself. A blogroll is a collection of links that the owner of the blog thinks are worth reading.

A blog differs from online diaries or web pages in that it is more collaboratively constructed, interactive, frequently updated and written in a conversational voice (Weil, 2006).

Categories of Blog   Herring, Scheidt, Bonus and Wright (2004) identify three basic categories of blog:

- Filter blogs deal with (or 'filter') external events, perhaps focusing on a specific topic and providing links to world news or online events.
- Personal blogs are written by individuals or groups who like to share thoughts, interests and activities. Their content typically comprises personal diaries, accounts of travel experience, or personally-sourced information on a particular topic such as a hobby, children, nutrition, etc.
- Knowledge blogs are repositories of information about a specific topic.

Additionally, corporate blogs are created by companies to present information to customers and stakeholders and build a relationship with them. Companies need to change their controlled one-way communication and be open to learn, to listen and to ask people what they think (Weil, 2006). They should come across as passionate and authentic and be able to acknowledge their mistakes. A blog is not 'corporate speak', instead it is like a window through which a company allows its customers to see inside (Wright, 2006). Furthermore, blogs have to speak the 'language' of the target audience (Zerfass, 2005).

Crucially, companies need to have something to say; customers can choose what they want to read, what they want to talk about and with whom they want to build up a relationship. The reality of the marketplace is that consumers have a choice, and they can choose to ignore you! Thus companies have to give their customers something real, new and exciting enough either in their own blog or in other blogs related to the company or its products. If they are compelling enough, ideas and messages can spread like viruses do (Scoble and Israel, 2006; Gladwell, 2000).

Table 12.1   Categories of Corporate Blog

Analyst and advisor blog	Written by a person that knows the market and the customer very well
Inside blog	Written by a person that knows the industry well and shares its expertise with the employees
Bridge blog	Makes connections and brings people together
Window blog	Talks about things happening inside and outside the company
CEO blog	Through this blog the CEO shows his interest in speaking with his customers and building a connection between the company and its clients
Product blog	Focuses on a company's products, product features, how products can be used, what experiences clients have had with this product and other product-related topics
Service blog	Deals with customer service issues
Campaign blog	Used for viral marketing campaigns
Community blog	Builds up an active virtual community with people discussing topics of interest to them

Corporate blogs can be divided into categories as shown in Table 12.1, although often a blog cannot be assigned to one category exclusively, but is a combination of two or three different categories.

Before starting up a blog a company has to have a strategy and a goal, and needs to know exactly what value the blog should bring to the organisation. For example, it could be to increase the visibility of the organisation or its product/service, to spread news, to enlarge the customer base, to deal with complaints, to manage customer relations, for internal communication or to build up a loyal customer base. Diagram 12.5 summarises these options.

Internal blogs can be further categorised as follows:

- *Knowledge management*—Employees can be kept informed about the company, its products and the industry, even if they are away. The unique knowledge of every single employee can be shared and people can learn form each other.
- *Project management*—All project members can share their information on a project blog. Important discussion points can be raised and ideas can be shared among all project members. Everybody gets the same information and can easily contribute.

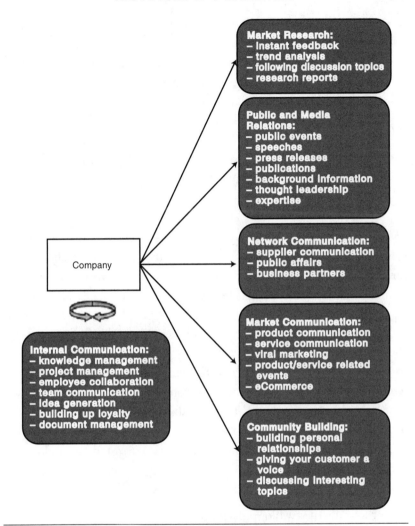

Diagram 12.5 Uses of corporate blogs

- *Employee collaboration*—Employees can build up relationships with their colleagues around the world. They can discuss problems on a global basis, gather new ideas and discuss issues. Like-minded people can find each other and exchange thoughts on topics they are interested in.
- *Team communication*—Team-related topics can be discussed and documents shared. This can help reduce e-mail traffic and make sure everybody has the latest information.

- *Idea generation*—Blogs can be used for brainstorming or as a 'bottom-up' idea generation tool.
- *Building loyalty*—Because employees get more involved, informed and connected with other employees their loyalty towards the company can be increased.
- *Document management*—Blogs can also be used for sharing documents. This again will decrease e-mail traffic and make sure everybody has the newest version of a document. Moreover, people can post comments and inputs which are viewable by everyone.

The Role of Blogs in Market Research We discussed online market research in Chapter 3. Increasingly, the virtual world is being monitored by search and tracking sites looking for keywords being mentioned in posts. Monitoring blogs is a very effective means of market research, allowing marketers to see what people are talking about. All categories of blogs can serve as market research platforms. Blogs should be monitored systematically by defining a strategy for how to search, what to search, where to search, how often to search and which blogs to read. By doing so a company does not only analyse past behaviour but gets real-time feedback and sees what trends are developing.

A few blog search engines and directories devoted to cataloguing this global network are listed below:

1. Search engines
   Blogpuls (www.blogpuls.com)
   Daypop (www.daypop.com)
   Feedster (www.feedster.com)
   IceRocket (www.icerocket.com)
   Blogrolling (www.blogrolling.com)
   Blogcount (www.dijest.com/bc)
   Technorati (www.technorati.com)
   Google (www.google.com—add the word 'blogs' to the search topic)
   Yahoo! (www.yahoo.com)
   PubSub (www.pubsub.com)

2. Directories

Blogarama (www.blogarama.com)

Globe of Blogs (www.globeofblogs.com)

The Open Directory (http://dmoz.org/Computers/Internet/ On the Web/Weblogs/).

Technorati is a blog search engine tracking over 100 million blogs. Technorati's main purpose is tracking the number of links to a specific blog and monitoring what blogs are talking about a specific topic. It also ranks the blogs based on their authority. The more links that point to a blog the higher is its authority.

BlogPuls helps to measure online word of mouth and customer recommendations. It helps companies to answer several key questions: Which people, and in what numbers, are talking about our brand or our competitor's brand? Exactly what is being said? What issues seem to be important to customers? The four tools of BlogPuls can provide this information:

- 'Trend Search' and 'Featured Trends' allow the creation of graphs that visually track 'buzz' over time for companies, products or other topics. They also allow comparing of search terms against others.
- The 'Conversation Tracker' follows a whole conversation starting from the original post.
- The 'BlogPuls Profile' displays information about a specific blog or blogger.

Public and Media Relations The main blog categories that serve public and media relations are analyst and advisor, window and CEO blogs. Blogs allow for more visibility, as general public and media see what organisations are doing on a daily basis and companies can put their own version of a story out there and get feedback on it. Blogs could go along with a public event and speeches publicising reports and feedback related to them. Press releases can be uploaded to blogs and allow for feedback and additional information. A blog can also be used as a channel to build up an expertise and thought leadership and share the viewpoints of a company. Furthermore, blogs can be used as another place to publish papers and discuss their findings with the readers (Wright 2006; Weil 2006).

Market Communication Blogs that focus on market communication can be categorised as product, service and campaign blogs. Blogs can enhance communication to customers by providing a dynamic FAQ with a comment section where customers can add their ideas and thoughts, sharing information about products and services, providing service updates and industry news. It also allows uploading of white papers, company presentations and dynamic user guides.

A company can also sell products and services directly from a blog. A blog with quality content will naturally have a greater attraction for readers and thus a greater effectiveness as a vehicle for spreading the intended promotional messages. Because of this vehicle/message function, blogs can be seen as a viral marketing tool, but with the huge advantage that they provide multi-directional communication. Traditional viral marketing campaigns, using contests, games or video clips as content are one-way instruments which might spread well for a certain period of time but ultimately lose their impact because no relationship has been formed (Weil 2006; Wright 2006).

Return on Blogs (ROB) 'Return on blogs' cannot be measured the same way as 'return on investment'. There are, however, measures which can be applied to blogs. When people comment on posts, blogs generate member-based content. This member-based content increases the attractiveness of the blog and can thus draw more people to it, which builds yet more content. The content of the blog becomes more and more attractive and builds member loyalty. If companies listen carefully to what is discussed in blogs they might be able to target their products and services more precisely to their customers needs. This again will increase profitability as customers get the products they are really looking for. With a direct link to the company's web page the customer can be encouraged to purchase a product directly in an e-shop.

Furthermore, 'hits' and 'return visits' can be measured and the amount of comments and trackbacks tell how popular a blog is. Services like Technorati or BlogPuls can be used to analyse trends of topics a company is discussing on its blog, or how many people are discussing the company and its products.

Credibility of Blogs   Despite all the bravado of blogs one question that needs to be asked, however, is whether the information found on blogs can be trusted. A blog is a disclosure of the blogger's biases in that it does not undergo any peer review or editing to eliminate misinformation, and is not governed by any professional standards. However, it is precisely this freedom to express thoughts without restriction that makes blogs so successful. There have been some studies examining the credibility perceptions of blogs among bloggers, where weblogs were judged significantly more credible than any traditional medium (Johnson and Kaye 2004). The authors argue 'Blogs do rely on peer review of other bloggers to point out mistakes that can be easily and prominently corrected. Users may find Weblogs more credible because they are independent rather than controlled by corporate interests....' If a blog is written by a trusted newspaper or company the information should be expected to be credible because the originator has an image to maintain. Another indication of content credibility is the ranking on a search engine and how many readers comment on it. Technorati, for instance, rank a blog according to its authority, meaning that the more links point to a blog the higher is its ranking. It can be said that if many people read a blog and link to it, the blog is highly likely to have trustworthy and interesting content.

Case Study: Cox Communication

Cox Communication, which is one of the largest US communication companies, produces a blog called Digital Straight Talk, as illustrated in Diagram 12.6. This blog provides news and information on the many issues affecting the broadband industry. With the Digital Straight Talk blog the company is addressing topics on which it wants to provide its own point of view and invite readers to discuss and debate. The authors do not fear any negative comments and are prepared to respond to any customer question.

Diagram 12.6   The Digital Straight Talk blog.

Case Study: ING

ING is one of the largest financial services companies in the world, with its Asia/Pacific insurance, banking, asset management, and real estate operations headquartered in Hong Kong. See Diagram 12.7 in which Jacques Kemp, CEO of ING Asia/Pacific provides a CEO blog in which he shares insights into ING's activities and his experiences in the Asia/Pacific region, and hopes to establish a good dialogue with his readers.

The Future of Blogs

Over the next few years, company blogs will become less of a novelty and more of an integrated fixture on the corporate website. Technologies evolve rapidly and new forms of blogging will emerge. Nowadays, people usually access the Internet from a computer, either from home, the office or an Internet cafe. As discussed in Chapter 7, changes will occur as people increasingly access the Internet while on the move. Mobile blogging, which is blogging from a mobile phone, will allow

Diagram 12.7 ING blog.

bloggers to stay connected with their community anytime and any-where. Companies will also have to think about how to use audioblogs (podcasts) and vlogs (video blogs), for communication purposes.

Podcasts

Podcasting is an automatic mechanism by which computer files are transferred from a server to a client which pulls down XML files containing the addresses of the media files. In general, these files contain audio or video, but also could be images, text (*e.g.* PDF), or any file type. The BBC define a podcast as '…a way to "subscribe" to radio programmes and have them delivered to your personal computer'. Podcasts can be free or you can buy a subscription to the most popular content. Subscribers receive the latest edition of the programme transferable to an mp3 player.

To make the system work, you need an Internet connection and a piece of podcast software which can check for new episodes of the subscription programme and automatically download them to your player.

The publisher issues a list of permanent URLs or feeds directing the recipient to the location of the programme, which are then selected using a podcatcher or newsfeed receiver. Podcasting is not currently covered by the broadcast regulatory bodies so it is possible for podcast content to include, for example, product endorsements which are not permitted on traditional radio broadcasting.

Although podcasting is relatively new, a diverse number of applications have so far been developed:

• *News organisations*— as an addition to their existing text.
• *Education*— for audio revision and homework.
• *Politics*—in the US both major political parties have podcasts, as does the Conservative party in the UK.
• *Religion*—podcasting (or 'godcasting') has been used by many religious groups.
• *Cultural sites*—for unofficial and official audio tours.
• *Professional bodies*—to update members with summaries of important articles and research.

One of the leaders in this field has been Angela Merkel, Chancellor of Germany, who not only publishes a regular podcast but also a video version (known as a vidcast or vodcast; see www.bundeskanzlerin.de for the latest political news from Germany).

More bizarrely, podcasts have also been made from space. On 7 August 2005 American astronaut Steve Robinson claimed the first space podcast during the Space Shuttle *Discovery* mission STS-114. There was no subscription feed, only an audio file that required manual downloading.

Online Networking

There are a number of fundamental insights and technologies that allow technically literate individuals to take advantage of Web 2.0 tools to make themselves appear larger, more competent and more important than their peers (and maybe than they really are). With the rise in usage of the Internet, many social networks are now being formed and carried out wholly in cyberspace, making geographical location far less important for effective business networking than

Table 12.2 Membership Numbers of the Main Social Networks

NETWORK	NUMBER OF MEMBERS (01/07)
WAYN	7,000,000
OpenBC/Xing	1,000,000
Linked-in	8,500,000
Ecademy	100,000
My Space	130 million
Friendster	29,1 million
MSN Spaces	30 million
Orkut	36.5 million

Source: 'A friend in every city' by Thomas and Penny Power with Andy Coote (2006) and updated from Wikipedia in January 2007.

before. With Internet sites developing rapidly in the field of networking, and other related technologies such as e-mail and VOIP creating easy, fast and low-cost methods of maintaining and developing new contacts on a world-wide basis, online networking is an area that could impact upon small businesses quite significantly. Some approximate statistics are shown in Table 12.2.

FirstTuesday was an early site aimed at top executives, venture capitalists and entrepreneurs where membership was by invitation only and limited to one hundred people, making it very desirable to become part of this community. For the more open business market the main players are currently LinkedIn and OpenBC. Another good example is Ecademy (www.ecademy.com), an online networking platform which uniquely combines a substantial offline face-to-face networking component to its offer. The most sophisticated social networking sites incorporate software to hold online discussions and meetings, allowing many people to login without having to move from their desk. Internet networking maintenance can be easier than face-to-face or telephone interaction due to the online tools that are accessible any time of day and night; web pages, e-mail and chat rooms. These technologies provide instant access to a diverse network of individuals around the world which allows networks to be broadened and strengthened, thereby overcoming many of the limitations of traditional face-to-face networking such as small network size and diversity. In 2007, Facebook has taken the market by storm with membership numbers of 35 million and rising.

MySpace is also active offline; for example, it has run a series of intimate concerts by major bands in small venues exclusively to audiences of MySpace users. In the summer of 2006 it made a deal with Google to place advertising on MySpace pages for a guaranteed return of $900 million.

In his e-book *Flipping the Funnel* (2006), Seth Godin outlines his strategy of creating a platform to allow advocates to 'tell a good story'. He has created a platform to allow others to build this structure in an online network called Squidoo (www.squidoo.com). This is a content aggregation tool which allows participants to build a "lens" so that they can focus their expertise and build credibility with prospective customers. It is essentially an additional one page site which can be used to drive traffic back to the main website. There are three innovative aspects to this:

- It is designed to pick up RSS feeds from, for example, special interest clubs on a networking platform like Ecademy. This is very important for the small 'knowledge economy' business wanting to promote itself.
- The company is able to create an 'HQ lens' under which other lenses can be aggregated. In addition to using this to build an 'empire' of knowledge, the cunning marketer can create a template to sit under his headquarters, to be made available to customers and other advocates to tell the 'story' for them in a rather sophisticated approach to viral marketing (as discussed in Chapter 8).
- The Squidoo lens can be 'rated' on a five star system according to the extent of its usefulness to readers, rather like the video rating system deployed on YouTube and discussed in Chapter 9.

The key point is that this material can be easily created by businesses with free blogging software and effectively fed to strategic points such as the website front page using RSS where interested parties can pick up the feed and automatically receive any further words of wisdom or other communication that originate from that source. Some of the key spaces for amateurs to 'dip their toes' into the world of blogging are already 'RSS-enabled' in this way. So it is possible to pick up a discussion thread that is going on in a club in Ecademy and reproduce it in a content aggregation tool like a Squidoo lens. This effectively means that the 'switched on' user can make the same information appear in various different locations, all of which can be arranged to point back to the same source. This boosts traffic to their website and hence the Google page rank is enhanced and it makes the business appear bigger and more influential than it might actually be. As a bonus, if links with the appropriate anchor text keywords are embedded in the blog material, for example, in an autosignature, it has the effect of improving the page rank of the site to which it is directed, since the locations available tend to be well connected themselves so there is a 'halo effect' that reflects back to the business's own site.

You can see how the autosignature works from Diagram 12.8 which is a screenshot of a blog posting on the networking site Ecademy. The writer of the post, Dr Alan Rae, has signed it off with his name, company and a clickable link to his own website, www.howtodobusiness. com. Postings such as this which Alan has made on Ecademy (and anywhere else on the web) can be picked up and aggregated in his Squidoo lens to provide a 'one stop shop' for all his blogging activity.

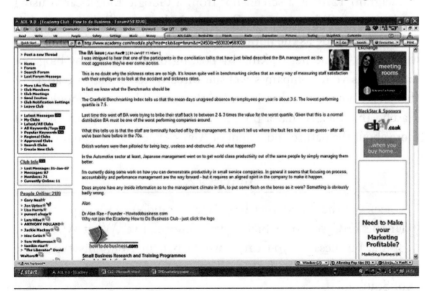

Diagram 12.8 Posting on Ecademy Blog.

Diagram 12.9   Listing of blog postings on Squidoo.

You can check this out by locating the above posting from Ecademy (titled 'The BA issue') in www.squidoo.com/howtodobusiness listed in date order with Alan's other blog postings, as shown in Diagram 12.9.

Diagram 12.10 is a screenshot from a Google Blog Search using the key words 'BA issue Alan Rae' which displays a link to the original Ecademy blog as the number one search result. This demonstrates that active online networking by posting on the Ecademy blog not only makes your company's website directly accessible to readers of that blog, but also makes it indirectly accessible via a Google Blog search. This means that a potential client could very easily find out more about the nature and extent of Alan's expertise by 'googling' him

Activity 12.2

Check out the Squidoo website (www.squidoo.com), in particular the FAQ section which is very informative. What types of online business do you think would benefit from this type of website? What do the FAQs tell you about the emerging culture of Squidoo?

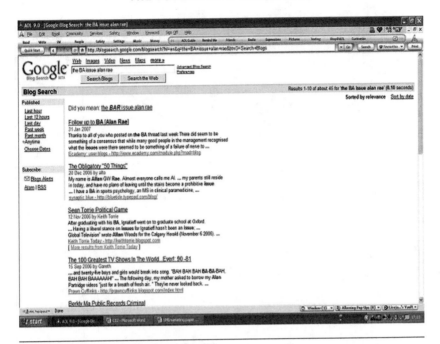

Diagram 12.10   Google Blog Search Results.

and pulling up results like this. As discussed in Chapter 8, the Squidoo average rating for the How to Do Business lens is five stars, which gives an indication of brand quality for the benefit of people who may be new to the company, and are visiting its Squidoo Lens for the first time to seek reassurance as to its credentials.

Where Are We Now? Successes and Failures

Diagram 12.11 indicates, in general terms, how the scope of e-business has developed over the past 10 years. It is interesting to note that despite the dotcom crash, the business impact of the Internet (as evidenced by the arrow) has done nothing but increase throughout this time. It is clear that brochure websites tend to be a peripheral aspect of business strategy, but that more recent iterations of e-business are increasingly central to company strategy. Don't forget, however, that for certain types of business the face to face sale is always going to dominate and e-business may never become critical in such circumstances (on the customer-facing side at least—remember also from Chapter 6 that the

Brochureware	Ecommerce	E-Procurement	E-Marketplaces	Digital Economy
Stand-alone advertising & product information	Stand-alone retailing B2C	Tightly-coupled buying B2B	Dynamically-coupled buyers & sellers	Dynamic business ecosystems: Interconnected e-marketplaces User generated content
	First e-tailers			
				Peer-to-peer collaborative value chains & knowledge management
	Sell-side transactions	Buy-side transactions	Communities & commerce	Click & mortar digital corporations
1996	1997	2000	2003	2006+

Business Impact of the Internet

Diagram 12.11   The business impact of the Internet

Internet is becoming increasingly important for intranets within businesses and for extranets between business partners).

While there is no doubt that the Internet has had a discernible impact on the speed, location and volume of information communication, it remains debatable whether there are as yet many concrete examples of *radically new* commercial structures. Many of the successes of the Internet so far have been unexpected; for example, the marketing applications of text messaging, as discussed in Chapter 7. Additionally, Chapter 1 discussed how the early forecasts of dis-intermediation on a global scale as sellers and buyers communicated directly, now appear exaggerated in view of innovative re-intermediation in many industries. Note the ascent of 'white van man' (traditional road-based delivery operations) as a direct consequence of the growth in online retail shopping! UK government transport statistics appear to support this development, showing that goods vehicle traffic increased on major roads in urban areas by 9.2 per cent between quarter 2 of 2003 and the same quarter of 2004. Light van traffic represents 18 per cent of all motor vehicles (Department for Transport, 2004).

On the negative side there have also of course been some high profile failures. We discussed the lessons to be learned from Boo.com in Chapter 1. Other online businesses which failed to live up to the hype include www.pets.com, which raised $35 million in 1999 only to go bankrupt a year later, despite the backing of Amazon. Ill-advised marketing spend by the company included a single advert during the Super Bowl which cost $2 million. The children's toy retailer www. toysrus.com was caught out by the first rush of public interest in e-commerce at Christmas 1999 and was unable to deliver large quantities of toys on time. After a large fine by the US Federal Trade Commission for breaking promises, Toys-R-Us partnered with Amazon for a more successful Christmas the following year. The partnership is still intact today. Other companies which have joined forces with Amazon to 'piggy-back' their e-business systems rather than compete directly include the long-established bookseller Borders. If you visit www.borders.com you will find joint branding but the website looks and feels very similar to the Amazon site.

For more details on success factors and supporting articles see www.insightexec.com.

What Does the Future Hold?

So what of the future? A lot of 'hype' has been written about the 'revolutionary' business implications of the Internet to the extent that some authors have argued that a new business 'paradigm' has emerged due to the scope of the potential applications of Internet technology.

There seems little doubt that most, if not all businesses will become e-businesses, in the sense that Internet-based technologies will become near universal. Those organisations not using the Internet in some capacity in their operations will be considered exceptional, if not a little eccentric. Waters (2005) argues that many of the predictions made during the dotcom boom were actually correct, just 'time shifted'. Think, for example, of VOIP technology, which is now starting to achieve critical mass alongside the take-up of broadband (high speed Internet and download services). Millions of people have now downloaded the

---
Activity 12.3

Take a look at the Skype website (www.skype.com). What is the attraction of this product to users?

---

software for Skype (www.skype.com) an Internet telephone service which allows free calls between users anywhere in the world.

Durman (2005) notes that a new type of Internet advertising is currently being developed by a UK company called espotting (www. espotting.com) which makes the Internet relevant to the needs of a wide range of traditionally offline small businesses such as plumbers, child-minders, dressmakers, electricians, etc. The service is called 'pay per call' and is an enhancement of 'paid search' advertising (as discussed in Chapter 9). Searchable directories listing the telephone numbers of these small businesses will be created and the advertiser only pays when prospective customers call through to them. The Internet is therefore used to locate the required service but the sale is conducted over the telephone, so the advertiser does not need to have its own website. Google is working on a similar development to supply eBay with web-search advertising, and for the two companies then to jointly offer 'click to call' services whereby online shoppers who click on an advertisement will initiate an Internet voice call to participating eBay merchants or Google advertisers using Skype (which was purchased by eBay in 2005) or to Instant Message (IM) using Google Talk.

However, despite the extent of innovation, in the years since the dot-com crash there has actually been little change in underlying business beliefs and values. It also seems likely that the completely online (i.e. pure-play or dotcom) business will be rare indeed. E-businesses operate within the same business environment as conventional businesses and hence are subject to the same rules. Dutta and Biren (2001) proposed that the key role of Internet technology was not to revolutionise business practices but instead to seek efficiency improvements through 'e-nabling' the current activities of the firm in a 'low risk' approach to innovation that is consistent with existing organisational culture. Even where established businesses have embraced the Internet, online trading revenues currently represent only 13 percent of total sales revenue, although this percentage is growing rapidly year by year. Forrester Research (www.forrester.com) predicts that online sales could double by 2010, a compound annual growth rate of 14 percent.

The vast majority of businesses will always require some kind of 'real world' presence, in their back office if not their front office operations. As such, all business will have to learn how to manage e-business. At present though, many companies are struggling to implement e-business practices that effectively support their business strategies. Contrary to the early rhetoric, the reality is that there appears to be no 'one best way' for organisations to implement and manage e-business processes. As with many other facets of business activity, e-business seems to operate on a contingency model; its management depending on factors specific to each case.

According to Hitwise (www.hitwise.com) the following categories of online businesses grew most significantly in 2006:

- Net communities and chat (34 percent)
- News and media (24 percent)
- Search engines (22 percent)
- Food and drink (29 percent)
- Education (18 percent)
- Business and finance (12 percent).

Among the growth categories, the rise of social networking is not surprising in view of the discussion earlier in this chapter. We noted that community sites such as MySpace, Facebook and YouTube are growing rapidly and fundamentally changing the relationship that businesses have with their customers.

Google accounted for 25 percent of the access points to all categories of websites, meaning that one in four UK Internet visits to websites came from Google. More generally, Hitwise notes:

- Total search engine access (including Google) accounted for 35 percent of visits, up 13 percent year on year.
- Web-based e-mail services accounted for 7 percent, up 16 percent year on year.
- Net communities and chat accounted for 7 percent of upstream visits, up 64 percent year on year.

- News and media accounted for 5 percent, up 26 percent year on year.

A useful online resource to check out for keeping tabs on Internet trends is www.informationarchitects.jp which has published a guide to the top websites for 2006, against a range of criteria and in a variety of categories. It also highlights some likely developments for 2007 and beyond.

Case Study: The Long Tail

We introduced the principle of the long tail in Chapter 4. This case study provides a number of practical examples that are particularly relevant to this discussion of the future of the Internet.

The Internet is changing the entertainment business from one that is driven by 'hits' to one that will make most of its money from 'misses'. This is good news for consumers, because it means more choice, and this 'new economics of abundance' is already the basis of success for such e-business luminaries as Amazon, eBay and Google. Companies are now asking one another: 'Are you long tail?' The phrase was popularised by *Wired* magazine's Chris Anderson in 2004.

The long tail is named after the power law curve obtained when the sales of CDs, computer games and other products, or the popularity of websites, or the frequency of word use in a language is plotted on a graph. Taking the usage of words as an example, there are a small number that appear very frequently: (the, of, to, and, a, in, etc.) After that, there is a steep decline, followed by tens of thousands of words that appear relatively rarely. These rare words form a long tail that tapers off to the right of the graph.

Moving on to an e-business example, it is tempting to think that since all websites are more or less equally accessible, visitors should be evenly distributed. But, a small number of websites have tens of millions of visitors each month—Google, Yahoo!, MSN, etc.—but millions of sites attract only a handful each, forming the same long tail as in the previous example. Counter-intuitively, the more choices there are the more extreme the curve becomes. As the winner takes all, it seems that accepted notions of the Internet as a 'level playing field' or 'global shop window' are misplaced. However, for digital products such as music or films there is potentially business value in the tail, because there are physical limits on how much choice a retail shop can stock or a cinema can show. With the move to digital downloads, Anderson argues that the misses can be as important as the hits: 'With no shelf space to pay for, no manufacturing costs and hardly any distribution fees, a miss sold is just another sale, with the same margins as a hit. Suddenly, popularity no longer has a monopoly on profitability', he wrote in *Wired*. Where a retailer might offer, say, 30,000 songs on CD, an online music store can offer a million. The hits will still sell far more than the misses, but since almost every download finds someone willing to give it a try, the long tail could provide the majority of sales.

Anderson also cites Google as a long tail business, because of its contextual advertising. The first big Internet sites aimed to attract millions of users so they could sell banner advertisements to major brands. Google's AdWords, by contrast, are so cheap almost anyone can buy them, and they can be targeted at a handful of users. Google's financial success therefore comes from aggregating lots of small adverts shown to small audiences—a long tail effect; eBay is another long tail business. It is not about auctioning a few old masters for £20m apiece, but providing a market where huge numbers of people can sell almost anything for a few pounds.

Mass market advertising is clearly out of the question for niche products, but Internet retailers have already developed ways to make them visible, particularly Amazon. One example is the social software that does 'collaborative filtering' as discussed in Chapter 9. Getting buyers to write reviews and create their own hit lists and wish lists also helps buyers to find people with similar tastes, and perhaps to try their recommendations. The process only works if a website offers a full range of products, because the hits are needed to attract mainstream buyers. After that, recommendations can encourage them to try niche products, driving them down the long tail. Offering only hits, of course, does nothing to expand the market and change consumer behaviour.

Source: Adapted from Schofield, J. (2005) 'A miss hit'
The Guardian, 24th March.

Activity 12.4

Go to Amazon (www.amazon.co.uk) and either create an account, or login (if you've already got an account). Browse through a particular category of books or CDs and add items of interest to your wish list. The more you use it, the more the page will become accustomed to your tastes and make recommendations to you. Do you feel this is accurate and effective? Does it make you want to purchase these other products?

Conclusion

Having completed this book it should now be clear what distinguishes good and bad e-marketing practice. The key success factors can be summarised as follows:

- Integrating old and new marketing strategies in creative ways (as discussed in Chapter 7).
- Adopting a 'marketing orientation' throughout the business which puts the needs of the customer first (as discussed in Chapter 1).
- Using the Internet to control costs (but not at the expense of customer value; for example, by forcing queries through a website rather than through support staff, as discussed in Chapter 7).
- Treating online channels as broad enablers of customer relationships (for example, from initial enquiries through to post-sales support as discussed in Chapter 6) rather than focusing solely on transactions.
- Ensuring that chosen marketing strategies drive the implementation of appropriate technologies, (such as CRM systems) and not the other way around (as discussed in Chapter 4).
- Making use of user generated content on discussion boards, chat rooms, or blogs in order to build trust and hence the value of the brand (as discussed in Chapters 8, 9 and 12)

- Keeping up to date with rapid developments in technology and key trends in Internet use (as emphasised in Chapters 3 and 12).

We tend to assume that contemporary changes are the most significant because we are closest to them and do not have the clarity accorded by distance from the phenomenon. It is evident that earlier innovations have had radical impacts on society, but perhaps not always in ways expected at the time. The perspective lent by distance is necessary to comprehend the full extent of the changes taking place over a significant period. The value of this historical thinking centres upon the additional insights it provides to analysis of the current business environment. Our capacity to plan for the future can be enhanced by understanding how earlier innovations appeared at the time, so that we do not apply the standards of the present to the past through the 'rosy glow' of hindsight. If the existing process is a significant building block for innovation, then perhaps we should not be too quick to abandon traditional business principles in our enthusiasm for new ideas, but rather to 'mix and match' as customer needs and market conditions dictate.

The amount of rhetoric dedicated to the 'Internet revolution' in recent years means that it is tempting to regard it as a unique challenge, acting both as a driver of change and as a provider of the tools of change. Throughout this book we have dug deeper than this to demonstrate the enduring value of core business principles and emphasise the key role of the Internet in integrating rather than replacing more traditional business activities, regardless of the size of the organisation.

Questions

Question 12.1

What lessons can we learn from recent developments in the online travel industry that have broader relevance to other businesses in their utilisation of new technologies?

Question 12.1 Feedback

Intermediaries in the traditional travel value chain face significant dangers of being circumvented by new technologies, in this case the threat comes from customers dealing directly with airlines or tour operators and cutting out the travel agent. However, this threat does not mean that the game is up for the travel agent—by using new technologies effectively themselves, in this case to create value for customers through 'dynamic packaging' of hotels, flights and car hire for example, the threat can be turned into a business opportunity. So the general lesson is that new technology can be treated as either a threat or an opportunity, and for every type of business that new technology replaces, it also creates another. Think, for example, of www.lastminute.com which has successfully positioned itself as a new intermediary in the travel industry.

Question 12.2

To what extent does the Internet 'level the playing field' in terms of providing new marketing opportunities for businesses of all sizes?

Question 12.2 Feedback

While it is tempting to think that all websites are potentially equal in terms of online visibility and ease of customer access through search engines, the section in this chapter called 'A Miss Hit' demonstrates that inequalities in the offline world are equally prevalent online. A small number of websites have tens of millions of visitors each month—Google, Yahoo!, MSN, etc.—but millions of sites attract only a handful of visitors apiece. So, regardless of the size of the business, just because it has a website it does not mean that customers will immediately flock to it if the brand is unknown. This book has demonstrated ways in which businesses of all sizes can raise their brand profiles online; for example, by choosing and implementing an appropriate e-business strategy, interacting with customers through a variety of channels, building relationships with those customers and promoting the business effectively to a targeted audience. Finally, it is worth noting that the businesses mentioned in this article, namely Google, Yahoo! and even MSN, were themselves just small businesses only a few years ago!

Question 12.3

In what ways are RSS feeds a less intrusive marketing communication tool than e-mail?

Question 12.3 Feedback
Recipients have to actively request an RSS feed, and if it is not useful then the link can simply be removed. Therefore there is no possibility of passing on viruses or clogging up the e-mail inbox of someone who is already experiencing e-mail overload.

Question 12.4

What types of promotional activity do you think are well suited to podcasting and why?

Question 12.4 Feedback
Entertainment industries have made good use of podcasts to provide tasters for new albums, movies or comedy shows. The BBC makes a number of its radio shows available as podcasts after their official broadcast, so they can be listened to at the recipient's convenience. It is also possible to subscribe to a video cast of BBC's 'A Question of Sport' but the picture quality is currently uninspiring over a standard broadband connection!

Question 12.5

What recent technological innovations do you think are likely to have an impact on the future of e-marketing?

Question 12.5 Feedback
While it is impossible to predict the exact direction of new technology, the role of mobile technology such as 3G within everyday life will certainly have some impact. One particularly interesting area is the integration of all of this technology, from PCs and laptops to mobile phones and PDAs. Also, with the growing success of You-Tube, now owned by Google, online video has become a hot topic. Don't forget that so far, many of the most successful technological

innovations have been unexpected and a surprise to everyone, including their producers!

Feedback on Activities

Activity 12.2

If a company's website includes a blog, a Squidoo lens is a good way of highlighting the best posts and pointing to the products and services that it writes about, reads about, enjoys, or wants to see succeed. Charities can benefit from the Squidoo commission share system specifically and from the philanthropic culture generally, which encourages participants to share proceeds and resources. A company which produces podcasts can list the details of the podcasts and include the RSS for subscribing to the podcast. The lens would also have a set of links for getting started with podcasting and getting a podcast reader. An author could include links to relevant books and reviews of his work on Amazon, and to conferences where he is speaking.

Activity 12.3

Obviously there is a considerable cost-saving involved in using Skype. For Skype users the easiest thing to do is to get your friends to use the service as well, thus making it even cheaper for you to use. Thus Skype's strategy of allowing free calls to other Skype users helps explain the exponential increase in the number of users as the 'network effect' kicks in (a strategy used to good effect in the past by Hotmail).

Activity 12.4

While some of the recommendations can be inappropriate, particularly if you have been in the habit of buying a range of book categories for different people, the 'recommended products' option works well for Amazon. The technique they use to customise recommendations is known as 'collaborative filtering'. The wish list is also a useful feature, not only does it allow customers to keep track of potential purchases, but it also allows Amazon to keep track of them as well and customise future promotional messages accordingly.

Bibliography

Aldisert, L. (1999) 'Branding and legacy', *Bank Marketing*, November, 31 (11): 36

Allegra Strategies (2006) *How Women Shop*, Allegra Strategies

Ang, S. H., Leong, S. M. and Lim, J. (1997) 'The mediating influence of pleasure and arousal on layout and signage effects', *Journal of Retailing and Consumer Services*, 4 (1): 13–24

Ansoff, H. (1957) 'Strategies for diversification', *Harvard Business Review*, September–October: 113–124

Areni, C. S. and Kiecker, P. (1993) 'Gender differences in motivation: Some implications for manipulating task-related involvement', ed. Costa Janeen Arnold, *Gender Consumer Behaviour*, Salt Lake City, Utah, University of Utah, pp. 30–43

Ayios, A. and Harris, L. (2005) 'Call centres: Sweat shops or massage parlours?' *International Journal of Qualitative Marketing Research*, Special Issue on Marketing Ethics

Babin, B. J., Darden, W. R. and Griffin, M. (1994) 'Work and/or fun: Measuring hedonic and utilitarian shopping value', *Journal of Consumer Research*, 20: 644–56

Baker, S. (2004) 'The Online Ad Surge' *Business Week*, 22nd November

Berry, L. L. (1969) 'The components of department store image: A theoretical and empirical analysis', *Journal of Retailing*, 45 (1): 3–20

Beynon-Davies, P. (2004) *e-Business*, Basingstoke: Palgrave

Boddy, D. and Buchanan, D. (1992) *The Expertise of the Change Agent*, Hemel Hempstead: Prentice-Hall

Boulding, K. E. (1956) *The Image*, Ann Arbor, University of Michigan

Brown, M., Pope, N. and Voges, K. (2003) 'Buying or browsing? An exploration of shopping orientations and online purchase intention', *European Journal of Marketing*, 37 (10/11): 1666–84

Brynjolfsson, E., Hu, Y. and Smith, M. (2006) 'From niches to riches: Anatomy of the long tail' *MIT Sloan Management Review*, 47 (4): 67–71

Buellingen, F. and Woerter, M. (2004) 'Development perspectives, firm strategies and applications in mobile commerce', *Journal of Business Research*, 57 (12): 1402–08

Buss, D. N. (1989) 'Sex differences in human mate preferences: Evolutionary hypotheses tested in 37 cultures', *Behavioural and Brain Sciences*, 12: 1–14

Cabinet Office (2006) 'Transformational Government Enabled by Technology' TSO (The Stationery Office) Norwich.

Campbell, C. (1997) 'Shopping, pleasure and the sex war', eds. P. Falk and C. Campbell, *The shopping experience?* London: Sage

Chaffey, D. (2004) *e-Commerce and e-Business Management*, 2nd edn, London: FT Prentice Hall

Chaffey, D. et al. (2006) *Internet Marketing*, 3rd edn, London: FT Prentice Hall

Chaston (2004) *Knowledge-based Marketing: The 21st Century Competitive Edge*, New York: Sage

Chen, L., Gillenson, M. L. and Sherrell, D. L. (2002) 'Enticing online consumers: An extended technology acceptance perspective', *Information and Management*, 39 (8): 705–19

Chen, S. (2001) *Strategic Management of e-Business*, Chichester: Wiley

Cheung, C. M. K., Chan, G. W. W. and Limayem, M. (2005) 'A critical review of online consumer behaviour: Empirical research', *Journal of Electronic Commerce in Organisations*, 3 (4): 1–19

Chicksand, L. and Knowles, R. (2002) 'Overcoming the difficulties of selling "look and feel" goods online: Implications for website design', *IBM E-Business Conference*, Birmingham University

Childers, T. L., Carr, C. L., Peck, J. and Carson, S. (2001) 'Hedonic and utilitarian motivations for online retail shopping behaviour', *Journal of Retailing*, 77: 511–35

Citizens Online (2007) *Statistics*, available from: http://www.citizensonline. org.uk/statistics (accessed 7 February, 2007)

Cox, J. and Dittmar, H. (1995) 'The functions of clothes and clothing (dis)satisfaction: A gender analysis among British students', *Journal of Consumer Policy*, 18: 237–65

Cross, M. (2006) 'The tangled web of e-government', *The Guardian*, 2nd November

David, P.A. (1991) 'Computer and dynamo: The modern productivity paradox in a not-too-distant mirror' in *Technology and Productivity: The Challenge for Economic Policy*, Paris: OECD

Davis, F. D. (1989) 'Perceived usefulness, perceived ease of use, and user acceptance of information technology', *MIS Quarterly*, 13 (3): 319–40

Davis, F. D., Bagozzi, R. P. and Warshaw, P. R. (1992) 'Extrinsic and intrinsic motivation to use computers in the workplace', *Journal of Applied Social Psychology*, 22 (14): 1109–30

De Kare-Silver, M .(2001) *e-Shock: The New Rules*, Basingstoke: Palgrave

Denison, T. (2003) 'Men and women arguing when shopping is genetic', *News Shop*, Exeter University, available from http://www.ex.ac.uk/news/news-shop.htm (accessed 22 September 2003)

Dennis, C. (2005) *Objects of Desire: Consumer Behaviour in Shopping Centre Choice*, Basingstoke: Palgrave

Dennis, C. E. and Hilton, J. (2001) 'Shoppers' motivations in choices of shopping centres', *8th International Conference on Recent Advances in Retailing and Services Science*, Vancouver, EIRASS

Dennis, C., Harris, L. and Sandhu, B. (2002) 'From bricks to clicks: Understanding the e-consumer', *Qualitative Market Research—An International Journal*, 5 (4): 281–90

Dennis, C. E., Patel, T. and Hilton, J. (2002) 'Shoppers' motivations in choices of shopping centres, a qualitative study', *9th International Conference on Recent Advances in Retailing and Services Science*, Heidelberg, EIRASS

Dennis, C.E. and Pappamatthaiou, E-K. (2003) 'Shoppers motivations for e-shopping', *Recent Advances in Retailing and Services Science, 6th International Conference*, The European Institute of Retailing and Services Studies, Portland, Oregon, August 7–10

Dennis, C. E., Fenech, T. and Merrilees, W. (2004) *e-Retailing*, London: Routledge

Dholakia, R. R. (1999) 'Going shopping: Key determinants of shopping behaviour and motivations', *International Journal of Retail and Distribution Management*, 27 (4–5): 154

Dholakia, R. R. and Uusitalo, O. (2001) 'The structure and determinants of consumer intention to switch to electronic shopping formats', *Recent Advances in Retailing and Services Science, 8th International Conference*, Eindhoven, the European Institute of Retailing and Services Studies

Dholakia, R. R., and Uusitalo, O. (2002) 'Switching to electronic stores: Consumer characteristics and the perception of shopping benefits', *International Journal of Retail and Distribution Management*, 30 (10): 459–69

Dholakia, R. R. and Chiang, K-P. (2003) 'Shoppers in cyberspace: Are they from Venus or Mars and does it matter?' *Journal of Consumer Psychology*, 13 (1–2): 171–76

Donovan, R. J., Rossiter, J. R., Marcoolyn, G. and Nesdale, A. (1994) 'Store atmosphere and purchasing behavior', *Journal of Retailing*, 70 (3): 283–94

Donthu, N. and Garcia (1999) 'The Internet shopper', *Journal of Advertising Research*, 39 (3)

Durman, P. (2005) 'Net destroyer', *The Sunday Times*, 24th April

Dutta, S. and Biren, B. (2001) 'Business transformation in the Internet: results from the 2000 study' *European Management Journal*, 19 (5): 449–62.

Economist, The (2005) 'Profiting from obscurity,' 5th May

Eisenberg, B. (2005) *Call to Action: Secret Formulas to Improve Online Results*, New York: Future Now

Elliot, R. (1994) 'Addictive consumption: Function and fragmentation in postmodernity', *Journal of Consumer Policy*, 17: 159–79

Eroglu, S. A., Macleit, K. A. and Davis, L. M. (2003) 'Empirical testing of a model of online store atmospherics and shopper responses', *Psychology and Marketing*, 20 (2): 139–50

eTypes (2001) *Who's Buying Online? UK Online 2001*, London: eTypes/CACI

Fasolo, B., Miscuraca, R., McClelland, G. H. and Cardaci M. (2006) 'Animation attracts: The attraction effect in an on-line shopping environment', *Psychology and Marketing*, 23 (10): 799–811

Feinberg, R. (2001) 'Correlates of Internet shopping customer satisfaction', *Recent Advances in Retailing and Services Science, 8th International Conference*, Eindhoven, the European Institute of Retailing and Services Studies

Fischer, J. (1999) *Understanding the Internet Economy: A Companion Guide to the Motley Fool's Internet Report*, New York: Motley Fool

Fishbein, M. and Ajzen, I. (1975) *Belief, Attitude, Intention and Behaviour: An Introduction to Theory and Research*, Reading, MA: Addison-Wesley

Forrester, *The Technographics Brief*, accessed July 31 2001 (http://www.forrester.com)

Freedman, L. (2007) 'Are you listening?', *Internet Retailer*, (http://www.internetretailer.com), January

Gale, J. and Abraham, D. (2005) 'Toward understanding e-business transformation', *Journal of Organizational Change Management*, 18 (2): 113–16

Gibson, B. (1999) 'Beyond shopping centres - e-commerce' *British Council of Shopping Centres Conference*

Gibson, P. (2004) 'The new communications mix', *Financial Times*, 17th November

Godin, S. (1999) *Permission Marketing*, New York: Simon and Schuster

Godin, S. (2001) *Unleasing the Ideavirus* New York: Hyperion

Godin, S. (2006) *Flipping the Funnel*, http:// www.sethgodin.typepad.com

Greenley, G., Hooley, G. and Saunders, J. (2004) 'Management processes in marketing planning', *European Journal of Marketing*, 38 (8)

Gulati, R. and Garino, J. (2000) 'Getting the right mix of bricks and clicks for your company', *Harvard Business Review*, May–June: 107–14

Gummesson, E. (1991) *Qualitative Issues in Management Research*, Newbury Park, CA: Sage

Gummesson, E. (2004), 'Return on relationships (ROR): The value of relationship marketing and CRM in business-to-business contexts', *The Journal of Business and Industrial Marketing*, 19 (2): 136–48

GVU (1997–2000) 'WWW user survey', *Graphic, Visualization, & Usability Center*, Available http://www.gvu.gatech.edu/user.surveys/survey

Hackbarth, G. and Kettinger, W. (2000) 'Building an e-business strategy', *Information Systems Management*, , 17(Summer): 78–94

Haig, M. (2003) *Brand Failures*, London: Kogan Page

Hansen, W. (2000) *Principles of Internet Marketing*, New York: Thompson Learning

Harris, K. (1998) 'Women on the Net II: The female-friendly site', *Sporting Goods Business*, 31 (13): 16

Hoffman, D., and Novak, T. (1997) A new marketing paradigm for electronic commers. *Information Society: An International Journal*, 13 (1): 33–54

IBM Global Services (1999) *Building a Successful E-business* New York: Caspian

IMRG (2007) *e-Christmas Sales Exceed Expectations with 54 Percent Rise*, London: Interactive Media in Retail Group/Forrester Research

Internet Retailer (2007) 'Forty-one percent of shoppers less likely to shop stores after bad online experience', *Internet Retailer* (http://www.internetretailer.com), January 30

Jackson, P. and Harris, L. (2003) 'e-business and organisational change', *Journal of Organizational Change Management*, 16 (5): 497–511

Jardine, L. (1999) 'The future began in 1455', *Spectator*, 16th October

Jayawardhena, C., Wright, L-T. and Dennis, C. (2006) 'e-Shopping Determinants: CAMI', *Academy of Marketing Conference*, Middlesex University

Jayawardhena, C., Wright, L-T, and Dennis, C. (2007) 'Consumers online: Intentions, orientations and segmentation', *International Journal of Retail and Distribution Management*, 35 (6)

Jevons, C. (2005) 'Names, brands, branding: Beyond the signs, symbols, products and services', *Journal of Product and Brand Management*, 14 (2): 117–18

Jones, P., Clarke-Hill, C. Shears, P. and Hillier, D. (2001) 'The eighth 'C' of (r)etailing: Customer concern', *Management Research News*, 24 (5): 11–16

Johnson, T. and Kaye, B. (2004) 'Wag the blog: How reliance on traditional media and the Internet influence credibility perceptions of weblogs among blog users', *Journalism and Mass Communication Quarterly*, Autumn

Kahn R. and Kellner D. (2004) 'New media and Internet activism: From the "Battle of Seattle" to blogging', *New Media & Society*, 6: 87–95

Kalakota, R. and Robinson, M (1999) *e-Business Roadmap for Success*, New York: Addison Wesley

Kanter, R. M. (2001) *Evolve!: Succeeding in the Digital Culture of Tomorrow*, Boston: Harvard Business School Press

Kaplan, R. S. and Norton, D. P. (1993) 'Putting the balanced scorecard to work', *Harvard Business Review*, September-October: 134–142

Kearney, A. T. (2000) *E-Business Performance*, Chicago: A. T. Kearney

Kelcoo/Nielsen/NetRatings (2006) *Nielsen/NetRatings Study Shows Shoppers Prefer the Internet over the High Street for Christmas Shopping*, Kelcoo (http://www.kelcoo.co.uk)

Kelly, E. and Rowland, H. (2000) 'Ethical and online privacy issues in electronic commerce', *Business Horizons* 43 (3): 3–12

Kim, J. and Forsythe, S. (2007) 'Hedonic usage of product virtualization technologies in online apparel shopping', *International Journal of Retail and Distribution Management*, 35 (6)

Kimber, C. (2001) *Researching Online Buying's Offline Impact*, London: CACI

Kittle, B. (2007) 'Online Christmas 2006: The long tail of e-tail', *Retail Education Today*, 27 (3): 5–10

Kolesar, M. B. and Galbraith, R. W. (2000) 'A services-marketing perspective on e-retailing: implications for e-retailers and directions for further research', *Internet Research: Electronic Networking Applications and Policy*, 10 (5): 424–38

Korgaonkar, P. K., Wolin, L. D. (1999) 'A multivariate analysis of Web usage', *Journal of Advertising Research*, 39 (2): 53–68

Kotler, P. (2005) 'Ten deadly marketing sins: Signs and solutions' *Journal of Consumer Marketing*, 22 (1)

Kotler, P. Armstrong, G. Saunders, J. and Wong, V. (2001) *Principles of Marketing*, London: Prentice Hall

Kumar, N. (1999) 'Internet distribution strategies: Dilemmas for the incumbent' *Financial Times*, special issue on Mastering Information Management, no 7, Electronic Commerce

Lauterborn, R. (1990) 'New marketing litany: 4Ps passé; 4Cs take over', *Advertising Age*, October 1

Lazer, W. and Kelly, E. J. (1961) 'The retailing mix: planning and management', *Journal of Retailing*, 37 (1): 34–41

Lee, M. K. O. and Turban, E. (2001) 'A trust model for consumer Internet shopping', *International Journal of Electronic Commerce*, 6 (1): 75–91

Li, H., Kuo, C. and Russell, M. G. (1999) 'The impact of perceived channel utilities, shopping orientations and demographics on consumers' online buying behaviour', *Journal of Computer Mediated Communication*, 5

Liff, S. and Shepherd, A. (2004) 'An Evolving Gender Divide?', *Oxford Internet Issue Brief*, 2 (July): 1–9

Lindquist, J. D. (1974) 'Meaning of image: a survey of empirical and hypothetical evidence', *Journal of Retailing*, 50 (4): 29–38, 116

Lindquist, J. D. and Kaufman-Scarborough, C. (2000) 'Browsing and purchasing activity in selected non-store settings: A contrast between female and male shoppers', *Retailing 2000: Launching the New Millennium, Proceedings of the 6th Triennial National Retailing Conference, the Academy of Marketing Science and the American Collegiate Retailing Association*, Columbus, Ohio, Hofstra University

Lindstrom, M. (1999) 'Rat race scurry', *ClickZ Network*, http://www.clickz.com, December 2

Lindstrom, M. (2004) 'Branding is no longer child's play!' *Journal of Consumer Marketing*, 24 (3): 175–82

Lindquist, J. D. and Kaufman-Scarborough, C. (2000) 'Browsing and purchasing activity in selected non-store settings: A contrast between female and male shoppers', *Retailing 2000: Launching the New Millennium, Proceedings of the 6th Triennial National Retailing Conference, the Academy of Marketing Science and the American Collegiate Retailing Association*, Columbus, Ohio, Hofstra University

Lucas, P. (2007) 'Come back here', *Internet Retailer* (http://www.internetretailer.com), January

Lumpkin, G. and Dess, G. (2004) 'How the Internet adds value', *Organizational Dynamics*, 33 (2): 161–73

Lynch, R. (2000) *Corporate Strategy*, Harlow: Pearson Education

McCarthy, J. (1960) *Basic Marketing*, Homewood: Irvin

McCarthy, S. (2000) 'Your web site is calling, please hold for your customer', *Call Center Solutions*, 18 (8): 70–73

McDaniel, C. and Gates, R. (2002) *Marketing Research: The impact of the Internet*, 5th edn, Cincinnati: South Western Publishing

McDonald, M. (2004) 'Strategic marketing planning: Theory and practice' ed. M. Baker, *The CIM Marketing Book*, 5th edn, London: Butterworth Heinemann

McGoldrick, P. (2002) *Retail Marketing*, 2nd edn, Maidenhead: McGraw-Hill

Macintyre, B. (2005) 'There, but for the grace of Google', *The Times*, May 14th

MacKinnon R. (2004) Blogging North Korea, *Nieman Reports* 58 (3): 103

Malmsten, E. *et al.* (2001) *Boohoo—A dot-com story from concept to catastrophe*, London: Random House

Martineau, P. (1958) 'The personality of the retail store', *Harvard Business Review*, 36 (1): 47–55

Meekings, A., Russell, C., Fuller, M. and Hewson, W. (2003) *Profit or Pain from Your User Experience*, London: Hewson Consulting Group

Min, S. and Wolfinbarger, M. (2005) Market Share, Profit Margin, and Marketing Efficiency of Early Movers, Bricks and Clicks, and Specialists in e-Commerce. *Journal of Business Research*, 58: 1030–1029

Miller, D. (1998) *A Theory of Shopping*, London: Polity

Mintzberg, H. (1994) *The Rise and Fall of Strategic Planning*, Saddle River, NJ: Prentice Hall

Miyazaki, A. D. and Fernandez, A. (2001) 'Consumer perceptions of privacy and security risks for online shopping', *The Journal of Consumer Affairs*, 35 (1): 27–44

Moon, J. W. and Kim, Y-G. (2001) 'Extending the TAM for a world-wide-web context', *Information and Management*, 38 (4): 217–30

Musgrove, M. (2006) 'Video visionaries meld traditional TV and the Web', *The Washington Post*, 2nd December

Nancarrow, C. *et al*, (2001) 'A new research medium', *Qualitative Market Research: an International Journal*, 4 (3): 136–49

Newell, F. (2000) *Loyalty.Com: Customer Relationship Management in the New Era of Internet Marketing*, New York: McGraw-Hill

NTIA (2000) *Falling Through the Net: Towards Digital Inclusion*, http:/www./search.ntia.doc.gov/pdf/fttn00.pdf

Olins, W. (1999) *Corporate Identity*, London: Thames and Hudson

O'Malley, L. and Tynan, C. (2001) 'Reframing relationship marketing for consumer markets', *Interactive Marketing*, 2 (3): 240–46

OxIS (2005) *Oxford Internet Survey*, Oxford Internet Institute

Palmer, R.A. (2001) 'There's no business like e-business', paper presented at *Business Intelligence and e-Marketing Workshop*, Warwick, UK, 6th December

Parsons, A.G. (2002) 'Non-functional motives for online shoppers: Why we click', *Journal of Consumer Marketing*, 19 (5): 380–92

Peppers, T. and Rogers, M. (2002) *One to one B2B: customer relationship management strategies for the real economy*, Oxford: Cupstone

Peppers, T. and Rogers, M. (2004) *Managing customer relationships: A strategic framework*, Chichester: John Wiley

Peppers, D. and Rogers, M. (2005) 'Return on customer: Creating maximum value from your scarcest resource' http://www.1to1.com

Peppers, D. and Rogers, M. (2006) 'Busting out of the inbox: Five new rules of 1to1 email marketing' http://www.1to1.com

Perea y Monsuwé, T., Dellaert, B. D. C. and de Ruyter, K. (2004) 'What drives consumers to shop online? A literature review', *International Journal of Service Industries Management*, 15 (1): 102–21

Phau, I. and Poon, S. M. (2000) 'Factors influencing the types of products and services purchased over the Internet', *Internet Research: Electronic Networking Applications and Policy*, 10 (2): 102–13

Phillips, F.Y. (2001) *Market-Oriented Technology Management*, Berlin: Springer

Porter, M. (2001) Strategy and the Internet, *Harvard Business Review*, March

Prince, M. (1993) Women, men and money styles. *Journal of Economics Psycology*, 14: 175–82

Retail Bulletin (2006) *Two-thirds of Retailers Missing out on Christmas Customers by not Trading Online*, Retail Bulletin (http://www.theretailbulletin. com), 28 November

Reynolds, J. (2000) 'Pricing dynamics and European retailing: Direct and indirect impacts of e-Commerce', *Proceedings of the International EARCD Conference on Retail Innovation* (CD-ROM), ESADE, Barcelona, European Association for Education and Research in Commercial Distribution

Rice, R. R. (2004) 'A comparative perspective from US surveys', *Oxford Internet Issue Brief*, 2.2, August: 13–15

Rogers, E. M. (1995) *The Diffusion of Innovations*, 4th edn., New York: Free Press

Rohm, A. J. and Swaminathan V (2004) 'A typology of online shoppers based on shopping motivations,' *Journal of Business Research*, 57(7): 748–47

Rowley, J. (2001) 'Eight questions for customer knowledge management in e-business', paper presented at *The Business Intelligence and E-Marketing Workshop*, IBM, Warwick, 6th December

Rowley, J. (2005) 'Building brand webs: Customer relationship management through the Tesco club card loyalty scheme', *International Journal of Retail*, 33 (3): 194–206

Royal Mail (2006) *Home Shopping Tracking Study*, Royal Mail (UK) http:// www.royalmail.com, accessed 2 March 2007

Sawhney, M. and Zabin, J. (2001) *The Seven Steps to Nirvana: Strategic Insights into e-Business transformation*, New York: McGraw-Hill

Schofield, J. (2005) 'A miss hit?' *The Guardian*, 24th March

Schramm, W. (1955) *The Process and Effects of Mass Communications*, Springfield: University of Illinois Press

Scoble, R. and Israel, S. (2006) *Naked Conversations: How Blogs Are Changing the Way Businesses Talk with Customers*, Hoboken, NJ: John Wiley

Shim, S. and Eastlick, M. A. (1998) 'The hierarchical influence of personal values on mall shopping attitude and behaviour', *Journal of Retailing*, 74 (1): 139–60

Shim, S., Eastlick, M. A. and Lotz, S. (2000) 'Assessing the impact of Internet Shopping on Store shopping among mall shoppers and Internet users', *Journal of Shopping Center Research*

Shim, S., Eastlick, M. A., Lotz, S. and Warrington, P. (2000) 'An online pre-purchase intentions model: the role of the intention to search', *Journal of Retailing*, 77 (3): 397–416

Simon, H. A. (1987) 'The steam engine and the computer: What makes technology revolutionary', *EDUCOM Bulletin* 22 (1): 2–5

Sit, J., Merrilees, W. and Birch, D. (2003) 'Entertainment-seeking shopping centre patrons: the missing segments', *International Journal of Retail and Distribution Management*, 31 (2): 80–94

Smith, P. R. and Chaffey, D. (2005) *eMarketing Excellence*, 2nd edn, Oxford: Butterworth Heinemann

Smith, R. B. and Sherman, E. (1993) 'Effects of store image and mood on consumer behaviour: a theoretical and empirical analysis, *Advances in Consumer Research*, 20 (1): 631

Spies, K., Hesse, F. and Loesch, K. (1997) 'Store atmosphere, mood and purchasing behaviour', *International Journal of Research in Marketing*, 14: 1–17

Sui, N. Y. and Cheng, M. M. (2001) 'A study of expected adoption of online shopping: the case of Hong Kong, *Journal of International Consumer Marketing*, 13: 87–106

Surowiecki, J. (2005) *The Wisdom of Crowds*, London: Abacus

Swinyard, W. R. and Smith, S. M. (2003) 'Why people (don't) shop online: A lifestyle study of the Internet consumer', *Psychology and Marketing*, 20 (7): 567–97

Tan, J. J. (1999) 'Strategies for reducing consumers' risk aversion in Internet shopping', *Journal of Consumer Marketing*, 16: 163–80

Tauber, E. M. (1972) 'Why do people shop?' *Journal of Marketing*, 36 (October): 46–59

Tiernan, B. (2000) *E-tailing*, Chicago: Dearborn

Turley, L. W. and Milliman, R. E. (2000) 'Atmospheric effects on shopping behavior: A review of the experimental evidence', *Journal of Business Research*, 49 (2): 193–211

Underhill, P. (1999) *Why We Buy*, London: Orion

Verdict (2000–2006) *Verdict on e-Shopping* and *e-Retail*, London: Verdict Research

Verdict (2006), *e-Retail*, London: Verdict Research

Vincent, A., Clark, H. and English, A. (2000) 'Retail distribution: A multi-channel traffic jam', *International Journal of New Product Development & Innovation Management*, 2 (2): 179–96

Vincent J. (2004) 'Social shaping of e-government—What can we learn from mobile mediated communications?' eds. L. Budd and L. Harris, *e-Economy: Rhetoric or Business Reality?* Abingdon: Routledge

Vrechopoulos, A. P., O'Keefe, R. M., Doukidis, G. I. and Siomkos, G. J. (2004) 'Virtual store layout: An experimental comparison in the context of grocery retail', *Journal of Retailing*, 80 (1): 13–22

Wagner, D. (2006) 'Throttling the customer' *MIT Sloan Management Review*, 4 (4): 10–11

Waters, R. (2005) 'It's the Internet, but not as we know it', *Financial Times*, 20th April

Webber, K. and Roehl, W. S. (1999) 'Profiling people searching for and purchasing travel products on the world wide web', *Journal of Travel Research*, 37: 291–98

Weil, D. (2006) *The Corporate Blogging*, New York: Penguin Group

Westbrook, R. A. and Black, W. C. (1985) 'A motivation-based shopper typology', *Journal of Retailing*, 61 (1): 78–103

Willcocks, L. and Sauer, C. (2000) *E-Business. The Ultimate Practical Guide to Effective E-Business*, London: Random House

Williams, R. (2005) 'Is this ethical marketing?' *Guardian*, 16th February

Wolfinbarger, M. and Gilly, M. C. (2002) *.comQ: Dimensionalizing, measuring and predicting quality of the e-tail experience*, Working Paper No. 02-100. Cambridge, MA: Marketing Science Institute

Wolfinbarger, M. and Gilly, M. C. (2003) 'eTailQ: Dimensionalizing, measuring and predicting etail quality', *Journal of Retailing*, 79 (3): 183–98

Wright, J. (2006) *Blog Marketing*, New York: McGraw-Hill

Xu, G. and Guitierrez, J. (2006) 'An exploratory study of killer applications and critical success factors in m-commerce', *Journal of Electronic Commerce in Organisations*, 4 (3): 63–79

Zwass, V. (1998) 'Structure and macro-level impacts of electronic commerce: From technological infrastructure to electronic marketplaces', ed. E. Kendall, *Emerging Information Technologies*, Thousand Oaks, CA: Sage

Index